HANDBUILT POTTERY TECHNIQUES

REVEALED

The secrets of handbuilding shown in unique cutaway photography

Jacqui Atkin

A QUARTO BOOK

Published in 2005 by Silverdale Books
An imprint of Bookmart Ltd
Registered Number 2372865
Trading as Bookmart Limited
Blaby Road
Wigston
Leicester LE18 4SE

ISBN 1-84509-151-5

Conceived, designed, and produced by
Quarto Publishing plc
The Old Brewery
6 Blundell Street
London N7 9BH

QUAR.HBPT

Senior project editor Nadia Naqib
Senior art editor and designer Julie Francis
Copy editor Mary Senechal
Photographer Ian Howes
Illustrator Sherri Tay
Assistant art director Penny Cobb

Art director Moira Clinch
Publisher Piers Spence

Manufactured by Pica Digital PTE Ltd, Singapore

Printed by SNP Leefung Printers Limited, China

9 8 7 6 5 4 3 2 1

Contents

Introduction 6
Tools 8
Clay 10
Kneading 15

CHAPTER ONE

coiling 16
Using rounded coils 18
Using flattened coils 24
Coiled bowl 28
Coiled dish 34
Coiled basket 40
Coiled surface decoration 46
Garden sculpture 52

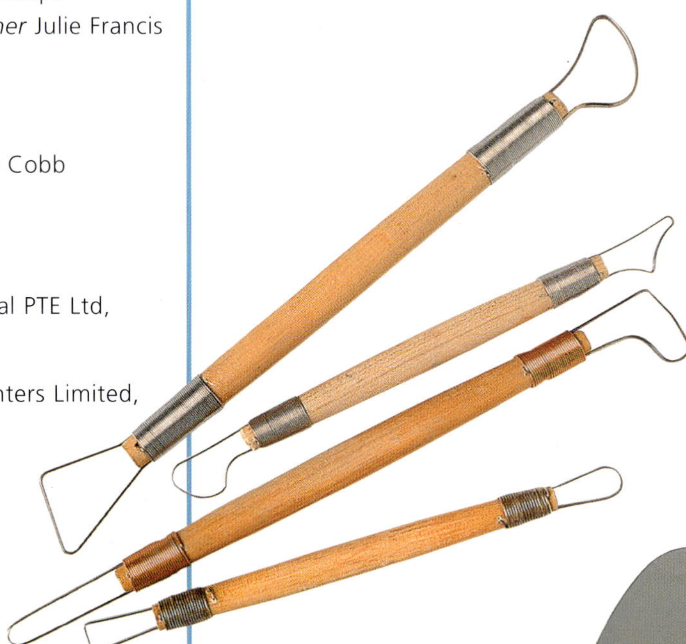

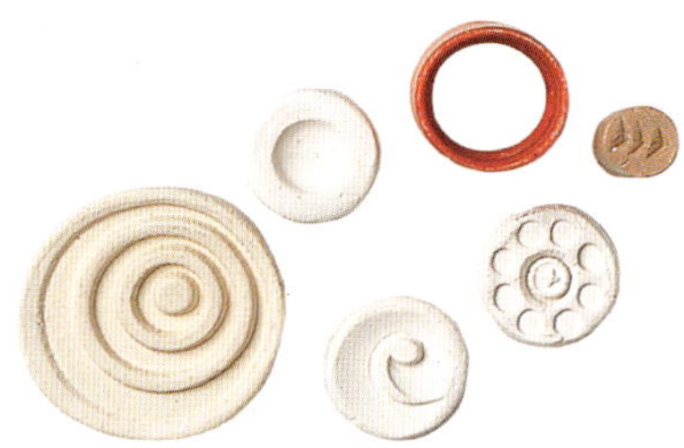

HANDBUILT POTTERY TECHNIQUES REVEALED

CHAPTER TWO

pinching 58

Pinching a simple bowl form 60

Joining two pinched bowls to make a simple pebble 64

Modelling a clay pod 66

Modelling a clay bird 72

Bowl set 78

CHAPTER THREE

slabbing 84

Using firm slabs to make a lidded box 86

Building a vessel with soft slabs 92

Making a decorated window box with large slabbing 98

Porcelain boxes 102

Butter dish 108

CHAPTER FOUR

moulding 114

Making a press mould 116

Making and using a low-relief tile mould with a simple repeat pattern 120

Making a two-part mould 124

Press moulding from a two-part mould 128

Using a two-part mould with casting slip to cast a form 130

Sprig mould 132

Dish with sprig decoration 138

Simple agate bowl 142

Laminated porcelain dish 146

Double-walled bowl 152

Index and credits 158

Introduction

Pottery has been made by hand since prehistoric times. Early uses of clay centred on the construction of functional vessels and figurative sculptures, and the clay was hardened by baking in the sun. The discovery that fire made clay harder encouraged the development of a more considered approach to the manipulation of the material, and pottery making became an important skill that was passed down from one generation to the next.

Early peoples would soon have discovered the amazing versatility of clay, but also its limitations. It can crack at both the making and firing stages, dry out too quickly, or be too soft and sticky to handle. Forms can sag when the clay is too wet, or collapse when its weight is too great to support a shape. Out of these limitations, however, grew an understanding of the material and the development of fundamental techniques. Methods of handbuilding pottery have changed little since those early beginnings. Some cultures continue to make pottery by exactly the same methods as their ancestors, using few tools and firing the pieces outdoors in pits and rudimentary kilns. The integrity and spontaneity of the work produced by these traditional ethnic potters have been powerful sources of

Technique

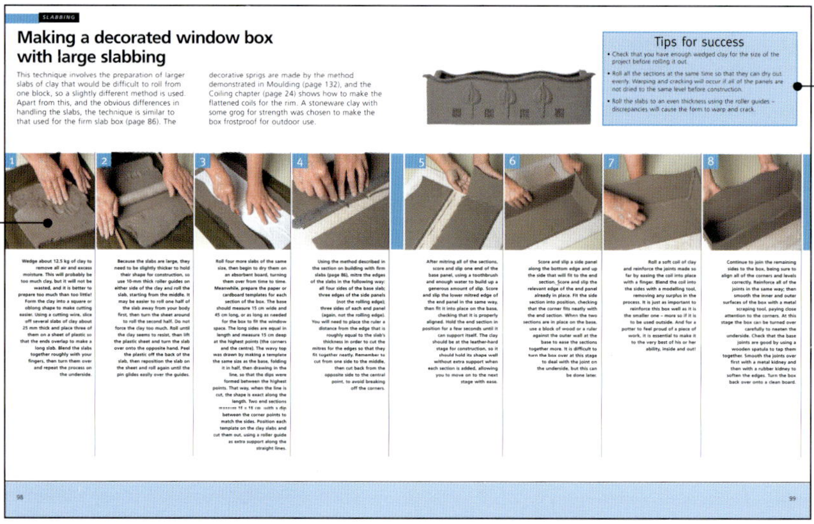

Each of the book's four chapters – Coiling, Pinching, Slabbing and Moulding – begins with basic techniques in a step-by-step format. The photographs show every part of the technique in clear, logical order.

Throughout the book, hints and tips help you to make the most of the handbuilding methods described in the step-by-step sequences.

The cutaway photographs show what is happening on the inside of the form, and reveal the hand positions that would otherwise be unseen during handbuilding.

The red and green arrows describe the hand movements appropriate to the technique being demonstrated.

Project

Variations on the basic form described in the step-by-step sequences are illustrated at the beginning of each project. These suggest alternative shapes or patterns that the potter can try.

Photographs of the finished projects show you what it is possible to achieve when you master the basic techniques.

inspiration to Western potters since the middle of the twentieth century.

This book aims to provide the potter with all the necessary technical information to complete the projects demonstrated, using a few basic tools and a minimum amount of equipment. It is by no means a definitive guide, since after initial training most potters gradually develop an individual approach to handbuilding. It is important to realize, therefore, that techniques are not an end in themselves but a starting point from which you can develop your own methods, ideas, and unique expression.

The book begins with information about the tools required for handbuilding and about clays: their types, properties, preparation and handling. The main body of the book is divided into chapters that cover the basic handbuilding methods of coiling, pinching, slabbing and making and using moulds. Each chapter includes an introductory section, which demonstrates one or more basic techniques, followed by several projects of varying degrees of difficulty that put the techniques into practice. All the relevant information needed to complete each task is demonstrated in a step-by-step format, with cutaway sections, where relevant, to show the position of the hands both inside and outside the pot.

All of the projects in this book are designed to help you develop your pottery skills and give you the confidence to adapt the techniques to your own creative style.

Beware

Certain colourants and materials can be added to clay for handbuilding, to change its properties or colour. Extra care must be taken when using the following materials:

Highly toxic

Lead, cadmium, antimony, barium.

Use with care

All colourants, especially copper oxide and carbonate, cobalt oxide and carbonate, chromium oxide, lithium oxide, zinc, strontium, nickel oxide and slip and glaze stains.

Borax, boron, boric acid, silica, quartz, flint, feldspar, china clay, ball clay, whiting, dolomite.

All of the above materials must be used with caution. Pottery suppliers can provide the relevant health and safety data for their products. Information relating to each material is printed on its container – be sure to read it.

Health and safety

Handbuilding pottery is not considered a dangerous pastime, but a few basic rules must be observed for safe practice.

1 Always work in a suitably ventilated room, with readily cleaned, impermeable work surfaces and washing facilities close by.

2 Never eat, drink or smoke in the workshop.

3 Avoid generating airborne dust – it is better to prevent dust than to try to control it. To minimise dust hazards:

- Clean up spillages when they occur. This applies to slurries as well as powders, because plastic clays and slips that dry become a source of dust. Spillages on floors also cause the risk of slipping.
- Clean all equipment and tools at the end of a day's work.
- Use a vacuum cleaner with a filter for fine dust, not a brush, to clean work surfaces and floors. After vacuuming, wash the surfaces.

4 Wear gloves when using any colouring agents or oxides.

5 Wear a respirator (face mask) when using any powders.

6 Wear protective clothing, but try not to wipe dirty hands on aprons because dried residue will flake off and cause dust. Wash aprons and overalls regularly.

7 If sanding or fettling (trimming or cleaning) dry or bisque-fired pots, wear a respirator and goggles.

8 Check that your tetanus immunization is up to date. Remember that clay is dug from the ground and may carry bacteria that can cause infection in open wounds.

9 Keep a first-aid kit on hand, and protect cuts and scratches from contact with any ceramic materials.

Tools

Handbuilding requires few tools. Some of these can be made at home – adapted from kitchen utensils and other everyday items; others can be purchased from pottery suppliers. Below are the most useful tools for handbuilding.

Metal kidney

The metal kidney is possibly the most useful tool. It is used to refine the clay surface. Kidneys come in various sizes, grades (thicknesses), and shapes – from oval to square. They can also have serrated edges for paring down rough surfaces.

Potter's knife

Potter's knives have long, narrow, pointed blades to make the cutting of wet clay easier. A hacksaw blade, sharpened at one end, works equally well, and the serrated edge makes a handy extra tool.

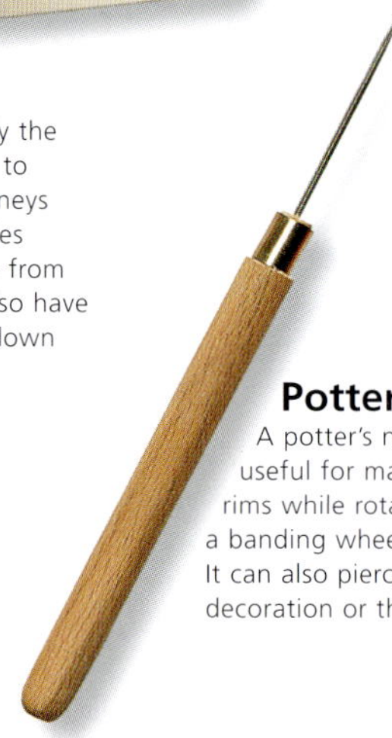

Potter's needle

A potter's needle is useful for marking levels on rims while rotating the work on a banding wheel before cutting. It can also pierce holes for decoration or the release of air.

Cutting wire

A wire is essential for wedging clay and cutting pots off a wheel head, whether they are handbuilt or thrown. Wires are usually about 18 inches (45 cm) long, with wooden toggles at each end. They can be made at home from coat toggle buttons and fishing wire of a suitable thickness.

Rasp (Surform) blade

This extremely useful tool can be used to pare down clay surfaces and level rims. The marks left by the blade can be used as a decorative surface texture.

Paint scraper

A household paint scraper is useful for cleaning work surfaces and boards. It is especially helpful in removing dry plaster splashes that occur during mould-making.

Bow harp

A tool used to slice slabs of clay.

Hole cutter

Hole cutters come in a variety of sizes, usually with a tapering metal blade. The cutter is turned as it is pushed through the clay to make holes of different sizes.

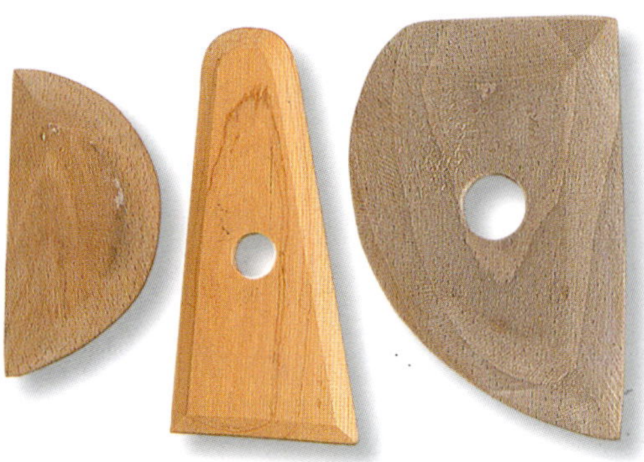

Wooden ribs

Ribs are primarily used for smoothing and shaping pots on the wheel, but they come in shapes to fit any kind of work.

Turning tools

These tools are most often used to trim the bases of pots on the wheel, but they are also useful for hollowing out handmade shapes, especially sculptural ones.

Rubber kidney

This is a flexible kidney, used for the very fine smoothing and compacting of clay surfaces.

Banding wheel or turntable

Although not essential, a turntable makes most tasks easier because it allows the work to be rotated and viewed from all sides. This is particularly helpful when coiling.

Wooden modelling tools

These tools are available from pottery suppliers in an enormous variety of shapes. Many potters use only one or two of them to serve many functions, so consider how much you will use the tool before making a purchase.

Roller guides

Roller guides of varying thickness are indispensable for slab building.

Rolling pin

This should be about 5 cm in diameter, preferably without handles, as long as possible, and of good-quality wood. The surface should not be varnished, or the clay will stick to it.

Brushes

Old toothbrushes are useful for roughening clay surfaces. They replace the need for scoring and slipping because they combine both tasks. They can also be used for spattering slip decoration.

Homemade tools for shaping and texturing/stamping

Useful tools can be made from old credit cards. These can be cut into a variety of shapes according to the form being made. Stamps for texturing clay can be made from bisque-fired clay or found objects, and are a valuable means of applying patterns.

Wooden spoons and spatulas

These tools are highly versatile and can be used for beating, smoothing and texturing clay.

Sponges

All potters need a selection of natural or man-made sponges. These are used to remove excess water from the insides and surfaces of pots, to smooth rims and to apply slip decoration. A sponge on a stick is useful for removing water and pieces of clay from the inside of tall or narrow forms.

Clay

The chemistry of clay is an interesting but complex subject. This is just a brief outline of the origins and composition of clays to enable you to choose a suitable clay for your intended technique.

Clay is a fine-grained earthy material, which in its natural state can be found almost everywhere in the world – often most obviously in gardens and riverbanks. Many potters still dig their own clay, but raw clay is not very pliable and can be difficult to work – other materials must be added to give it plasticity. Nevertheless, it contains properties unique to the place where it was dug, which causes many potters to value it above its standardised commercial counterparts.

The two essential components of clay are silica and alumina, which originate from igneous rocks. Naturally occurring clay is formed from feldspathic or granite rocks that decomposed through the action of glaciers and weather over millions of years. Clays that remain where they originally formed are fairly rare and are known as residual, or primary, clays, the most important of which is china clay (or kaolin). China clay is very pure and white, but its large particle size tends to make it too 'short' (nonplastic) for use on its own. Bentonite is another primary clay, but it is extremely fine and plastic; therefore, it is added to shorter clays to increase their plasticity. Because of their whiteness, primary clays form the main part of clay bodies such as porcelain.

Sedimentary, or secondary, clays have been further eroded and weathered, then moved from their original source by the action of water, wind or glacier, so that the eventual deposit has fine particles and is very plastic. This group includes the ball clays. In the process of travelling from their place of origin, secondary clays pick up certain minerals and impurities that give them different qualities depending upon their journey and their final resting place. Colour is one feature that is affected by movement, and this often makes the clay suitable only for low-firing temperatures. Terra-cotta clays, for example, acquire their characteristic colouring from iron – a mineral found the world over – and they are the lowest firing of all the clays.

Digging your own clay

Clay for handbuilding can be dug straight from the ground, which is an exciting way to start a project, but the clay is rarely suitable for use without considerable refining.

1. After digging, let the clay dry out thoroughly. Next, place it in a bucket and cover it completely with water – a process known as slaking down.
2. When the clay breaks down into a slurry, strain it to remove stones and other organic material, and allow the resulting slip to settle in a bucket over several days.
3. Siphon all of the excess water off the slip, using a sponge or squeeze bottle, then pour the slip onto a plaster bat and allow it to dry to the right consistency.
4. Finally, wedge and knead the clay, and seal it in a plastic bag to rest for a while before testing. This process is similar to that used for reclaiming clay (see page 14).

To test the clay, roll a little coil in your hand and then bend it into a curve. If it splits and breaks, it is probably short and will need the addition of a more plastic clay, such as ball clay, before use. Up to 30 per cent can be added, as required. If the clay is too sticky, it will need the addition of non-plastic clay to give it 'tooth'. This can be added in the form of grog (fired and ground clay) or sand, which is mixed into the clay in small amounts until it is workable.

Digging and processing clay is hard work, but the most difficult aspect is altering the clay body to make it useable. Practised potters who prefer to produce their own clay can call on considerable knowledge and experience when doing so. Beginners may find the entire process somewhat daunting, especially when they are unsure of the kind of clay needed for a particular handbuilding project. To begin with, then, it is preferable to buy ready-made clay from a pottery supplier. In time, if you want to explore the possibility of making your own clay body from locally dug sources, you will find many good books that explain the process in greater detail than is possible here.

Ready-made clays

All clays shrink as they dry, and shrink more during firing. On average, clay shrinks between 10 and 15 per cent, depending on its type. As a rule, the higher the temperature at which the clay is fired, the more it shrinks. Clay can also warp as it dries, and some clays are more prone to this than others, but additives, such as sand and grog, can usually solve this problem.

Pottery suppliers carry clays that are ready-made and refined. They can advise on the specific qualities of the clays, including shrinkage rates and whether or not a particular clay is likely to warp if used for handbuilding. Suppliers can also provide information on firing temperatures and can often help to resolve any problems that occur with a particular clay.

If you live near a supplier, it is preferable to collect the clay because its weight can make delivery charges expensive. If that is not possible, ask the supplier for samples of clay to test before purchasing large amounts. Suppliers usually have catalogues describing each clay's particular properties and giving examples of colour – raw and fired. If no catalogue is available, explain your requirements and ask for advice on clays for beginners that are reliable for various handbuilding projects. The clay will be supplied in sealed plastic bags, ready for use.

Shrinkage

Each of the clay tiles on the right had a 10-cm line drawn in the raw clay before firing. This is used to measure shrinkage after firing. Most clays shrink by 10 per cent between their raw state and their mature fired state. What seems like quite a large pot when it is first formed can look considerably smaller when fired.

Raw Clay

A very dark grey stoneware clay with flecks of iron dispersed throughout.

The high iron content gives red stoneware clay its colour.

Porcelain is a very white clay.

A standard, buff-coloured stoneware clay.

White earthenware is grey before it is fired.

Red earthenware.

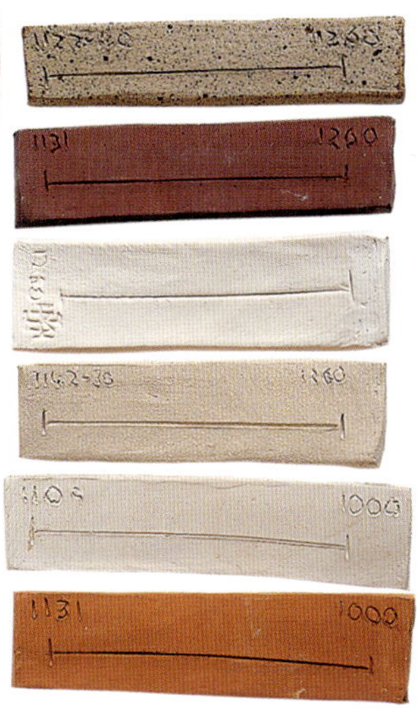

Fired Clay

The iron spots produce flecks of brown in the clay when it is fired.

The red stoneware becomes very dark when fired.

When fired, porcelain is white and smooth; it rings when struck.

The buff stoneware clay is a creamy colour when fired.

The white earthenware turns white after firing.

Fired red earthenware is a rich terra-cotta colour.

This white firing stoneware clay is particularly suitable for handbuilding. It is formed from a blend of low shrinkage clays and has the addition of molochite or calcined china clay, which gives the clay a medium grogged texture.

The grog in this stoneware clay is clearly visible, giving it great texture. It is good for many handbuilding techniques, particularly slab work.

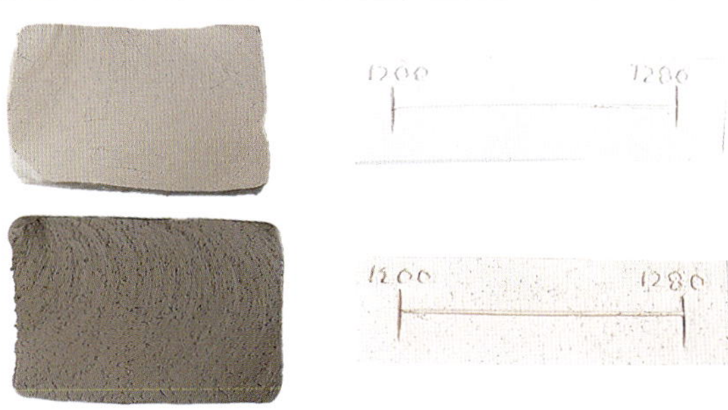

White stoneware fires to an ivory white colour.

This grogged stoneware fires to a speckled buff colour.

Clay types

There are many clays to choose from, and the array can be confusing. Before choosing, consider what you want to make, how it will be fired, and the final result you hope to achieve. For example, a smooth white surface could be needed for maximum colour response at the decorating stage, or a rough, textured surface for a more sculptural piece. If the piece is to be Raku-fired, the clay must have good thermal shock properties to withstand the rapid heating and cooling process involved in this technique. Ask your suppliers for their recommendations.

Broadly speaking, clays are grouped into three main categories.

Earthenware clays

Red earthenware, or terra-cotta, is the most common naturally occurring clay and, therefore, the least expensive. It is most often seen in flower pots, chimneys and tiles. The clay's high iron content gives it a rich, rusty colour.

Earthenware has a firing temperature of 1,000–1,180°C. The clay body does not vitrify (become glasslike) when fired, so if it is intended for domestic ware, it needs a coating of glaze to render it impervious to liquids. The glaze also needs to be craze-resistant to prevent foods and liquids from being absorbed into the clay body, and lead-free to prevent poisoning.

White earthenware is also commercially available, and increasingly popular because of its good colour response when decorated with slips or stains. It has a firing range of 1,060–1,180°C.

Both types of earthenware have limited use for handbuilders because of their low resistance to warping, but they are used to great effect by some potters, especially in the form of casting slip, which is a deflocculated (thinned) liquid form of the clay, generally used in moulds.

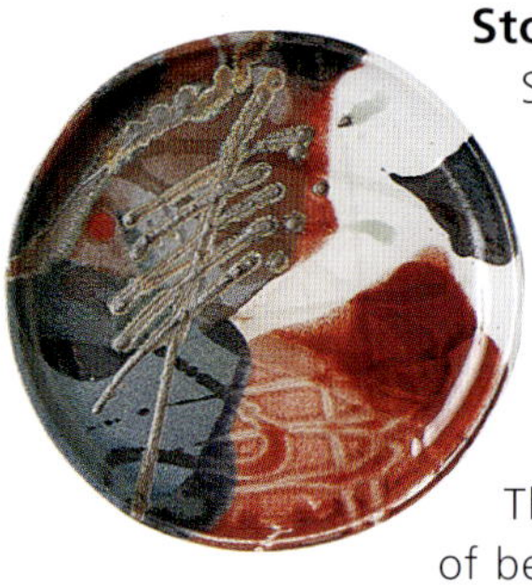

Stoneware clays

Stoneware clays are dense and hard when fired, and much stronger than earthenware. They are capable of being fired to much higher temperatures – usually 1,200–1,300 °C. At these temperatures, the clay particles fuse or vitrify, making the pot non-porous even without a glaze, and it is this stonelike quality that gives these clays their name. The addition of a glaze is usually for hygienic or decorative purposes only.

Stoneware clays are available in a number of colours, from white to dark brown. Most are bodies prepared from plastic clays and minerals; they can range from being very smooth to very coarse. Many suppliers have their own range of stoneware bodies for hand-building, although some bodies are multifunctional and can be used for throwing also; this includes a range of casting slips. It is important to be aware that many of the brighter colours available for earthenware decoration will burn out at stoneware temperatures, so the palette is more limited.

Porcelain

Porcelain is the whitest and purest of all clay bodies and is capable of being fired to very high temperatures – usually around 1,300°C. At this temperature, the clay can be quite translucent, if potted thinly, while remaining hard and nonporous. Many potters put this translucency to good effect by leaving the work unglazed to enable maximum light to pass through the form.

It should be stressed that porcelain is not the best material for a beginner. It is more difficult to use than other clays because it is less plastic and can change from being a sticky, putty-like material to being leather-hard and brittle in no time at all. In addition, the clay is prone to distortion in the firing. Only practice and a delicate touch will allow the mastery of this clay body, but for some potters there is no other clay.

There is only one project in this book that uses porcelain for the main form, but if the material proves a struggle, white stoneware or earthenware can be used instead. Porcelain is also available as casting slip; it is widely used in this form because the technique allows shapes to be made with a very thin wall section.

Clay consistency and storage

Clay for handbuilding must vary in consistency according to the item being made and the technique being used. For example, coiling is generally much easier if the clay is malleable, but hard slabbing calls for firm clay. As a general rule, all clays should be soft enough to mould in the fingers without sticking to them. If they are too soft, they can be firmed up by kneading on a plaster bat or other porous surface to remove some of the water. If the clay is too hard, it can sometimes be saved by wedging in some softer clay; otherwise, it should be dried out and reclaimed, using the method described on page 14.

Try the clay directly from the bag. If it already seems quite firm, it will not be improved by a lot of wedging (page 14) on a porous surface, so wedge it on a nonporous one to prevent additional water loss. Keep the wedging to a minimum because hot hands can dry the clay even more.

Store clay in tightly sealed plastic bags to keep it damp, and preferably in a dark, cool, but frost-free place. Even in these conditions, the clay will eventually dry out, so check it from time to time. If it overdries, it can sometimes be softened by wrapping it in an old wet towel and sealing it in a plastic bag for a few days. If not, allow it to dry out completely, then reclaim it (see page 14).

Colouring clay

Clay can be coloured using either metal oxides or commercially available stains. The best results are achieved when the colour is mixed into white clay, which allows a brighter response. Adding colour to clay alters the clay's chemical make-up, making it 'short' (less plastic) and more difficult to work, but this can be overcome by storing the coloured clay for a few months before use. Thorough tests should be carried out to check the response of all coloured clay before beginning a piece of work, because the firing temperature is lowered by the addition of oxides and stains. These materials can also be expensive, so coloured clay is generally used to make smaller items.

The colour can be added to the clay by mixing it into a dry clay body before adding water, or by massaging it into ready-prepared clay. If mixing several coloured clays, it is essential to clean up thoroughly after making each one, to avoid contamination. This includes thoroughly washing surfaces, gloves and any tools used in the process. Care must be taken when handling oxides and stains, because they can be poisonous or easily absorbed through the skin. Wear a mask and rubber gloves when handling them in their dry state.

Wearing a face mask to prevent inhaling any powder, and rubber gloves to protect your hands, mix the chosen colourant with a small amount of water to make a thick paste.

Cut a block of white clay (in this case, porcelain) into slices, and spread the paste onto the layers.

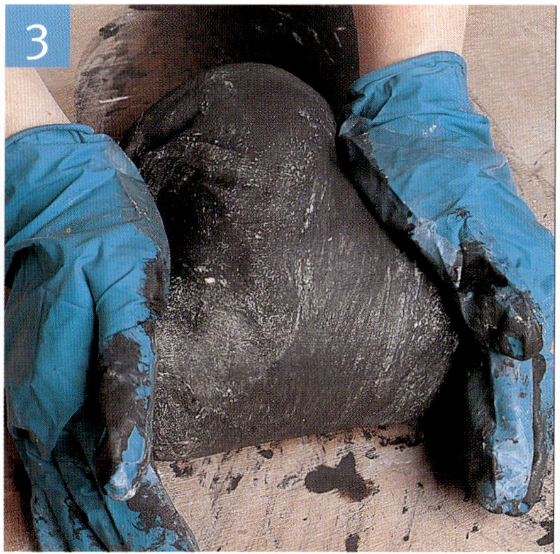

Stack the layers together; then knead them until the colour is thoroughly distributed through the clay body. Store the coloured clay in an airtight bag for at least two weeks before using it, to enable it to regain some plasticity.

Reclaiming clay

One of the great qualities of clay is that it never needs to be wasted, and until it is fired it can be reprocessed over and over again. Scrapings and pieces cut away from a pot in the making, and even unsuccessful pots, can be reclaimed and made back into a workable body. Different clays can be reclaimed in the same bucket to make a mixed body, and this frequently happens in schools where technicians do not have time to sort out the different clay types. It is important to test the mixed clay before starting a piece of work, however, because it could behave unexpectedly in both handling and firing.

Before clay can be reclaimed, it must be allowed to dry out completely. This can take some time, depending on the surrounding temperatures and the size of the clay pieces. When it is dry, break it down into small pieces and place it in a large plastic container. Cover the clay in warm water and allow it to break down overnight. This is called slaking down. The water should completely cover the clay.

Siphon off the excess water covering the clay. Mix the slurry with one hand and transfer it to a plaster bat to form an even layer about 5 cm thick. The plaster will absorb the water from the clay and allow it to firm up again. Check the clay from time to time, as it can firm up quite quickly. When the clay has dried to the point where it can be lifted easily from the bat, turn it over so that the wetter slurry on the surface comes into contact with the plaster to even up the drying process. As soon as the clay has firmed up to a workable consistency, remove it from the plaster bat and wedge it (see opposite). If the clay can be rolled and bent between the fingers without cracking, it can be reused immediately. If the clay does crack, it is 'short' and will benefit from storage to regain its plasticity. Either way, store the clay in sealed plastic bags until ready for use.

Wedging clay

Wedging is a process that prepares clay for building. It is necessary for several reasons, but chiefly to mix the clay thoroughly and remove air bubbles, which could cause the form to shatter during firing. The technique shown here is used to blend two or more clay types, or to make a clay more workable by combining soft and hard layers. Wedging is an ideal method of preparation for large amounts of clay. Smaller amounts are better prepared by one of the kneading techniques demonstrated on page 15.

A sturdy workbench or table is required for wedging because the process involves a lot of force. Ideally, the wedging bench should be below waist height to allow the clay to fall from a greater height and enable the potter to use less force and energy.

Slice the two blocks of clay to be combined into sheets, using a cutting wire. Pile up alternate layers of the clays on top of one another. Give each layer a little slap once it has been positioned over the last one. This action forces out air that may be trapped in pockets between the layers. When all the clay has been layered, neaten the pile into an oblong or brick shape by beating it with your hand. Lift the clay in one hand and allow the front end of the brick shape to fall onto the workbench. The clay should stay in this position with the back end raised from the surface. Position the cutting wire beneath the brick as close to the center of the mass as possible and cut it in half lengthways.

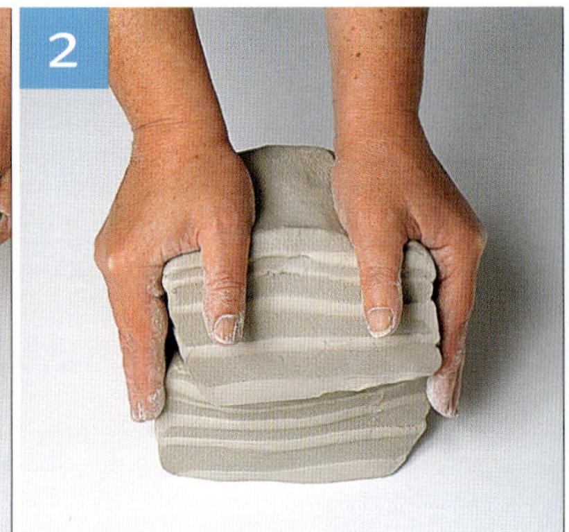

Take one-half of the clay and lift it up to about shoulder height; then forcibly throw it down on top of the other half. Allow the weight of the clay to do the work for you. This action should flatten the clay mass to its previous size, but neatening the clay to a brick shape will make the job much easier. Keeping control of the mass in this way allows you to work much faster. The action of throwing the clay halves together forces out air bubbles trapped in the layers. Repeat the cutting and throwing process, remembering to keep control of the shape. After only a few repetitions, the clays will mix together as the layers become thinner. Repeat the process until the clay mass is even in colour and consistency, and is air-free. This will require at least 20 cut-and-lift sessions. The clay is now ready for use.

Kneading

All clay, from whatever source, must be prepared for use. Kneading is essential to even out the clay and remove any air bubbles, which would cause bloating or explosions during firing. Badly prepared clay can lead to very disappointing results in handbuilt forms. Commercially produced clay often seems wet around the edge of the bag and much drier in the middle. This is because the process of evaporation draws water to the plastic covering. Kneading the clay distributes the water evenly again, but it does not stay that way for long because evaporation starts again almost immediately. That is why you should only prepare enough clay for one project at a time. There are two methods of kneading – choose the one you find most suitable.

Ox-head kneading

This method of kneading owes its name to the shape that is formed in the clay as the kneading is done. Many potters find this the easier of the two techniques described here.

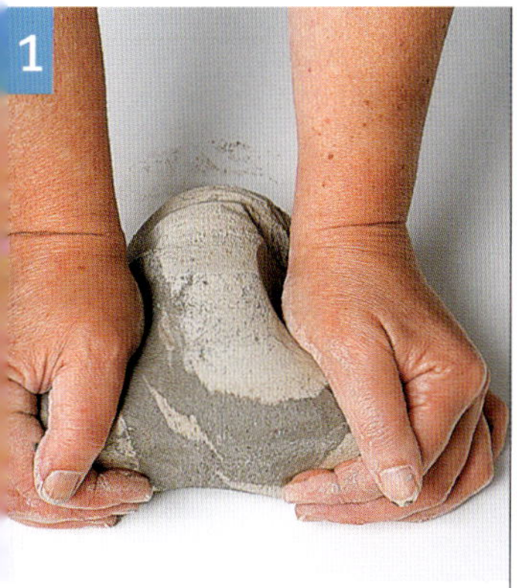

Place the hands on opposite sides of a rounded block of clay. Holding the sides as though to contain them, push the clay forcibly downwards and away from the body. The palms of the hands will dig into the clay on either side to form a raised mass in the middle. Roll the clay towards the body and move the hands slightly forwards on the clay.

Repeat the downward and forward motions, trying not to fold the clay, as this will reintroduce air into the clay. The clay now vaguely resembles an ox or ram's head, the positions of the hands forming the eye sockets. Repeat the action of pushing down and then rocking the clay forward until it is thoroughly mixed. A cut through the kneaded clay shows how well the two different clays have combined.

After kneading

A batch of clay should be used immediately after kneading to avoid it drying out. Leaving it unnecessarily exposed to the air or standing it on a porous surface will have a detrimental effect. Wrap all clay in soft plastic until ready for use, but be aware that, even then, the clay will sweat over time, creating unevenness and making it difficult to handle.

Spiral kneading

This technique is so-called for the spiral shape that forms as the clay is processed. It is the more difficult of the two techniques to master, but is useful for larger pieces of clay.

Place your hands on opposite sides of a rounded block of clay. The right hand is used to push down on the clay as it is rolled forward. The left hand retains the shape by preventing the sideways movement of the clay, and rotates it after each forward movement. This creates the spiral. Using the weight of your upper body rather than just your wrist to aid the movement, push down on the clay with the right hand, keeping the left hand in position on the side of the clay.

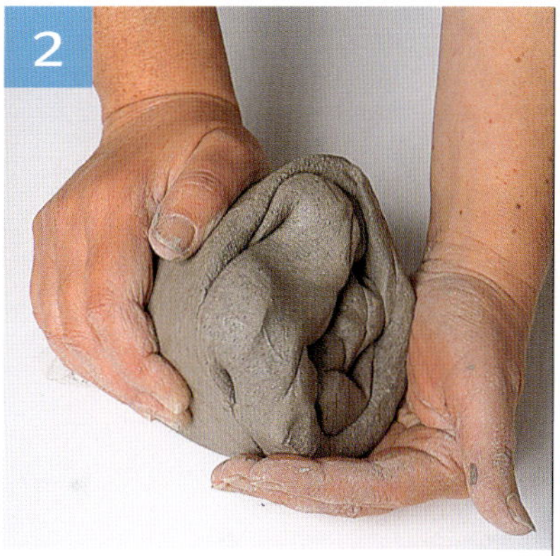

Rotate the clay with the left hand by lifting it counterclockwise; then move the right hand into position for the next downward push. A natural rhythm is created as the body rocks forward for the downward push and then backwards as the clay is lifted and turned. It helps if the work table is below waist level because this allows for efficient use of body weight. As with ox-head kneading, the clay must not be folded in the process but compressed against the table to squeeze out any air. The spiral can clearly be seen as the two clays mix together. Knead the clay until the two clays are throughly combined. There is no way of knowing how many rotations this may require, so you should cut through the clay at regular intervals to make sure there are no air bubbles or variations in clay colour. If either are present, the whole process should be repeated.

Coiling

Coiling is perhaps the most versatile of the handbuilding techniques because it allows the potter to build forms of any size and scale, unlike other methods, which have their limitations. It is also a technique that can be used to produce a range of work, from vessels to sculptural or even architectural forms. Contemporary potters have adapted and refined the ancient building methods but these remain essentially the same. Almost any clay is suitable for coiling, but the size and shape of the intended form should be taken into consideration, along with the firing temperature and function. It is preferable for the clay to be lightly grogged. Larger forms need a clay that is more heavily grogged, to give greater mechanical strength.

Coiling is a relatively slow and contemplative method of handbuilding, which is more suitable for some people than for others. It needs patience, but it can be very rewarding. Coiled pots are rarely totally symmetrical, and therein lies their beauty — they retain an element of the handmade, which renders each one unique.

Using rounded coils

Building pots using coils is a contemplative way of working. It demands some skill and attention to detail, but mostly it requires patience. Rounded coils are the most traditional way of using clay to construct form. Making them requires practice, but it is worth taking time to perfect the technique before starting to build. The beauty of clay is that it is never wasted. If it dries out, it can simply be slaked down and re-wedged to use again. You can, therefore, practise rolling coils just as long as you need. A heavily grogged clay was used to make this vessel because the form is fairly large and needs additional strength. Check before starting that your clay is the right type for the size pot you plan to make. Knead the clay well before beginning, and wrap it in plastic when not in use to prevent it from drying out.

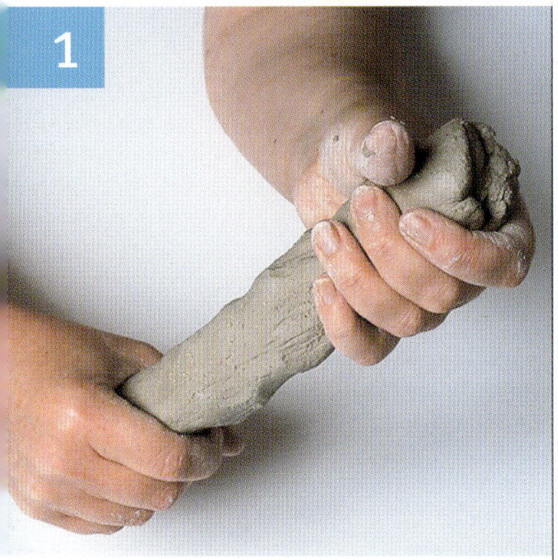

Roughly form the clay into a thick coil shape, using both hands and working from the middle towards each end. The more even the shape at this stage, the easier it will be to roll later. Work the coil until it is a manageable size for rolling.

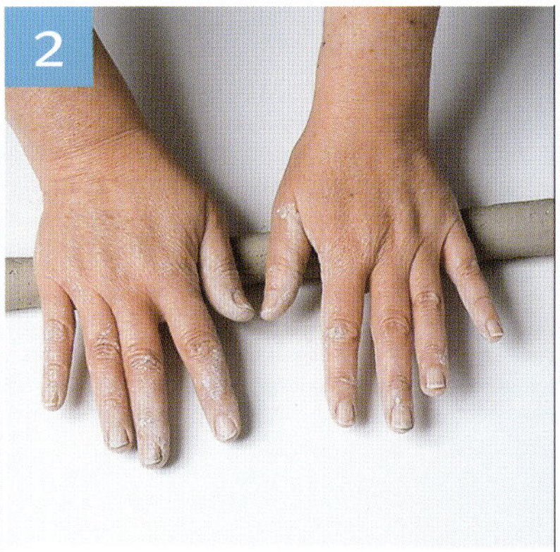

Roll the clay on a clean, nonabsorbent surface. Rolling can dry the clay, so it is important not to use a surface that would draw even more moisture from it. Dry coils are hard to work and are more likely to separate in the firing process. Using the palms of both hands rather than the fingers, roll the coil gently but firmly back and forth from the middle outward to each end. Each coil should be about 13 mm in diameter.

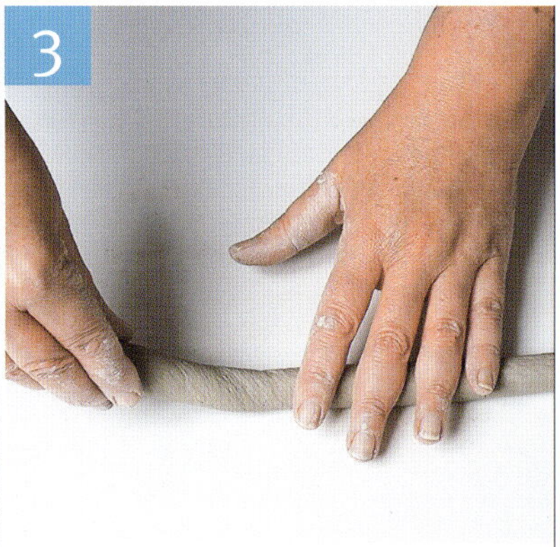

Coils tend to lose their shape and flatten out in the rolling process. To correct this, place one hand gently on the coil (25 mm or so from the distortion) to hold it in place, then twist the coil, either away from or toward the body, until it looks rounded again. Re-roll the coil back into shape. This process can be repeated as many times as necessary to achieve a satisfactorily even coil. If the entire coil is misshapen, hold it at each end and twist in opposite directions until it returns to a rounded shape; then re-roll to size. Roll a number of coils and keep them wrapped in thin plastic to prevent them from drying out before use. Having them ready will help in the continuity and rhythm of building the form.

From a 225-g ball of clay, pinch out a shallow dish shape. Use the thumb to pinch the inner surface and the fingers to pinch the outside, while supporting the clay in the other hand. Pinch the bowl to about 13-mm thickness, working from the centre outwards and back again. The pinching action should be firm and even, working each pinch next to the last. Pinching outward in this way is relatively easy for the beginner, because the angle of the hand naturally pulls the clay away from the centre.

KEY

Pulling, lifting and supporting movements

Pushing, shaping and reinforcing movements

Tips for success

- Roll as many coils in advance as you can. Keep them wrapped in thin plastic to prevent them from drying out.
- Try to roll out all the coils to the same size. This helps to keep the thickness of the wall even.
- Check the shape regularly, using the template, and make corrections immediately.
- Use a hairdryer to firm up the clay if it starts to become floppy, but don't overdry it. The form needs only to be able to hold its shape.

5 If, after pinching the clay to the required thickness, it remains too wet to support its shape, dry it off a little, using a hairdryer. Keep the dish supported in your hand as it is dried, but do not overdry it. Once the dish can support its shape, transfer it to a bat and even off the rim, using a rasp blade. Do not shave away too much – just enough to make the dish round and level. The rasped edge is a good surface on which to build the first coil.

6 Once the rim of the dish is corrected, refine the thickness by scraping away any lumps and bumps, using a metal kidney. Support the dish in one hand as you scrape the underside smooth. The inside can sit on the bat as it is smoothed, but must remain supported with one hand around the edge at all times, to prevent the shape from distorting. Run a rubber kidney over the inner and outer surfaces to smooth them finely.

7 Because the base section was dried off a little to support its shape, the first coil must be added to a scored and slipped edge. This process can be done in one action, using an old toothbrush and some water. Supporting the dish with one hand, gently work the wet toothbrush around the edge, using the same action as brushing the teeth. The edge should have a good amount of slip worked up on it before moving to the next stage.

8 The first coil is positioned on the outer edge of the scored base rim to maintain the outward flare of the form. The form will continue to flare out until it is about 30 cm high. While supporting the coil in one hand, use the other to position the coil, pressing it firmly into place around the scored edge.

Remove any surplus coil by overlapping the beginning and end and cutting through both at an angle, using a potter's knife. Support the wall with one hand as close as possible to the cut, allowing for safety, as you cut through the coils. Discard the cut piece of coil and ease the cut ends together, trying not to trap air in the joint. Smooth the joint over with a finger to make a continuous ring.

Supporting the form from underneath with one hand, gently but firmly blend the coil onto the base, using a finger or thumb of the other hand. Push the clay onto the base using downward strokes evenly applied around the edge. It helps to have the work on a turntable for blending in the coils, because it allows for even, rhythmic action. The process speeds up significantly with practice, and working in this way can show quick results.

To blend in the coil on the underside, lift the base off the bat slightly, using one hand. The same downward action of the thumb is used to blend in the coil while the rest of the hand acts as extra support for the base. An alternative is to turn the entire base over onto the bat and lift it with one hand as the other blends in the coil in an upward direction – effectively the same procedure in reverse. Ultimately, every potter develops his or her own approach from a selection of learned techniques, and gradually you will find the way of working that is most effective for you.

Supporting the side opposite the one being worked on, redefine the outline shape by scraping away any surplus clay with a metal kidney. Try not to remove too much clay but use the kidney to smooth the joint, which will also reinforce it. Some potters prefer to build up several coils or even the entire form before carrying out this process. For the beginner, however, smoothing and refining after the addition of each coil allows greater control of the form, and any mistakes can be immediately corrected.

The left hand holds the base section securely while the right hand blends the outer side of the coil onto the base. It is important not to distort the shape too much.

The base could be lifted to blend in this coil, providing it is well supported.

The first coil was fixed into position and blended into the base section.

One hand supports the outside of the form to prevent the shape from distorting as the excess clay is removed from the inside.

The other hand scrapes away excess clay, using a metal kidney.

The form sits firmly on a bat as the surface is refined.

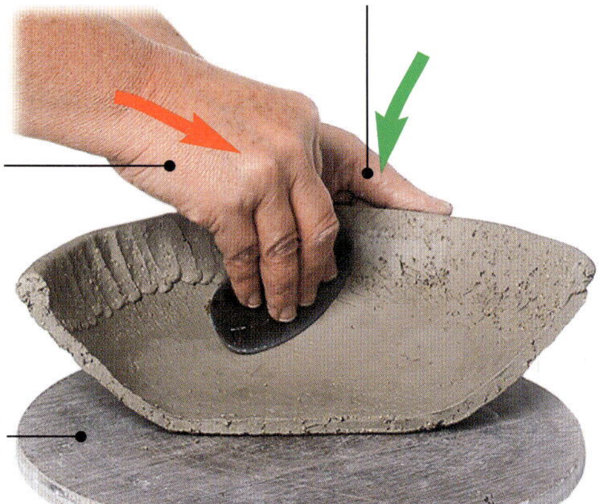

Continue to build up the form in the same way, adding coils to the outer edge to maintain the flare of the form. It is not necessary to score and slip each coil if it was wrapped in plastic and is soft enough to work with easily. Just add one coil onto the last, making sure that each is well blended in. It is essential to support the form at all times as you work on it to prevent the shape from distorting.

A check is kept on the shape of the pot, using a template – an outline shape cut from heavy cardboard, plywood or similar material. Stand the template on the bat at the base of the pot so that it fits neatly into the shape. Holding the pot securely in one hand, drag the template around the outside with the other hand. If the template does not fit because the shape has distorted, cut a V-shaped section of clay diagonally from the wall of the pot at the point where it is most out of shape. Rejoin the cut section using the toothbrush and a little water to score the surface first. If the pot is too small for the template to fit correctly, pinch out the wall between your forefinger and thumb until the correct shape is achieved.

When the pot is built up to about 30 cm, or to the first level of the template, scrape the rim flat. Holding a potter's knife at a 45-degree angle pointing down into the bowl, mitre the rim carefully, supporting the wall continuously with the other hand. Take care to keep the supporting hand well clear of the knife as you cut. Alternatively, the rim can be mitred from the inside, with the knife pointing upwards and the wall supported on the outside, with the hand well away from the knife. Any method is acceptable providing it is carried out safely.

Score and slip the mitred edge, using the toothbrush and water, and position the next coil on the angled rim. The direction of the coil will now have moved inwards. Extra support will be required as the coil is fixed into place because it has none from underneath. Join the coil at the overlap in the same way as before to complete the circle.

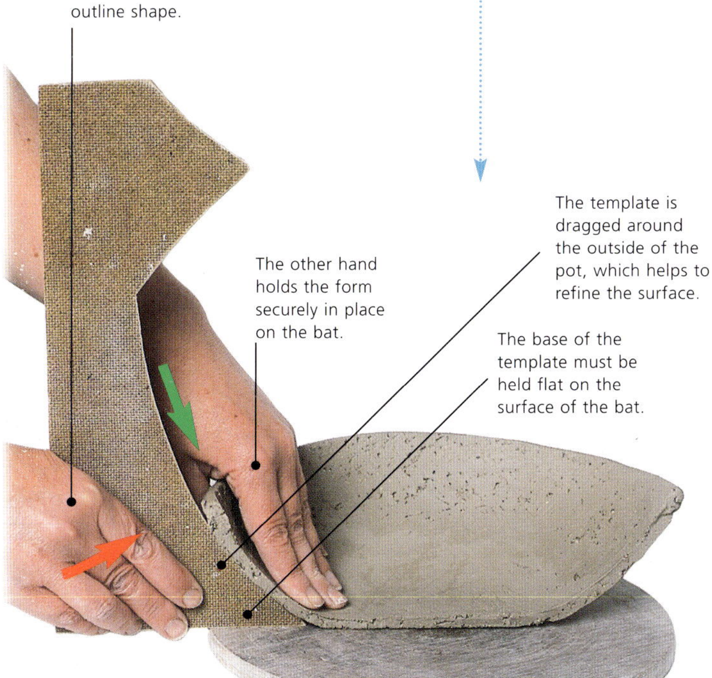

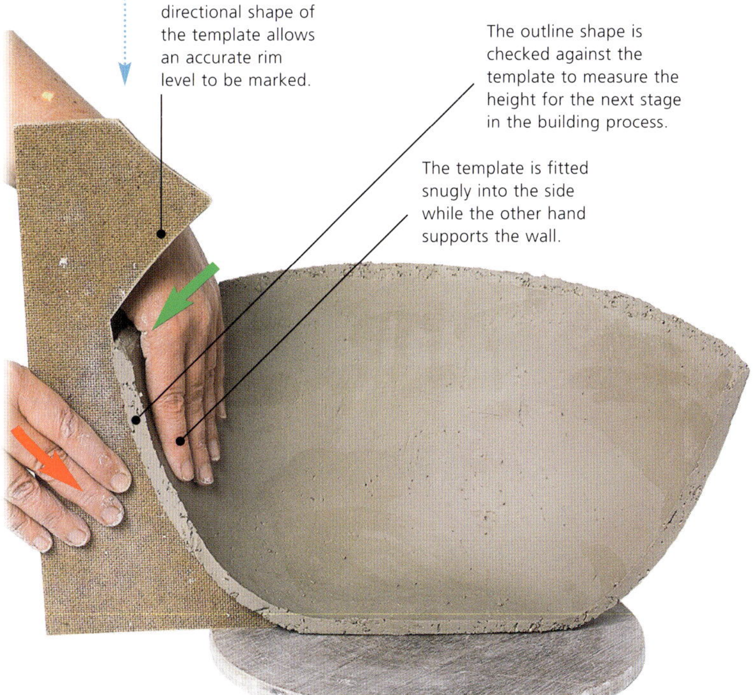

17

Blend the coil into place, as before. Support the coil underneath as you blend it in above, using a thumb and the rest of the hand as extra support. Blending the coil at this angle reinforces the change of direction. Try not to push the clay too far over so that the angle is lost. It is easy to distort the shape at this stage, so control is vital.

18

When the coil is thoroughly blended in on the upper side, reinforce the angle and the joint by paddling (a gentle beating action with a wooden spatula or paddle) around the rim. Support the underside of the coil as you paddle. There is no need to smooth this surface with a kidney because paddling evens it sufficiently. Refinements can be made later.

19

Paddling can cause some of the coil to squeeze over the side of the pot. Remove this excess by running a metal kidney around the side, scraping down and away from the edge so as not to disturb the line. When all of the surplus clay is removed, turn the kidney on its side and smooth the surface. Finally, run a finger around the edge to take the sharpness off the angle.

20

Holding the pot with one hand so that the thumb and palm support the outer wall and rim, blend the coil in on the underside, using the same downward action. It is slightly more difficult to blend the coils on the inside of the pot because the hand is angled awkwardly, but take the time to do it properly because this is a potentially vulnerable joint.

21

Blend the clay deeper into the main body of the pot, using the rounded end of a metal kidney. Some clay will be removed in the process, but again the purpose is to compress and smooth. A little extra thickness of clay at angles helps strengthen the joint and support the next coil. Check the shape against the template and make any necessary adjustments, as before. It can be helpful to firm up the clay more often with the hairdryer as the form shapes inwards, because there is less support from underneath.

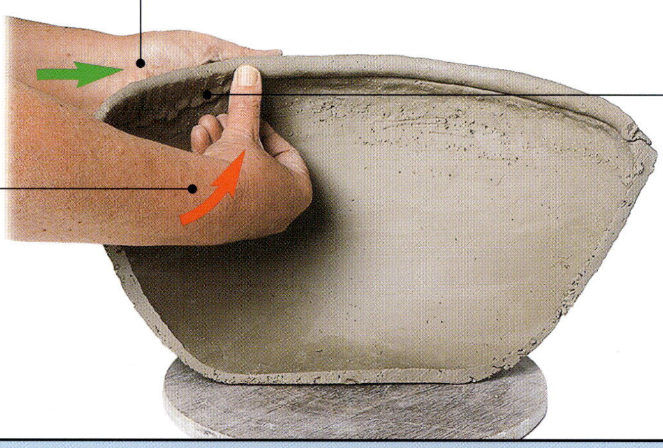

One hand supports the outer wall of the pot, with the thumb and palm resting on the rim.

The other hand blends the coil onto the base section, using the thumb in a downward direction.

Extra care is needed when blending the coils on the underside, because the hand is working at a difficult angle and it can be hard to see what it is doing, especially as the shape closes.

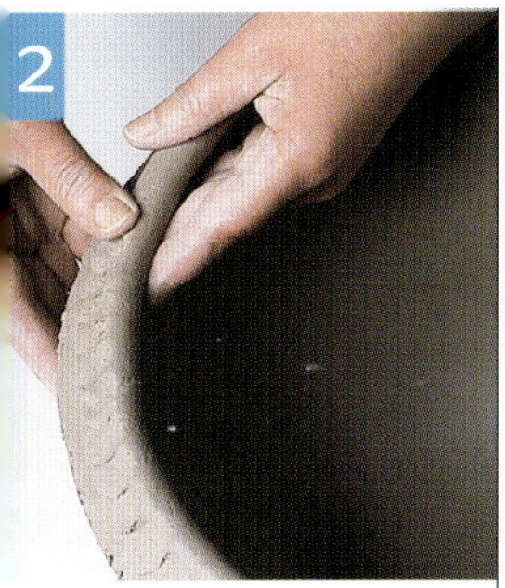

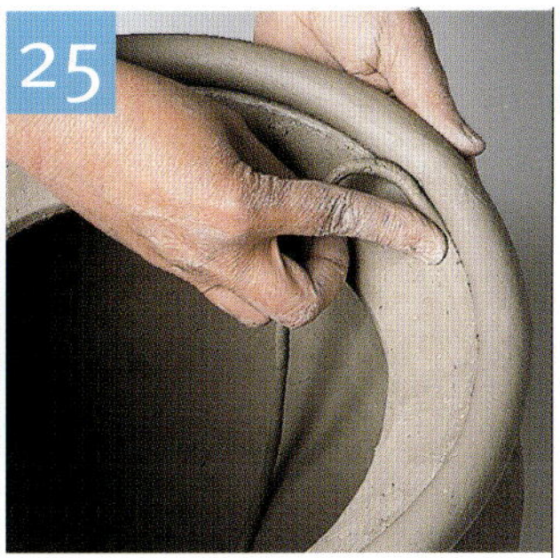

2 Continue coiling inwards by placing each successive coil in line with the last to maintain the angle. Take time to blend the coils very thoroughly, especially on the underside where it becomes increasingly difficult to see where you are working. Use a wooden modelling tool if it helps. When the pot is built up to the second level of the template, level the rim, then firm it with the hairdryer so that the shape can support another change of direction.

23 Score and slip the level rim and fit the next coil onto it. Blend the outer side of the coil vertically. The inner side is blended in a slightly outward flare again, but this happens almost naturally because of the angle of the hand while working. It is possible to blend this coil into place using one hand. The thumb blends the coil while the rest of the hand supports the underside of the rim. It is still important, however, to support the outer side of the pot with the other hand as you work.

24 Continue to build onto the last coil so that the rim flares outwards again. Measure the final section against the template and build until the upper level is complete. Firm up the clay a little using the hairdryer, then thoroughly smooth the surface with a kidney or a wooden rib, removing irregularities in the clay's thickness as you do so. Make sure the rim is supported as it is neatened, especially on the underside when finishing the upper surface. Sit back and take a look at the pot while rotating it on a turntable. It should be a good shape if it was checked against the template regularly.

25 Level the rim with a rib or a modelling tool to provide a flat surface on which to position the last coil. Roll a fatter coil than that used for the body of the pot – 25 mm diameter instead of 13 mm. Check that the coil is long enough to fit all the way round the rim. Score and slip the rim, as before, and fit the coil into place centrally. It should look too big. Cut the overlap diagonally, as before, and join the ends of the coil, taking care not to distort the shape. This is a decorative coil, which should look like a continuous ring once in position. Finally, reinforce the coil where it sits on the main body, using a thin coil of soft clay, inside and out.

26 The pot is now ready to finish, using whichever method of surface decoration you prefer. Dry the pot slowly to avoid warping or cracking.

One hand firms the clay a little with a hairdryer to enable the rim to hold the weight of the final decorative coil.

The other hand supports the rim to prevent it from relaxing out of shape.

Rotate the work on a turntable to avoid overdrying some areas and stressing the clay.

One hand holds the thin coil, using the forefinger to fix it into place under the larger coil.

The other hand supports the outer side of the rim to prevent the fat coil from moving while the reinforcing coil is blended into place.

A finger fixes and smooths at the same time.

Using flattened coils

There are many ways of coil building and most potters eventually adopt a method to suit their own particular style. This technique of making coils by flattening them is an adaptation of the rounded coil method; it allows the potter to build up a form much faster but it still demands precision. You should be prepared to spend time on the details of construction to avoid splits and cracks in the clay at a later stage. A clay mixture of a grogged, white-firing stoneware body for strength, and porcelain for whiteness was used in the technique shown here. The white-firing clay has good thermal shock properties, making it excellent for extreme forms of firing such as Raku.

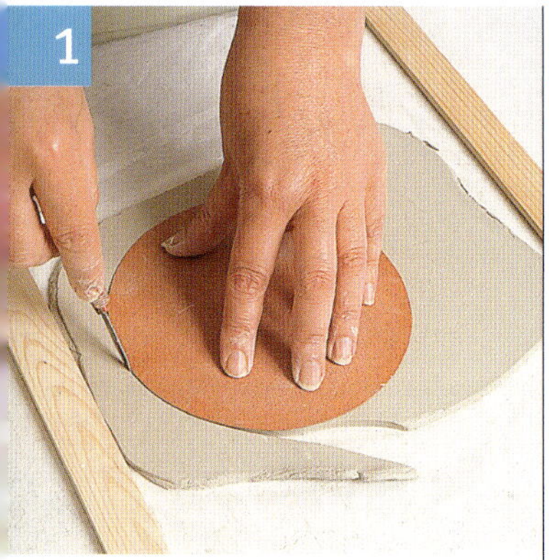

1

Refer to the chapter on slabbing (page 86) and roll out a piece of clay large enough to cut a section to form the base of the pot. Use a sheet of plastic to roll the clay on. This makes handling much easier and prevents the clay from drying out too quickly. Leave the clay on the plastic sheet and, using a cardboard template, carefully cut out the base shape.

2

Keeping the base on the plastic sheet, lift off the template and transfer the base slab onto a wooden bat, removing the sheet only when the slab is in the correct position. Using the plastic sheet in this way prevents the slab from distorting when it is transferred from one surface to another.

3

Roughly form the clay into a thick coil using both hands. When rolling the coil, use the palms of the hands in a long, smooth rolling action beginning at the middle of the coil and working outwards. Try not to use the fingers, because this can make the coil uneven and difficult to handle. Your aim is to produce a thick coil about 25 mm in diameter and 30 cm long. If the coil flattens in the process of rolling, it is possible to correct it by twisting at one end in an outward direction while twisting inwards at the other end and then re-rolling. The shape of the coil can be corrected as many times as necessary. In fact, this process adds some strength to the clay.

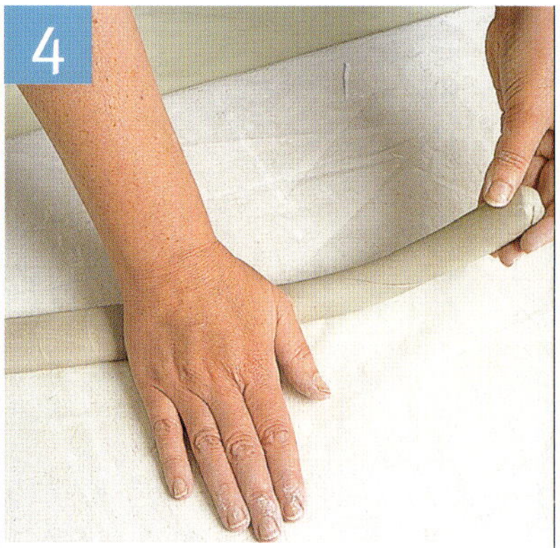

4

Working again on the sheet of plastic, hold the coil in a slightly raised position at one end while flattening the other end with the heel of the other hand. Work along the length of the coil in this way using a firm and even pressure at all times, but not flattening the coil too much to begin with. Repeat the process by lifting the coil from the plastic and turning it over to flatten the other side. To help form the shape of the pot, the coil can be manipulated into a curved shape during the final part of the flattening process.

KEY

Pulling, lifting and supporting movements

Pushing, shaping and reinforcing movements

Tips for success

- Coiling is a relatively slow method of construction and the pot may not be finished in a day. Have some soft plastic ready to wrap the work up if you need a break. Don't leave it uncovered for any length of time if you are not working on it.
- Use the hairdryer at regular intervals to even out the drying process, but don't overdo it. The clay should be firm enough to hold the next coil, but not too dry.
- If the clay dries out too much in the making, dampen an old cloth and wrap it around the pot, then wrap the whole thing in plastic for a while. The clay should be soft enough to work on again within half an hour.

5 When the coil is then placed onto the base section along the outer, longer edge, it will naturally curve inward. Similarly, if the coil were to be placed using the inner edge, it would curve outwards. Using an old toothbrush and water, score the outer edge of the base slab. (This is an easy way of scoring and slipping because the action of the toothbrush will do both jobs in one.)

6 Position the longer edge of the curved coil slightly in from the outer edge of the base slab, overlapping the coil where the ends meet. Cut through the overlapped sections of coil at a diagonal and discard the excess clay. Using the toothbrush and water, score the cuts and join the overlapping sections of coil together securely, trying not to distort the shape too much in the process.

7 Supporting the work on the inside with one hand, use a wooden tool to blend the clay from the base section, extending out from the point where the coil was positioned, up and into the wall of the coil. Set the bat on a turntable to do this, because it allows for a smooth and even action as the work turns. When all of the base clay is blended into the coil, a metal or wooden scraper can be used to smooth the surface and remove any excess clay.

8 Roll out a thin coil of soft clay and place it around the inside join of the base. Using a wooden tool (or a finger if you prefer), blend the reinforcing coil into the base and press it firmly onto the wall of the flattened coil. Support the outer edge at the base at all times to prevent the shape from distorting. Smooth off with a rounded tool or finger.

One hand feeds the coil while the other gently presses it into place.

The outside of the form is supported with the thumb to prevent distortion.

The soft coil on the inside of the form serves to reinforce the join.

It is important to get the base of the shape absolutely right before continuing. Use the pre-cut template to check that the first coil is at the correct angle by placing the template flat on the wooden bat at the base of the pot. Support the inside with one hand while rotating the template around the edge with the other hand. This process helps to smooth the outer surface and compact the clay. At this point it may be useful to firm up the clay a little with a hairdryer to give it some strength on which to build.

It is always easier to maintain the shape of the pot if the next coil is added onto a level-surfaced edge. Using a rasp blade, shave off any irregularities on the upper edge of the coil. Rotating the pot on the turntable while doing this will make the job much easier, but don't get carried away. There is something very satisfying about shaving the clay in this way, so make sure just the bare minimum is removed to level the edge.

Roll out the shape of the next coil as before. Using the toothbrush and a little water, score the upper edge of the pot. Position the coil around the rim, gently pushing the clay into place with one hand while supporting the rest with the other. As with the first coil, overlap the ends and cut diagonally through both sections, then secure them together.

Using the template again, check that the pot is maintaining its shape. If the shape has distorted and is found to be too wide, cut two or three V-shaped wedges on the diagonal around the rim of the pot and join the clay back together in the same way as the ends of the coil. Make sure these joins are very secure and, if necessary, reinforce with some little coils of soft clay, blended in well and smoothed off. If these second or subsequent coils narrow in too much, it should be possible to pinch the coil out slightly until the correct shape is achieved. Often simply smoothing the inside wall of the pot with a metal kidney will stretch the clay a little, especially if the clay is very soft. If you do not want the clay to stretch, then supporting the outer wall of the pot while smoothing the inside will help to prevent this, but scraping and smoothing at a leather-hard stage is the safest way to prevent distortion.

The hand positioned on the inner surface supports the clay and rotates the pot.

A turntable allows the pot to be rotated smoothly and evenly.

The template is held in position flat on the surface of the bat and dragged around the outer edge of the pot to check that the shape is correct and to further smooth the surface.

Having checked that the shape of the pot is correct, roll out some thin coils of soft clay. Blend one coil into the join on the outside of the pot, using your fingers to pinch it into position and then a wooden tool to smooth it out. Make sure that the inner surface is supported at all times with one hand. When the coil is thoroughly blended in, use a metal kidney to finely smooth the surface. Repeat the process on the inside join, making sure you support the outer surface at all times.

Continue to build up the pot in the same way as before, using the template at each stage to check the shape and make any necessary corrections. When the midpoint of the form is reached, roll out a slightly thicker coil, flattening it straight instead of curving it. Join the coil to the form in the usual way, making sure that it is fixing to a level rim. Reinforce the join inside and out and smooth the surfaces.

Pinch the upper edge of the coil in an outward direction, rotating the pot on the turntable to maintain an even section. Use one hand to support the shape while pinching with the other. Pinch only a little at a time and check the shape regularly with the template. Excess clay can be removed with a metal kidney at the refining stage and an uneven rim can be levelled with a rasp blade before attaching the next coil. Any adjustments to the form should be made before continuing.

Continue to build the pot as before, but position the coils using the inner rim of the curve for an outward lean. When the pot has reached the required height, level off the rim with a rasp blade. Then, supporting the form with one hand, refine the edge by gently running a metal kidney around the rim at an angle – inside first, then out. Continue to do this until the rim is rounded and level. It is worth spending time to get this right.

The left hand supports the work in order not to distort the shape. This is a very important element in the building of a pot because an uneven clay section creates tensions in the drying process, which may lead to cracking or even explosions during the firing process.

Once the coil has been reinforced, the right hand scrapes away any surplus clay with a metal kidney to give a smooth surface.

Constant reference to the template ensures that the shape of the pot stays on track.

The left hand supports the form at the neck and rotates the turntable.

The right hand drags the template around the body of the pot to detect any irregularities in shape and help smooth the surface.

Coiled bowl

This project combines several techniques and uses both rounded and flattened coils. A plaster mould is needed to form the first part of the bowl. This mould is made using the method described on pages 116–119.

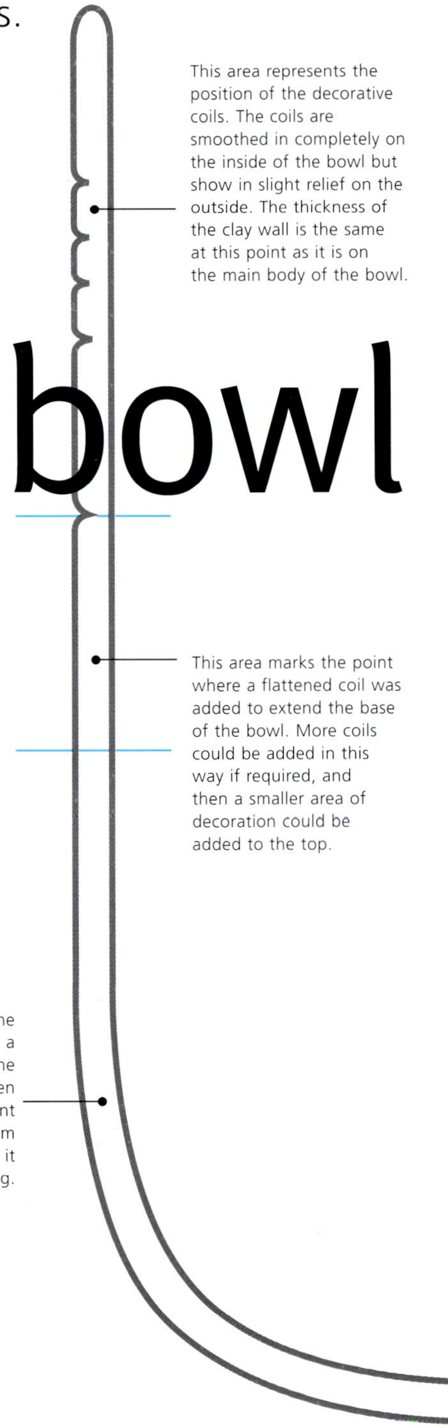

The design possibilities for this kind of bowl are endless, and relatively quick to produce. By following the basic building methods, you can use the technique shown as a starting point for working your own coil pattern into the design. A relatively smooth buff clay with a wide firing range was chosen for this bowl because it allows good definition for the decorative coils, but any all-purpose clay would be suitable.

This is a simple bowl shape with a sturdy, wide base that gives the form stability. The walls are vertical from the moulded base section upwards and can be built up quite high before the form loses its visual balance.

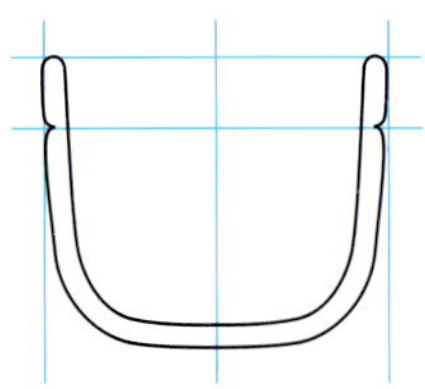

As an alternative to the original shape, the bowl can be made in the same way up to the point where the decorative coils are added. Then, instead of working the pattern vertically, you can build it inwards to close the form a little. This demands extra internal reinforcement at the point where the angle changes.

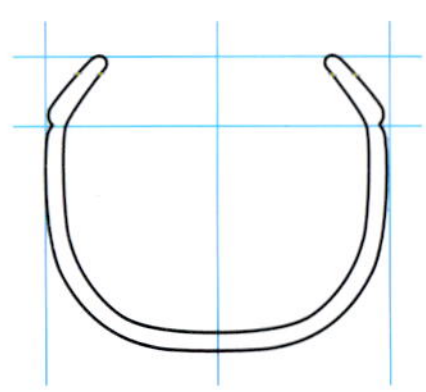

Working on from the previous shape, the form can be changed further by making a second change of direction outwards from the closed version. A form like this has an open, generous visual balance.

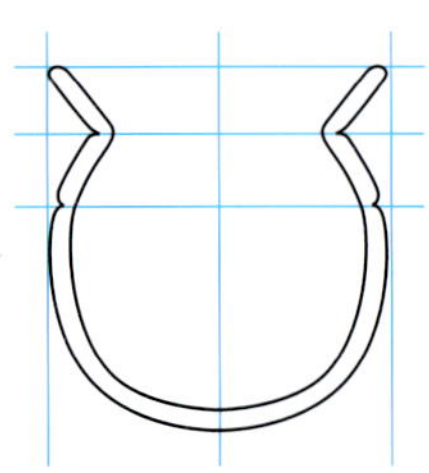

One mould, used creatively, can produce many different forms. In this version, a neck has been extended upward from the decorative collar of the second diagram. This could be extended outwards again, if required, to form a flared rim. Similarly, a decorative coiled foot ring could be added to give the form visual lift. This would also balance the decorative areas on either side of the main body of the bowl.

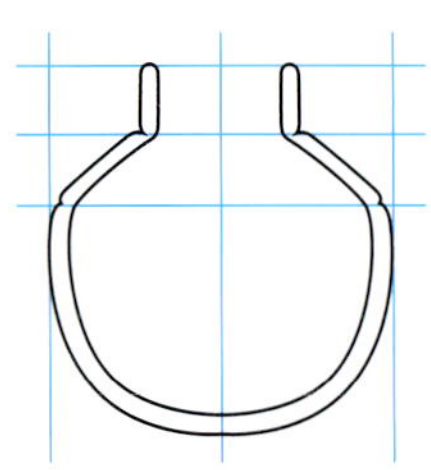

KEY

Pulling, lifting and supporting movements

Pushing, shaping and reinforcing movements

Slice about 5 cm from a lump of clay and knead this piece of clay thoroughly to remove trapped air. Place the clay on a clean plastic sheet and position a roller guide on either side. Beat the clay flatter with the rolling pin before rolling. Be careful not to beat deep furrows into the clay – aim to make each stroke evenly weighted as you move across the slab. Beating the clay in this way reduces the bulk and makes rolling much easier. It also removes any air that remains trapped in the clay. If the slab is still a little bulky for rolling, turn it over, rotating it a quarter turn, and beat it again.

When the clay slab is at a size to roll, reposition the roller guides on each side so that the ends of the rolling pin rest on them when the slab is rolled out. Start to roll the clay from the middle of the slab, pushing away from the body and then back again, applying moderate pressure. Lift the plastic sheet with the clay in place, then turn the slab over and off the sheet onto the other hand. Peel the sheet from the back of the slab and return it to the work surface. Turn the slab a quarter turn and replace it on the sheet, so that what was the underside now faces up. The slab will now be rolled in a different direction and on the other side.

Reposition the roller guides and roll the clay as before, working from the middle, away from the body. Check that the plastic sheet remains flat on the surface. If it gathers up, it will cause wrinkles in the clay, which are undesirable and will need to be repaired. Roll the clay until the slab is level with the roller guides and the rolling pin moves easily across them. It may be necessary to turn and roll the clay again before it is the same thickness as the roller guide; if so, follow the same procedure as before.

Keeping the slab on the plastic sheet, cut out a half-circle large enough to fill half of the plaster mould. To remove the piece from the sheet, lift the plastic and allow the cut section of the slab to fall away onto the opposite hand. This prevents the clay from stretching too much before it is fitted into the mould. Never try to peel the clay off the plastic while it is still on the work surface, because it will almost always tear.

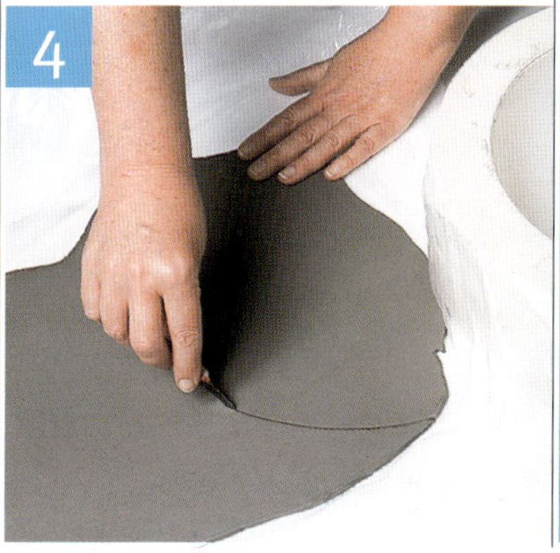

Tips for success

- Consider how you want the bowl to look before you start. Make a few simple line drawings of patterns for the coils.
- Check that no air bubbles are trapped in the slabs after rolling. If air can be seen in the clay, burst the bubbles with a potter's pin to avoid explosions in the firing.
- Blend the coils meticulously to avoid cracks developing later as the bowl dries, or in the firing.
- Allow the bowl to dry out very slowly before firing by wrapping it loosely in thin plastic. It may take several days to dry this way, but slow drying will help prevent warping and cracking.

Using a damp sponge, ease the clay section carefully into place to fill half of the mould. Use of a sponge helps to avoid stretching the clay, whereas fingers could easily pierce it. Apply the sponge in small dabbing movements, easing the clay from the base to the top of the mould to force out any air that may be trapped behind the slab. There should be some overlap at the rim of the mould; this will be removed later, when the second half has been fitted.

Cut out a second semicircle of clay and lift it from the plastic sheet in the same way as before. Ease the slab into the mould, using the sponge and allowing a 13-mm overlap of clay where the two pieces meet along the centre. Take extra care to ease out any air that may be trapped between the mould and the slab when fitting the second half. Using one hand to steady the mould, gently but firmly blend the overlapped sections together with the fingers. Work the clay by pressing away from the underlying edge out to the upper edge. Make sure that the sections are thoroughly blended to avoid cracking at a later stage.

When the two sections are well blended, scrape away any excess clay using a metal kidney. Do not remove too much clay. It is important to maintain an even section to the slabbed wall, because any discrepancies will cause the work to distort in the drying and firing process. Finely smooth the surface using a rubber kidney. This will further compact the joint.

To remove the excess clay above the mould, hold a roller guide sideways and position it flat onto the plaster rim. Drag the guide back towards your body as it moves around the rim. Use the other hand to steady and rotate the mould as the clay is removed. Levelling the rim in this way provides an even surface on which to build the next stage of the bowl. **Do not** use a knife to remove the surplus clay. It could chip away plaster from the mould, which would contaminate the clay and cause explosions in the firing. Before removing the bowl from the mould, you may need to firm up the clay a little to enable it to support its shape. Dry the bowl with a hairdryer while continually rotating the mould on a turntable.

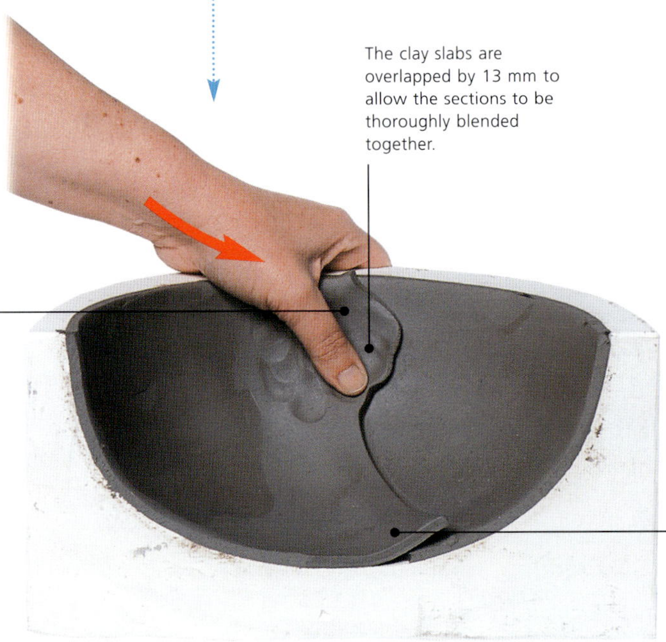

The clay slabs are overlapped by 13 mm to allow the sections to be thoroughly blended together.

The overlapping clay at the rim is removed using a roller guide to keep the edge level and flat.

To avoid trapping air in the overlap, the clay is blended from the underside edge across to the upper edge, using a finger or thumb.

When the clay starts to shrink away from the side of the mould, the bowl is ready to be removed. Place a wooden bat over the top of the mould, then turn both the bat and mould over so that the bowl drops out onto the bat. It is much easier to remove the mould this way than to try to lift the bowl out of the mould the right way up. This process also reduces the risk of distorting the shape by over-handling.

Holding a thin, soft coil of clay in one hand, reinforce the joint where the two slab sections were fitted together in the mould by first pressing the coil into place with a finger. Blend the coil in with a wooden modelling tool, then smooth over the surface with a metal kidney, scraping away any surplus clay. Dry the outer surface a little with the hairdryer so that the bowl will hold its shape when turned the right way up. Place another bat over the base of the bowl. With one hand holding each bat, turn the bowl over. Again, this prevents the bowl from being distorted by too much handling.

Using the technique described on page 24, roll and flatten a straight coil about 5 cm wide and long enough to fit around the rim of the bowl. Score and slip the rim of the bowl, using a toothbrush and a little water. Secure the coil onto the rim. Reinforce the joint inside and out with thin soft coils of clay, easing them into place with a finger before blending in with a wooden tool. Even up the clay wall by scraping away any irregularities with a metal kidney. Support the wall at all times on the opposite side to the one being worked on. Level the rim using the rasp blade, making sure not to shave too much away.

Turn the bowl over onto a large sheet of paper and draw a circle around the rim. Turn the bowl back over and replace it on the bat. Cut out the paper circle, fold it into four, and draw a pencil line along each fold. This template can be used many times and divided into as many sections as you choose for different pots – a simple method of division without the need for maths! Place the template over the top of the bowl and carefully hold it in place with one hand. Mark the quarter positions on the side of the bowl, using a knife or wooden tool, to correspond with the pencil lines on the template.

9

10

11

12

Variations

- Decorative coils do not have to be added to a moulded base. Try building an entire pot by coiling onto a flat, slabbed base-section. Cylinders are a good shape to begin with and even if the form distorts a little, this adds to the organic look of the pot.
- Another option with this type of coiling is to make up patterned slabs or panels. This would mean working in much the same way as shown on page 35, but the pattern would be formed on an absorbent flat surface, for example, a plaster bat. Once the slabs have been smoothed on one side and firmed up, they can be cut to make any slabbed shape, but make particularly pretty boxes. (Follow the method described on pages 86-91.)

Position an old bottle top (or any suitable round object) on one of the marked quarter lines so that it forms a semicircle, and draw around the shape with a sgraffito tool or knife. Repeat the process three times to correspond with the other marked quarter positions. Holding the wall of the bowl steady with one hand, cut out the semicircles with a potter's knife. Wrap the bowl loosely in thin plastic and set aside.

Roll out a batch of round, soft coils, roughly 6 mm in diameter, and cover them in thin plastic to prevent them from drying out. Curl one of the coils into a circle that will fit into the semicircle cut from the rim of the bowl. Leave enough length in the coil to curl back another circle of the same size, in the opposite direction, to sit on top of the rim. Before fixing the circle into place, score and slip the rim and cutout area, using the toothbrush and a little water. Ease the curl into the semicircle with one hand, holding the rest of the coil in the other. Curl the remaining coil into a circle and set it on the rim, filling in the gap between the two curls with a tiny ball of clay.

Using one hand to support the outer wall and the newly added coils, gently but firmly blend the coils together on the inner surface, using a thumb or finger. Drag the clay in a downward direction to avoid pushing the wall out of shape. This process is much easier if the clay is not too dry, so keep the prepared coils covered while not in use. If they seem to be drying, spray them lightly with water and rewrap them for a few minutes. This will soon return them to workable use. Repeat the coiling pattern in the other three semicircles to match the first.

Fill in the spaces between the curls with straight sections of coil, and add tiny balls of clay where gaps appear. Score and slip the rim before adding the first coils; this is not essential for successive coils. Cut the ends of the coils neatly to fit against the curls. Repeat the pattern all the way around the rim if symmetry is your prime aim. If not, the pattern can be built up in a free style with only the original coils forming any continuity.

13

14

15

16

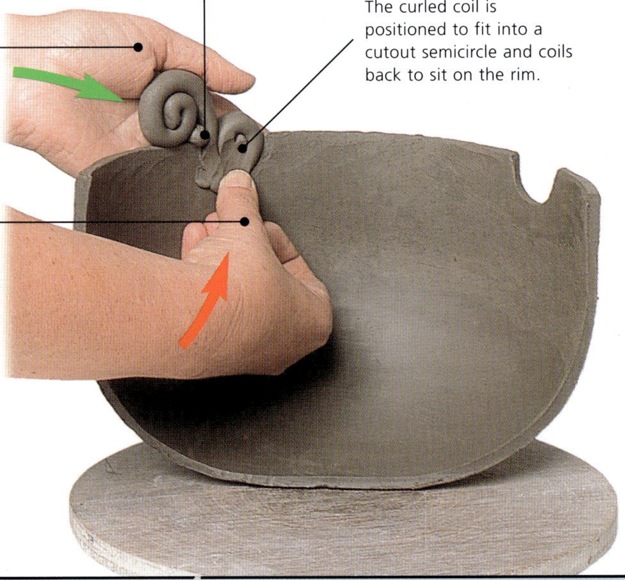

Vary the pattern by manipulating the coils into different shapes on the work surface before fixing them in place on the bowl. Make four coils at the same time in order to have them roughly the same size. Position the coiled shapes equally around the bowl to fit the developing design. Continue to build up the pattern with coils and tiny balls of clay until the design is satisfactory. Do not try to level the rim perfectly. This method of coiling has a free style despite the fundamental symmetry of the design, which lends itself to a rolling rim and enhances the finish of the bowl.

When all of the decorative coils are added and thoroughly blended on the inside, scrape away any lumps and bumps using a metal kidney. To prevent the coils from distorting, support the outer wall firmly as you work on the inside. Scrape the clay away in sideways sweeps instead of upwards, to avoid lifting the coils off the rim. When the thickness of the wall has been evened, run a wooden rib over the inside to smooth it. Hold the rib so that the long edge has the most contact with the wall. Wooden stamps can be used to add a finishing detail to the coiled design. Press the stamps into the balls of clay that were added to fill in spaces.

17

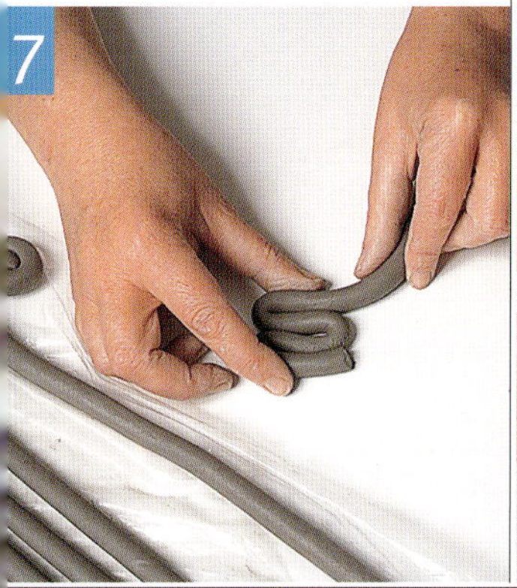

18

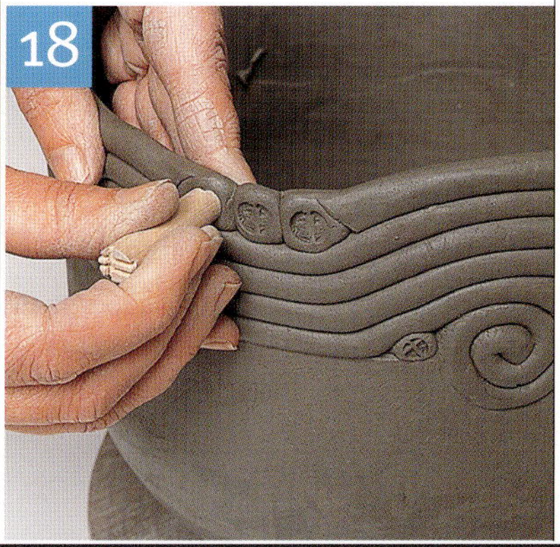

The finished bowl has been Raku-fired after coating in a high-alkaline glaze with the addition of tin and copper oxides. The Raku firing has been combined with post-firing reduction, a process whereby a still-hot object is placed into a covered container with combustibles, in this case sawdust. The container's oxygen-starved atmosphere generates smoke, which combines with the oxygen in the metals of the clay body and glazes to create dramatic effects and alterations of colour. Here, the post-firing reduction has created a copper lustre effect on some areas of the bowl. This accentuates the coiled decoration on the form but is particularly evident on the inside.

The key to making this dish is to prepare enough coils to complete the patterned section at one time. Plaster moulds dry the clay rapidly, so if you stop to roll more coils in the middle of the project, you will find yourself coiling wet clay next to much drier clay.

Coiled dish

A simple hump mould made in the shape of a shallow dish is a very versatile tool in moulding. It allows you to make bowls and other forms in a great number of shapes.

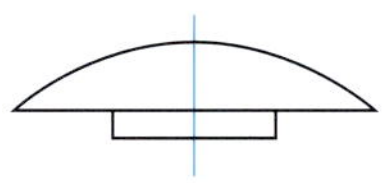

The shape of the dish is shown in plan form to show how the coils are arranged to create the pattern. Although the mould is round, the dish can be made in any shape. In this case, a square shape gives the dish an Asian look, particularly when raised on a foot ring.

This design is worked around the shape of the actual mould to make a round bowl. The ideal frame for holding the form is made of a flattened coil. There is no end to the different patterns you can design within the frame; the one shown here is simply a suggestion.

A variation on the square theme would be to indent each side slightly to create a petal-shaped outline. This would require the outer coil to be added on in eight, rather than four, sections.

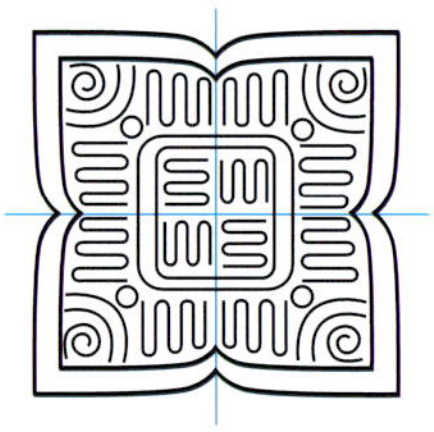

The outline shape of the dish can be as abstract as you want it to be. The only proviso is that the shape fit over the mould. In this design the shape is roughly triangular with two long sides and one short. It is important to position the feet correctly with this type of design to achieve the balance of the form.

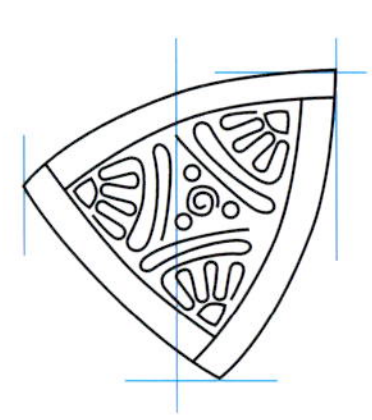

The discrepancy in dryness creates a potential problem, and the dish will almost invariably crack along this joint at a later stage. It is better to roll too many coils, which can always be used to make a smaller version of the dish when the larger one is finished.

A white clay with a wide firing range is used to make this dish to allow for a clear definition of colour in the pattern when it is glazed.

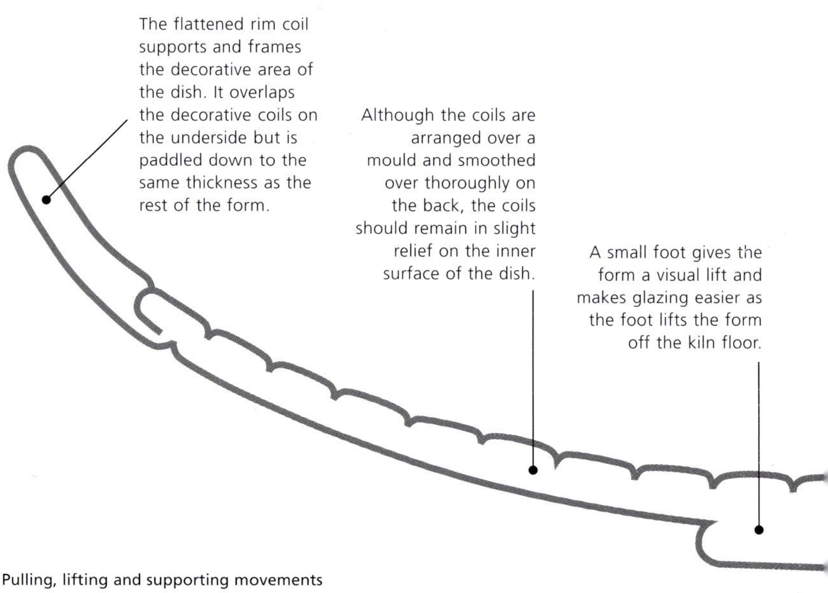

KEY

Pulling, lifting and supporting movements

Pushing, shaping and reinforcing movements

Roll a large batch of rounded coils, using the method described on pages 18–23. The coils should be about 6 mm in diameter and as evenly rolled as possible. Keep them wrapped in thin plastic to prevent them from drying out too quickly, and put them aside. Roll a thick strip of clay into a straight coil and flatten it to about 38 mm wide. The coil must be long enough to cut into four with an additional 25 mm at each end to form the rim of the dish. In this example, each section needs to be about 25 cm long. Beginning in the centre of the plaster mould, start to curl the coil in a circular pattern.

When the central curl is about three coils wide, change the direction of the pattern by coiling back and forth in a snakelike manner, fanning the shape outwards slightly towards the edge of the mould. Hold the coils in position with one hand as the pattern is built up with the other. The coils can be pulled off the mould easily at this stage, because the plaster draws moisture from the clay. Repeat the process three more times, fanning out from the central curl. Ease the coils together so that each fits closely to the one before. At the end of this stage, the pattern will look like a flower, with each petal matching.

On the work surface, use the rounded coils set aside in Step 1 to make a batch of small curls similar to the central one. Keep the curls wrapped in plastic until fitted into the pattern. Starting from the central curl, run another coil around the outside of each petal shape and back to the center. Hold the work in place with one hand as the pattern is built up, because the plaster will be drawing moisture from the clay, causing the coils to shrink away from the mould. Position the curls in the spaces between the petals and line them up in the same direction if you want symmetry in the design (see Step 4).

Tips for success

- Place everything you need to complete the dish within easy reach. Prepare all coils in advance – make too many rather than too few, and all the same size.
- Work as quickly as possible to position the coils decoratively without compromising the design.
- Make an even-numbered selection of shapes on the work surface, ready to place them in the design, and keep them wrapped in thin plastic until needed.
- Build similar dishes on a smaller scale to perfect the technique before committing yourself to making a large dish.

Build up the pattern by filling in the spaces with more curls and coils outlining the petal shape. Any area too small for a curl can be filled in with small balls of clay. Try to fit the balls in such way as to create an even pattern. The design is now developing an increasingly square shape. The dish should be built to within 25 mm of the mould's edge. The margin is needed for the rim. Complete the pattern by running a coil around each corner curl to contain the design and fully square off the shape, filling any gaps with more small balls, if necessary. The entire process to this point should not take more than 15 minutes.

The fact that the plaster drew moisture from the clay on the contact surface is now an advantage because the pattern will be less distorted when the coils are blended together on the outside, where they are still fairly moist and pliable. Holding the coils firmly in place over the mould, further square off the shape, using a wooden batten or roller guide. Gently push the coils into line, working around each side several times. The corners will remain slightly rounded but the general shape should look evenly square. The action of pushing the coils with the batten compacts them slightly, making the next stage much easier.

With one hand holding the dish firmly in place, start to blend the coils together, using a finger or thumb. Work from the outer edges towards the centre to prevent the coils from being dragged apart. Blend a line from each corner to the centre first, then from each side to the centre, before blending the spaces in between. This helps to hold all the coils together as each area is blended. Blending the coils can be tricky, so take the time to do it well. Now that all of the decorative coils are in place, there is less need for speed.

4

5

6

The arrangement of coils in this design develops in four sections separated by a coil cross. Coil curls are positioned centrally in each section to form a square, and the pattern fans out from each curl. Small balls of clay fill the spaces between the coils, and a flattened coil frames the design.

This design is arranged in simple lines contained inside a thin, square coil frame. From this point the frame is divided vertically into three panels. The centre panel has been filled with coil curls, aligned in opposite directions on either side of three central balls of clay. Each of the side panels is filled with a snakelike coil, and the whole design is framed by a flattened coil.

In this design, the pattern is again framed by a thin square coil. The arrangement develops with four coils fanned in from each corner towards the centre of the square. A small cross divides the space between the fans, which are then filled with coil curls and small balls of clay. The whole design is framed by a flattened coil.

When the coils are thoroughly blended, the surface will be fairly lumpy and uneven. Holding the dish firmly in place, smooth the surface with a metal kidney. Do not remove too much clay, but blend it back to an even thickness, holding the kidney on its side to work across the surface. The action of smoothing the surface compacts the coils more on the underside, so take great care not to apply too much pressure, and complete the process using as few strokes as possible to avoid losing pattern definition. Go over the surface lightly with a rubber kidney to finish.

From the flattened coils previously prepared, measure four lengths to fit along each side edge of the dish, allowing about 25 mm of overlap at either end. Before fixing the coils onto the rim, score and slip a 13-mm band around the edge of the dish, using the toothbrush and a little water. Fit the first coil onto one side, so that half the width is on the dish and the other half overhangs it, with the extra 25 mm protruding from each corner. Fit the other three rim coils into place in the same way, overlapping the spare length at each corner to complete the square.

When each rim section is fitted onto the dish and you are happy with the shape, paddle the strips with a wooden tool to make the two surfaces adhere securely. If the corner sections overlap the mould a little, support the underside of the rim with one hand while paddling the upper surface. Paddling the coils into place not only ensures a good joint but smooths out the coils, so that the surface needs no additional refinement.

The edges of the dish are loosely square to lend visual freedom to an otherwise controlled design.

The coils were thoroughly blended on the underside of the dish but remain clearly defined on the inside.

Each corner was finished with a decorative stamp detail to enhance the surface quality and complete the design.

The flattened coil is fixed into place so that half the width sits on the main body of the dish while the other half forms a frame for the inner design.

Apart from adding the feet, the dish is now essentially complete, but some small finishing details can help to lift the design, especially on the underside, which is fairly plain. A small clay stamp is used to impress a detail into each corner of the dish. Its pattern reflects the design of the decorative coils on the other side. Stamps like this are easily made from leftover scraps of clay into which patterns can be drawn or impressed from items such as buttons. The stamps are bisque fired before use.

10

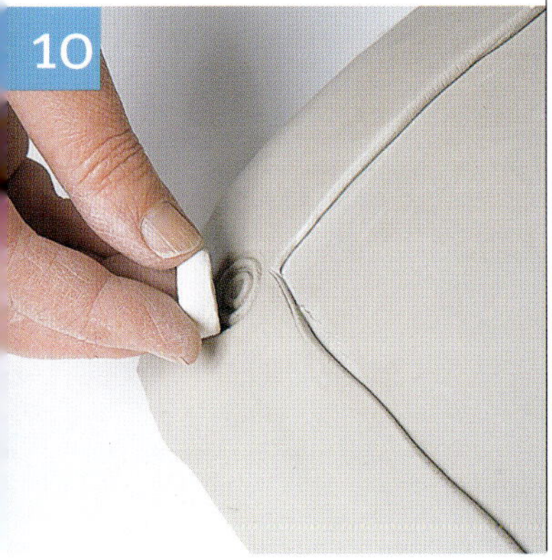

To make the feet, curl four more coils into the same shape as the pattern in the dish. Measure and mark a position for each foot squarely in the centre on the underside of the dish. Allow a finger space between each foot. Score and slip the marked points and the underside of each curl, then fit them into position. Match the alignment of the curled feet to the design in the dish. Such details demonstrate that although the finished dish has an unstructured look, the design was well thought out.

11

To be sure that the feet adhere well to the underside of the dish and that it will be level when turned off the mould, sit a wooden bat on the feet and, holding it carefully with one hand, give it a little thump in the center. This compresses the feet, so don't thump too hard. The feet provide a visual lift that enhances the rest of the form.

12

Carefully lift the dish off the mould and turn it over onto a bat. The plaster of the mould should have dried the clay out sufficiently to handle the dish, but if it feels too floppy to remove, dry it off a little first, using a hairdryer. Rotate the mould on a turntable when using the hairdryer to allow the clay to dry evenly. Remove the dish as soon as it can be handled; if it is left too long, the plaster will draw too much moisture from the clay and the dish will crack as it shrinks away from the surface.

13

The feet on the underside of this dish have been formed in a conically shaped plaster mould. When positioning feet like this, it is important to make an accurate measurement of the central position from the rim of the dish.

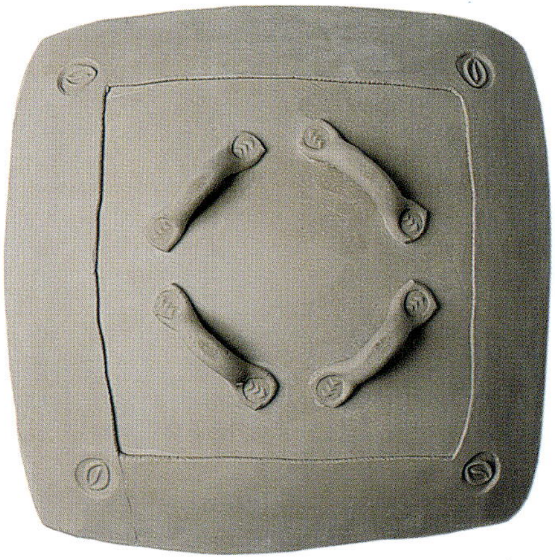

These feet have been made from coils left over from the patterned side of the dish. They have been positioned on the underside at an angle to the square of the dish. It is important to secure feet like this firmly to allow them to support the full weight of the dish when it is turned right side up.

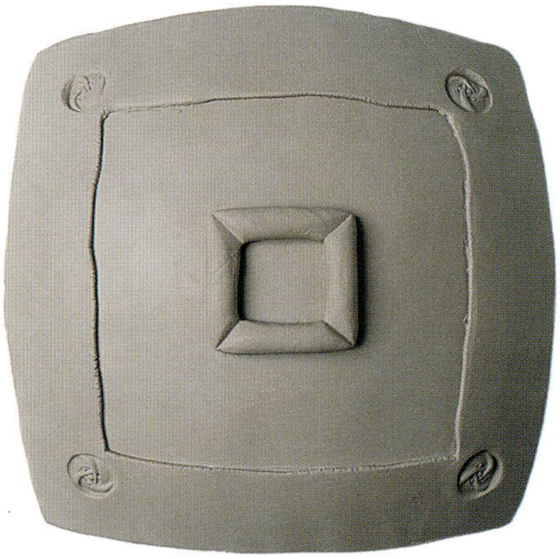

Here, a coil has been cut into four sections to make a simple square foot that echoes the shape of the dish. As a finishing detail and a reinforcement to the corners, a groove has been made along each of the foot's joints using a wooden tool.

After the dish is lifted from the mould, carefully stamp the same impression as before, at a point just above the one on the underside. The corner must be carefully supported underneath when stamping the top because the clay will have dried out considerably. Do not press the stamp in too hard, which could crack the rim. The dish is now ready to be finished in your preferred style, but it is best simply glazed, using oxides to define the pattern.

4

The dish was Raku-fired after the application of a copper lustre glaze. The rim of the dish was unglazed and blackened in the post-firing reduction period (see page 33) of the Raku process to create a contrast to the decorative coils. This firing process complements the style of the dish because the lustre effect reflects light, which in turn accentuates the pattern of the coils. The stamped areas in the corners of the dish were also glazed to form extra detail and complete the design.

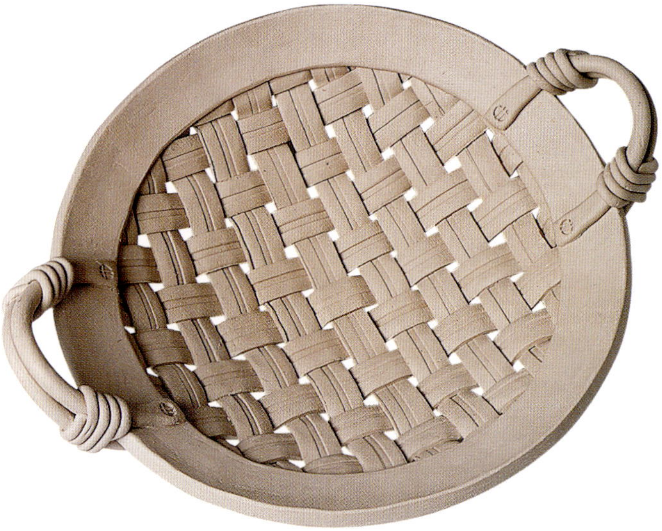

This project requires some dexterity, but the key to success lies in the preparation. Everything needed to complete the basket must be ready and within reach before beginning.

Coiled basket

The technique uses flattened coils with detail to add interest, and the preparation of these coils takes more time than the construction of the form. It is essential to prepare sufficient coils to complete the woven part of the form without stopping to make more. A white clay with a wide firing range is used to provide plenty of choices for the decoration of the form.

This shape is perhaps the easiest to make using the technique demonstrated here, as it is open and shallow and requires little manipulation of the clay. The bowl uses the simple hump mould used in many of the projects in this book.

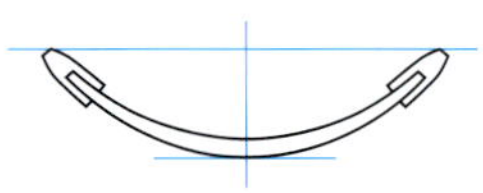

The same technique can be used around a cylinder template to make a container in the same style. You would need to add a slabbed base, but the rim could be finished off in the same way as for the basket. The woven part of the form should be made on a flat surface first, then wrapped around the template. The joint can be covered by a decorative coil.

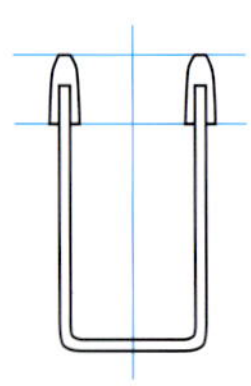

Instead of making the basket over a hump mould, the same technique can be used inside a press mould, allowing the form to be built up even further. The building process would be exactly the same.

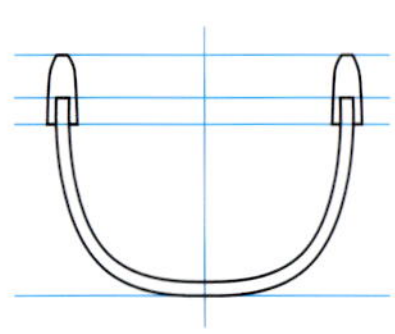

Long, shallow forms can be made using other containers as moulds, but these must be lined with material that allows for easy release when the form is complete. Thin plastic is always useful for this, and the kitchen is a good source of vessels to use as moulds.

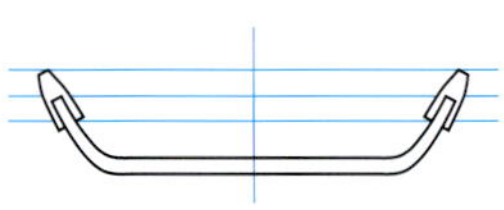

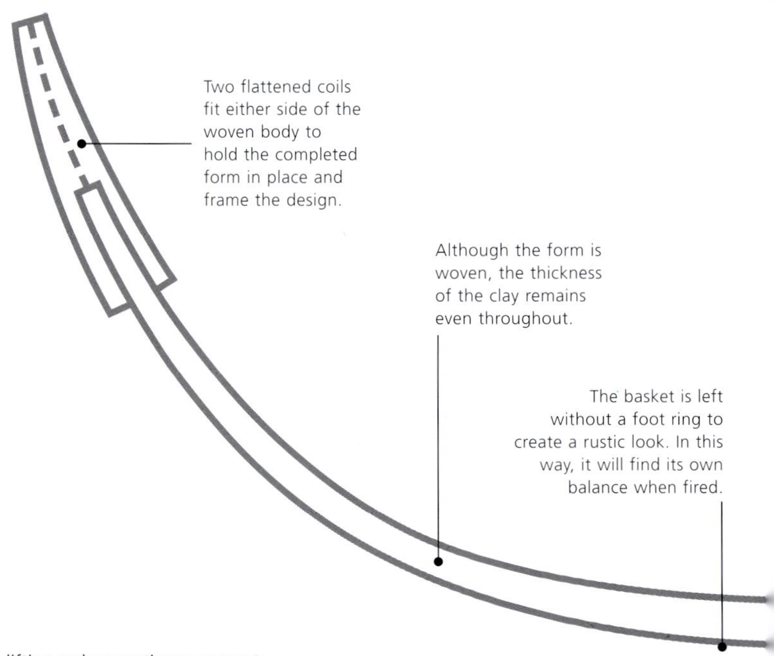

KEY

Pulling, lifting and supporting movements (green arrow)

Pushing, shaping and reinforcing movements (red arrow)

Roll at least 24 round coils, 13 mm in diameter and about 45 cm long. Flatten each coil using the technique described on page 24. Place a roller guide along the length of each coil and roll it over the surface, applying more pressure at the sides than in the middle. This should round the coil off, making it slightly dome-shaped. Cut away the clay that is squeezed out at each side of the coil, using the roller guide to cut a straight line. Each coil will eventually be uniform and the same width as the roller guide – about 20 mm.

Position the roller guide sideways along the length of one coil and apply a little pressure to create an indented channel. The grain of the wood in the roller guide will probably leave an impression in the channel, but this enhances the finish of the coil. Complete all of the coils in the same way. Line the coils up on thin plastic sheets and cover them over to prevent them from drying too much before use – they must remain very pliable.

Roll two thicker round coils, about 38 mm in diameter and long enough to fit around the circumference of the mould. Working on a sheet of plastic, flatten the first of the coils straight, then turn it over, and holding one end in your hand, flatten it further into a wide circle with the other hand. Leave the coil on the sheet of plastic and cover it over with more plastic to prevent drying. Flatten the second coil in the same way, and cover it until ready for use.

Place the first coil across the centre of the mould, with the channel side facing down. Position the second coil over the first to form a cross. Position the third coil next to the first and over the second. Each coil should be positioned as close to the previous one as possible. The basket could be built in a more open weave, but this would make it difficult to handle at a later stage and much more vulnerable, especially for the beginner.

1

2

3

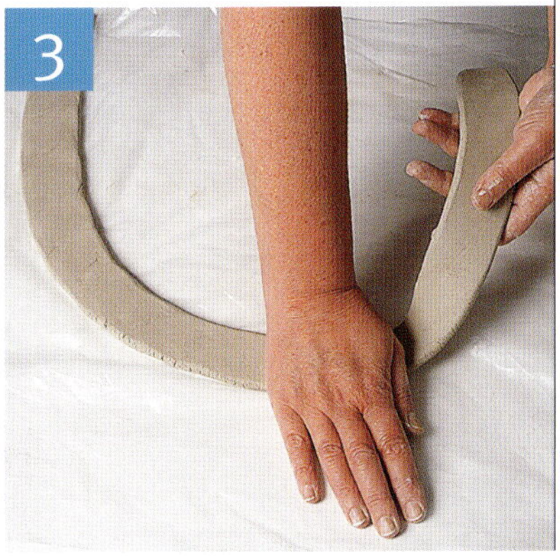

4

Tips for success

- Use soft clay incorporating a medium-sized grog, such as molochite, to give the clay strength.
- Practise weaving on a flat surface before attempting the project, to become familiar with the process.
- Have some help available to lift the basket off the mould – another pair of hands is useful for this tricky manoeuver. Weave over simple moulds to begin with, to make the process as easy as possible. You can attempt more advanced shapes as you grow in experience.

Continue to weave the coils, working squarely from the centre. Position the fourth coil over the third and under the first. The fifth coil goes under the fourth and over the second, and so on. Each coil should overhang the mould by several inches because some of the length is taken up in the weaving. Lift the coils carefully, supporting each coil securely and allowing them to fall back into place gently. As the basket starts to build up, use one hand to keep the work in place as the other settles the coils together. The plaster will dry the clay as soon as each coil is in place, so weave the coils as quickly as possible to avert cracks.

It becomes more difficult to weave the basket when several coils are in place and the shape develops. As more coils are woven over the hump of the mould, it is necessary to turn each individual one back on itself to enable another to be fitted underneath. It is especially important not to stretch the coils now, because they will have begun to dry and will be even more likely to crack. Make sure that each successive coil is neatly aligned to the last, running in the same direction. As the basket develops, ease the coils gently into place, using both hands. Work over the surface, applying even pressure using the palms of your hands.

The final coils are the most difficult to place because they are short and may overlap the edge of the mould. The angle of work is also awkward. Ignore the overlap for the moment – it is more important to weave the basket completely to the edge of the mould and all the way around. You will need to ease these coils together more carefully because they can easily fall away on the downward slope of the mould, but again, gentle, even pressure should be enough to secure them.

When all of the coils are woven into place, cut away the overhang with an old pair of scissors or a potter's knife. Check that the scissors are level with the underside of the mould as the clay is cut. Again, this is easier to do while rotating the work on a turntable. If using a knife, cut the coils in towards the mould to avoid dragging the clay off or distorting the weave.

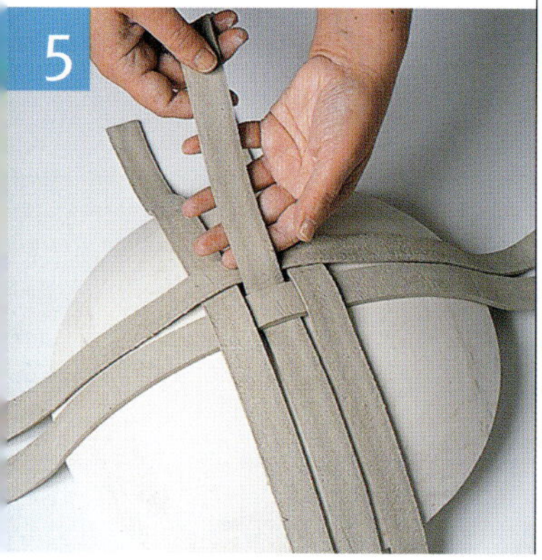

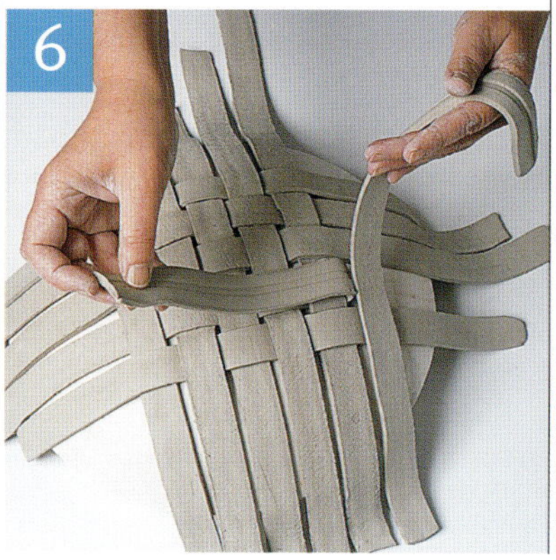

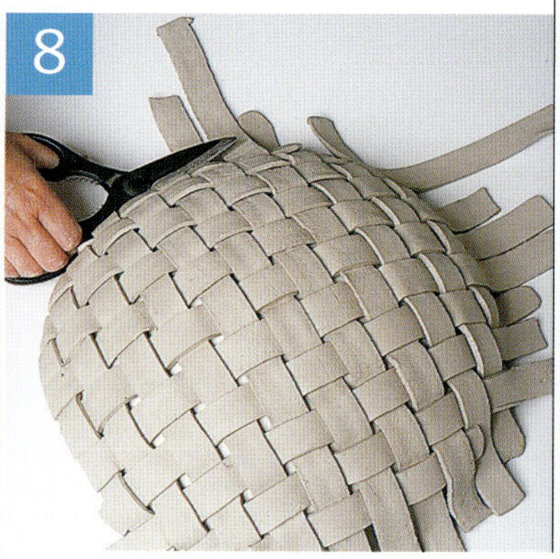

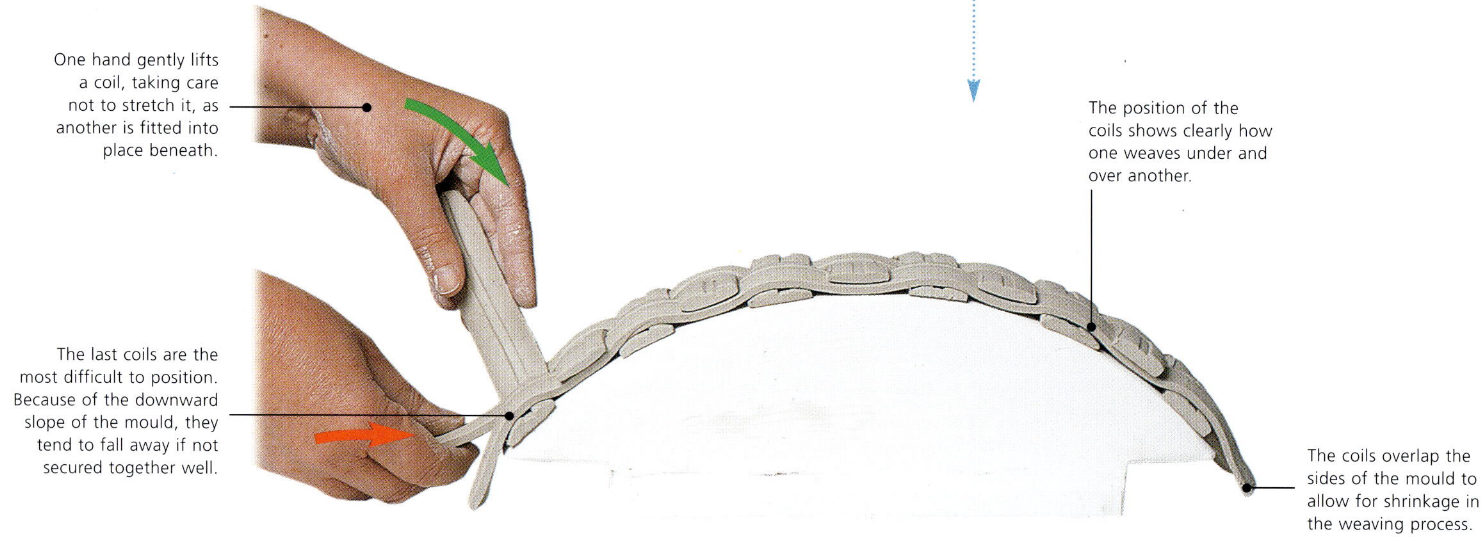

When the rim of the basket is cut level, score and slip a 13-mm margin all the way round it, using a toothbrush and a little water. Score the surface well but try not to distort the woven coils. This is a little tricky, but there is less emphasis on the timing now that all the weaving is complete. Have one of the round, flattened coils ready to fix in place when the rim is ready.

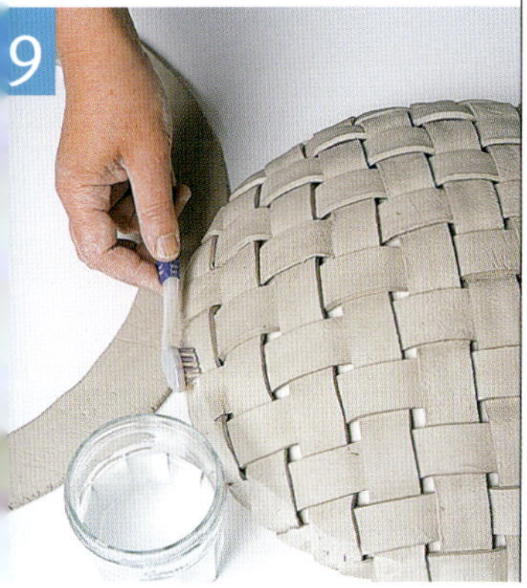

Position the rim coil around the scored edge so that half sits on the basket and the other half overhangs the mould. Overlap the coil where it meets back at the beginning and carefully cut through both sections of coil on the diagonal. Using a little slip, join the cut ends together and blend the clay to make a continuous ring. Support the coil protruding over the edge of the mould as the ends are fixed together. Smooth over the joint with a metal kidney to finish.

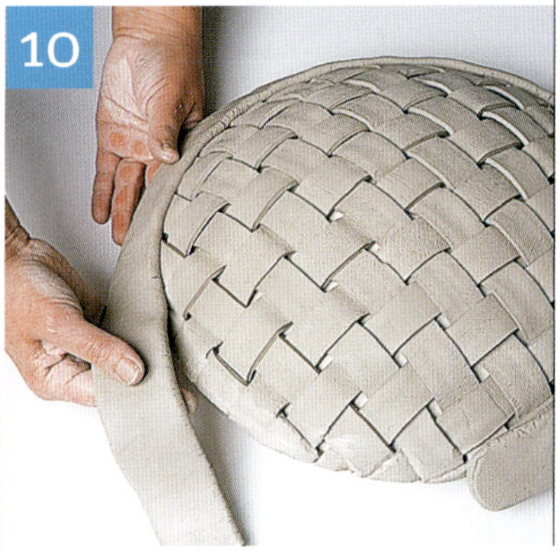

Ease the coil into place using a wooden paddle. Don't apply too much pressure – the aim is to secure the coil to the basket without distorting the shape. Work around the rim evenly, supporting the overhang from underneath with one hand at all times. The paddling action should help to dry the clay of the rim to the same stage as the clay of the basket, but if there is a great difference, dry the rim with a hairdryer until the two sections are the same and the basket is sturdy enough to be lifted off the mould safely. Rotate the work on a turntable to provide even drying.

Before lifting the basket off the mould, find a shallow bowl roughly the same shape as the basket, and pad it with thin plastic or bubblewrap. Check that the basket is dry enough to hold its shape, then carefully lift it off the mould, taking care not to distort the woven part, and turn it over to sit in the bowl. If the form seems to relax a little when sitting in the bowl, dry it further with the hairdryer until the shape is stable.

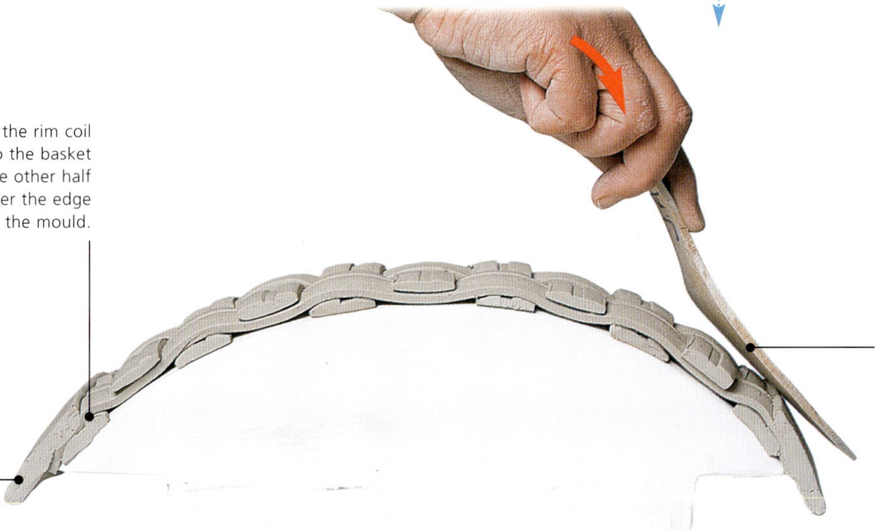

Score and slip a 13-mm margin around the inner rim of the basket, along with the extended section of flattened coil. Position the second flattened coil over the first. The basket is now sandwiched halfway between the two coils. Finish the coil by overlapping the ends, then cutting through both sections before joining them back together, using a little slip. Smooth the joint over with a metal kidney. Using both hands, gently pinch the two coils together with the basket in between. Work around the rim slowly, making sure that any trapped air is squeezed out. Scrape the inner rim smooth, using a metal kidney.

Dry the coil of the inner rim to the same level as the rest of the basket. Using a rasp blade, shave the outer edge of the rim until it measures equally all the way around. Work on a turntable to maintain smooth, even strokes, but don't remove too much. Hold the blade at a slightly tilted angle so that the underside of the rim is slightly wider than the inner side when finished. After levelling, run the flat side of a metal kidney around the edge to compact and smooth the clay. This will accentuate the angle and sharpen the edge. To soften the edge slightly, run a finger or a rubber kidney along the rim.

Roll four small coils of about 6-mm diameter. They need to be long enough to fit over the rim coil, extend around and out from the rim 38 mm, and back over the rim coil to form a semicircle. Measure and cut one coil to fit the basket, then measure the other three against the first. Position the coils in a semicircle on the work surface and dry them with a hairdryer until they can just hold their shape. Mark the position of the first coil by holding it against the inner side of the rim and scoring a line along each side. Score and slip the marked positions and the corresponding section at each end of the coil.

Fix the coil into position. Mark the position of the second coil on the underside of the basket to correspond exactly with the upper one. Score and slip the second position, the end sections of each coil, and a tiny area in the centre of both coils where they will meet in the middle. Fit the second coil into place under the first. Join the coils in the middle. Use a decorative stamp to impress a little pattern into each end of the coil where it was fixed onto the rim. Do the same on the underside. Dry the handle a little to prevent it from relaxing out of shape. Measure the position for the second handle on the opposite side of the basket, and repeat the process with the other two coils.

13

14

15

16

The techniques for weaving this example are the same as for the basket on page 45, but the coils are rolled much thinner before flattening and are positioned wider apart to produce a more open weave. A design like this must be quite firm and well supported when it is lifted off the mould to prevent distortion and cracking of the weave.

This woven design incorporates thin and thick flattened coils, positioned alternately and as close together as possible. The thicker coils have a central groove stamped into them for extra detail.

Roll four soft, round coils half as thin as the handle coils, making them as even as possible. Fit one end of a coil in the space between the inner and outer coils of the handle at the edge of the rim. Wrap the coil around the handle four times to create the impression that it is binding the handle together. Cut the coil so that the end fits back into the gap in the handle and secure it with a little slip. Repeat the process with the remaining three coils. Allow the basket to dry out slowly, wrapped in loose plastic and supported throughout in the padded dish. A slow bisque firing will help to prevent the clay from shrinking too quickly, but otherwise the basket can be finished off in your own style.

7

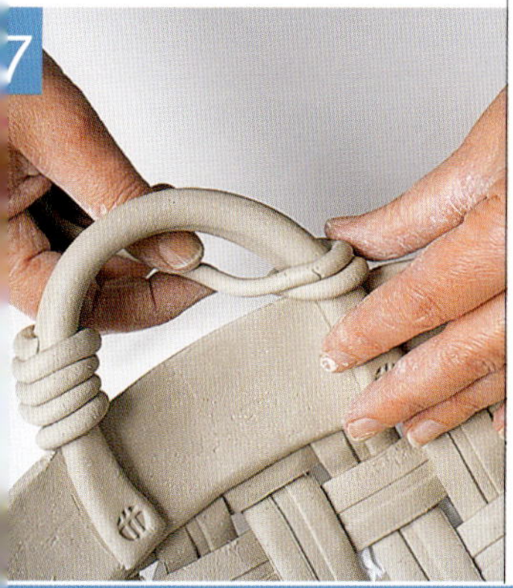

The basket has been finished with the brushing of a low-fire, semi-matte glaze that looks like wood or bamboo when fired. Because of the weave, there is a high likelihood that the shape will sag if fired at a high temperature, especially as it would need to be supported on a stilt if glazed all over. Brush-on glazes that fire to low temperatures are readily available in a vast range of colours and finishes from most pottery suppliers. Be aware, however, that not all of these are safe for use with food, so choose carefully if the form is to be used for that purpose.

Technically, this project is more slabbed than coiled, but it demonstrates another way of using coils – this time purely as surface decoration.

Coiled surface decoration

This simple, two-sided vessel shape provides the perfect surface for decoration. The shape is uncomplicated and does not require great manipulation of the clay slab once the decoration has been applied, an important factor to consider when deciding on a shape for the pot.

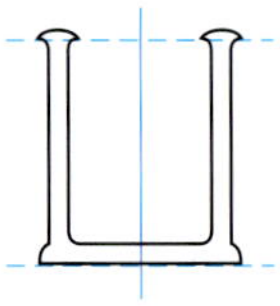

As an alternative to the two-sided vessel, the coils can be added to a single slab of clay, then wrapped around a template to make a cylinder. Consideration must be given to the position of the decorative coils to avoid disturbing them when the ends of the slab are joined.

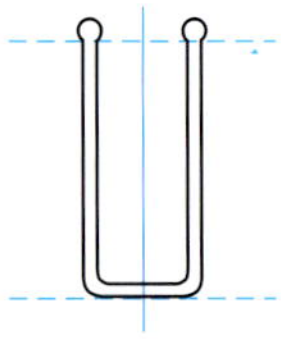

Other simple two-sided vessels can be made using the same technique of draping the slabs over a template to give them shape. Here, the slabs have been cut to give the outline of a simple vase form. The base has a slight lift at either side so that the form sits only on a small base section.

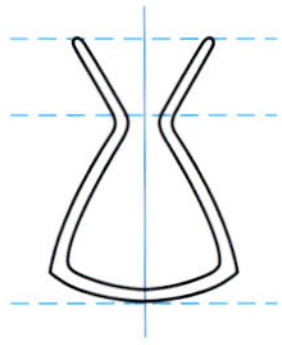

The technique lends itself well to any kind of slab work but looks particularly good as decoration on the inside of a bowl. A relatively shallow mould will be needed to allow you to position the slab on the mould in one piece. Otherwise, great planning is required to position more than one piece and to blend them together without disturbing the surface decoration.

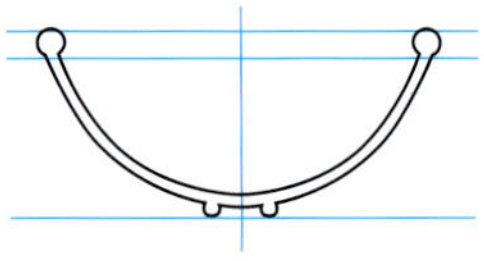

Two contrasting coloured clays show off the decoration to best advantage. The Keuper red clay has a higher firing range than traditional red earthenware and will fire to stoneware temperatures, making it more compatible with the porcelain coils used for the decoration. A small, hand-held extruder is used for the project, but this is not essential. You could achieve a similar effect with tiny, thinly rolled coils, but this would be more difficult and would add significantly to your work time.

KEY

- Pulling, lifting and supporting movements
- Pushing, shaping and reinforcing movements

Fit a multiholed die into the extruder, then roll a small coil of porcelain just a little thinner than the barrel. Drop the porcelain into the barrel as far as it will go and pinch off the surplus at the end. It is always better to fit single long lengths of coil into the barrel to allow for a continuous extrusion. If clay is added in smaller pieces, it will break at the points where additions were made, spoiling the flow of the coil. Fit the plunger into the end of the barrel and the extruder is ready for use.

On a clean sheet of plastic, using two 6-mm thick roller guides, roll and cut out two A4 slabs of clay, following the slabbing method described on pages 92–93. A third slab is needed for the base. Cover the two slabs in plastic and set aside. Then, using a brush and water, paint a 10-cm wide panel along the central length of the remaining slab.

Start to push the clay through the extruder so that the coils fall onto the slab from the top down the left side of the wet area. It may be necessary to use both hands to do this – one to hold the barrel and guide the flow while the other pushes the clay through. Try not to extrude the clay so quickly that it runs out before reaching the bottom of the slab. This is where practising the technique in advance pays off, because pushing the clay through the extruder can be hard work.

When all of the clay is through the extruder and covers the length of the slab, sit back briefly and assess the appearance of the coils on the surface. It does not matter that they look untidy, but if you are dissatisfied with the arrangement, use a wooden tool to ease the coils gently apart in places. Do not rearrange too much because the red clay will contaminate the porcelain and make the coils look very messy. When you are happy with the first coils, repeat the process along the right length of the wet panel. The process should leave the central area of the panel exposed for some different patterning.

1

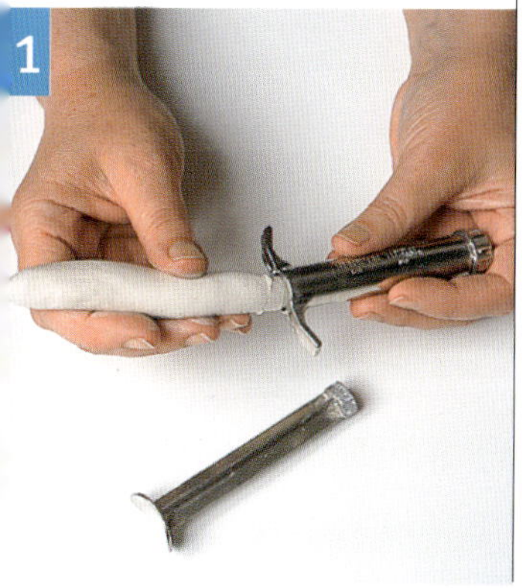

2

3

4

These small extruders (also known as clay guns) can be purchased from most clay suppliers.

Familiarise yourself with the different dies by experimenting with various combinations on test tiles before launching into the project. You'll find this to be a lot of fun!

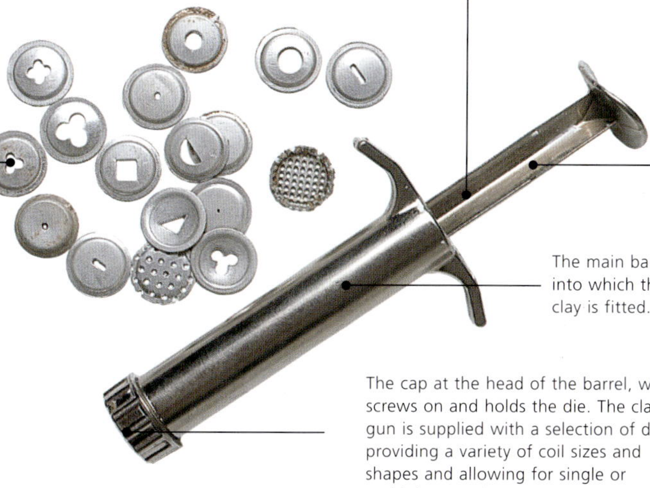

The plunger, which pushes the clay through the barrel.

The main barrel, into which the clay is fitted.

The cap at the head of the barrel, which screws on and holds the die. The clay gun is supplied with a selection of dies, providing a variety of coil sizes and shapes and allowing for single or multiple extrusions.

Reload the extruder with a single, medium-sized die and another coil of porcelain. Extrude a coil about 15 cm long, and start to add some order to the panel by curling the coils into place in the central space to form a random pattern. Keep the curls of clay fairly open, and position them to look as if they extended from the coils at the side.

5

When the central area of the panel is loosely arranged with curls, fill in some of the gaps with tiny balls of clay. These can be positioned along the outer area of the random coils and in between the central curls. The balls of clay look better in small groups, but don't place them too closely together or too near the coils, for reasons that will become clear later. It is not necessary to fill all of the gaps – less is definitely better than more!

6

The slab should still be on the sheet of plastic on which it was rolled. Reposition the roller guides on either side of the slab. Cover the slab with a piece of clean fabric, such as a length of old cotton sheet, which is slightly larger than the slab itself. Gently but firmly roll the porcelain coils onto the surface of the slab, beginning in the middle and rolling from end to end until the rolling pin glides easily over the guides. Lift one corner of the fabric to see if the slab is sufficiently rolled. If it needs more rolling, replace the fabric very carefully before continuing. The red clay stains the fabric, which will in turn stain the porcelain if replaced incorrectly.

7

Remove the fabric from the slab with extreme care. It will now be clear why some gaps were left between the coils. Many of the coils merged when rolled, leaving only some clearly defined areas. Add detail by stamping a few designs into the pattern. The process of adding the porcelain coils and rolling them onto the surface stretches the slab, so it must now be trimmed to size. Place an A4 sheet of paper over the slab and position a roller guide along each edge before cutting away the excess. Only the length of the slab should have extended, but check the size of the entire slab to be sure. With the finished slab as a guide, repeat the pattern on the second slab.

8

Tips for success

- Wash your hands more often than usual between stages to minimise the danger of contamination between the red and white clays.
- Keep the tools clean, wiping away clay residue immediately after use.
- Clean out the barrel of the extruder and all the dies used immediately after completion of the pot – dry clay is harder to remove and will frustrate the start of a new project.
- Wipe down the plastic sheets used for rolling the clay before using them with a different clay.

When both slabs are decorated, drape each one over a ridge tile, with the pattern side facing up. Leave the slabs to dry out on the tiles to the leather-hard stage. Each slab should be able to stand and hold its shape before the two are joined. When the slabs are dry enough to handle, turn each over to rest in one hand, then use a toothbrush and water to score and slip each long edge, including a 6-mm strip along the inside wall. Stand the slabs together on a wooden bat and join the sides so that one edge butts onto the inside wall of the other slab. The other side will butt join in the opposite direction.

Holding the slabs securely with one hand, pinch the edges together firmly between the fingers and thumb of the other hand. Work evenly along the length of the joint, making sure that the fit is neatly aligned. When the slabs are securely fixed, neaten the joints by running a metal kidney along the edge to remove any slip that oozed out. Holding the slabs firmly, work the kidney from the base up several times. This also strengthens the joint by helping to compact the clay and force out any trapped air, reducing the risk of the pot's cracking in the firing. Reinforce the inside of the joints with two soft coils of clay, using the method described in the section on slabbing (page 86).

Transfer the third slab of clay to a wooden bat and position the slabbed sections on top of it. Cut out the base shape, allowing 6 mm extra all the way round. Be as economical as possible when positioning the upper part of the form on the base slab. Any leftover pieces of clay could be used to make a small item, such as a box or a bud vase. Remember to wrap any useful leftovers in plastic to prevent them from drying.

Score and slip a 13-mm strip around the edge of the base slab. Turn the joined slab body over and score and slip the bottom edge. Turn the body back over and fit into place on the base slab, remembering that there should be 6 mm to spare all the way round. The body should stick immediately to the base, but to make the joint sound, lift the pot with the base attached and tap it gently on the bat a couple of times. Don't overdo this because it could distort the form.

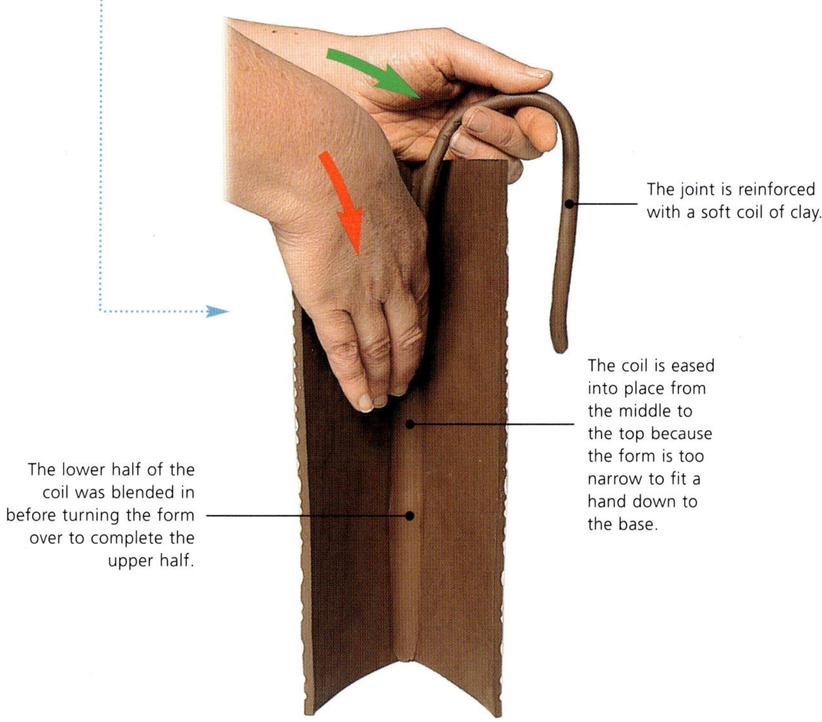

It is now almost impossible to reach down into the bottom of the form, so it must be reinforced on the outside. Roll out two small, soft, even coils of clay. Using a finger or thumb, ease the coils along the extended base so that they blend into the body of the pot. The coils serve a dual purpose, reinforcing the base joint and providing an additional decorative finish. It is important to take the time to make the coils look like an integral part of the form. Blend them in carefully, but don't overwork them to avoid contaminating the porcelain panel in the centre.

Using a rasp blade, shave a shallow semicircle from both sides of the rim to correspond with the patterned panel. This will be about 10 cm wide with 5 cm to spare on either side. Use a paper template cut from the short side of an A4 sheet to make the circle the same on both sides. Position the template against the rim and score the shape into the wall before cutting. Hold the pot firmly on the bat as the semicircles are cut out, and take care not to chip off the porcelain coils, because the surface can be delicate at this stage.

Roll a long, round coil about 13 mm in diameter to make the rim. Flatten the coil using the method described on page 24. Position a roller guide over the length of the coil and roll it gently but firmly forwards and backwards, applying more pressure at the edges and less in the centre. This will round off the coil, making it slightly domed. Cut away the squeezed-out clay on the sides of the coil, using the roller guide to cut a straight line.

Again using the edge of the roller guide, press a ridge into the coil, positioned just left of the centre. Press another ridge to the right of the centre to create a decorative raised central ridge. Cut the coil in half and measure one section along one side of the rim, allowing about 25 mm overlap at each end. Cut the coil to size, then remove it from the rim and cut the second half to match. Place the coil strips side by side on the work surface and cut a triangular section from each end. Together, the triangles of clay will resemble a cutaway V-shape. When the coils are attached to the rim, the cut sections join to form a point.

13

14

15

16

The coil is used to add decorative detail but also to reinforce the base joint, which cannot be reached on the inside.

A soft coil is positioned around the form on the extended base and blended into place with a finger.

The body is fixed to the base slab, allowing 6 mm extra all the way round.

Score and slip the rim of the pot, the underside of the rim coil, and each angled end. Position one section on the rim, checking that the coil is centrally aligned. Ease the coil into place gently but firmly, trying not to squash the central ridge. Fix the second section of coil onto the rim in the same way, easing the cut ends together, so that the ridges line up accurately. Using a thin, soft coil of clay, reinforce the underside of the rim on the inside of the pot. This is a little difficult and can only be done with one hand, but try to hold the rim in place with the thumb as the coil is eased into place with a finger.

A transparent glaze was used to seal the inside of the form and make it waterproof. The outside was washed with manganese dioxide, which was then sponged back to reveal the porcelain coil detail. A small amount of gold leaf was applied to certain textured areas to visually lift and complete the appearance of the form. An alternative to the oxide wash would be to simply glaze the whole form in transparent glaze, which would define clearly the contrast between the red clay and the porcelain. Precious metal lustre could then be applied to some of the textures to complete the form.

The inspiration for this garden sculpture comes from images of ancient standing stones and monoliths.

Garden sculpture

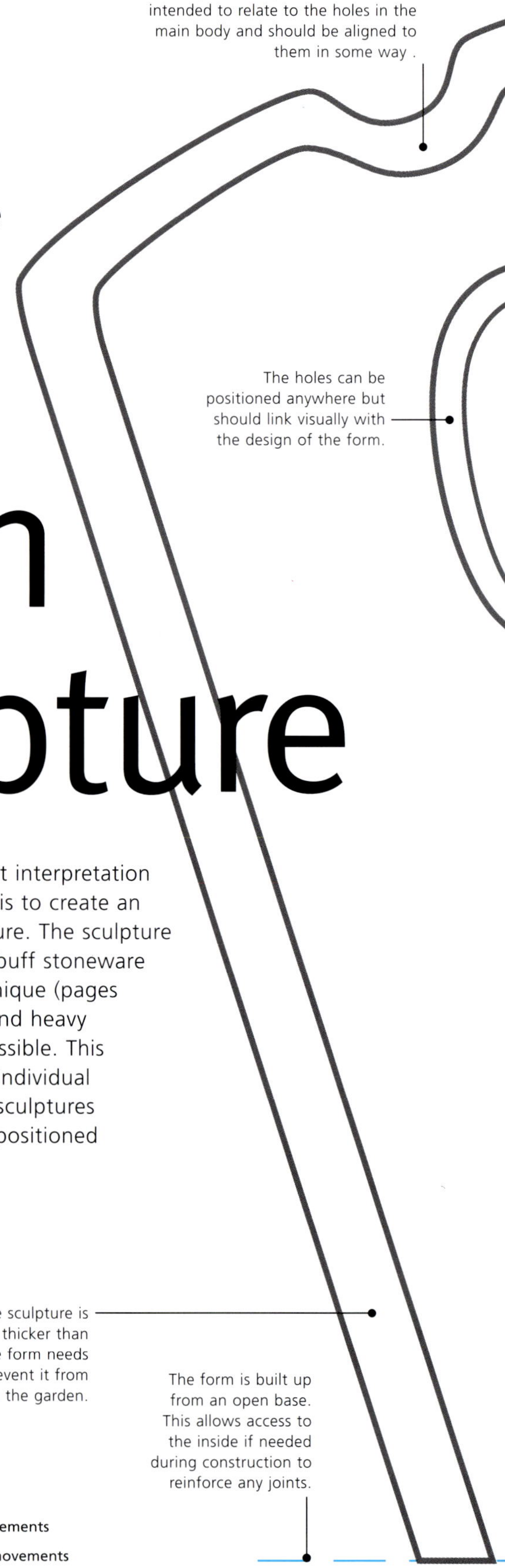

This is a scaled down and abstract interpretation of prehistoric monoliths; the aim is to create an elegant and timeless garden feature. The sculpture is made from a heavily grogged, buff stoneware clay using the flattened coil technique (pages 24–27). The coils must be thick and heavy to make the form as sturdy as possible. This sculpture can be displayed as an individual statement, or a small number of sculptures of varying sizes can be built and positioned together as shown on page 57.

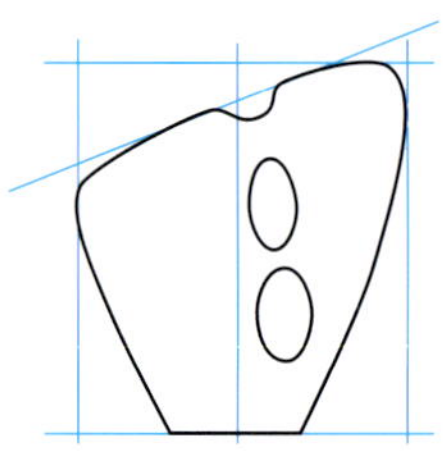

This shape is inspired by ancient standing stones or monoliths, but it is greatly reduced in size to fit into a small garden. The basic form flares out from a wide base, and the holes create the illusion of windows into a different world.

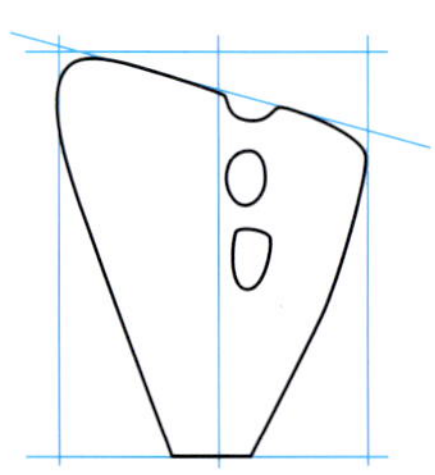

Narrowing the base and building the form higher alters the shape's visual balance while retaining its likeness to the first sculpture. These sculptures are often effective in groups of odd numbers.

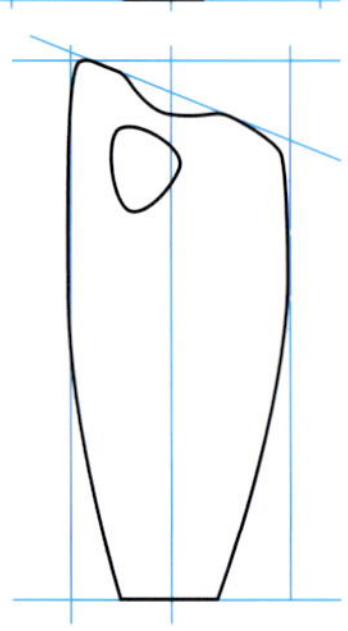

Another variation on the basic shape is to make the form almost straight on both sides, with the addition of just one strategic hole to relate it to the other sculptures in the group.

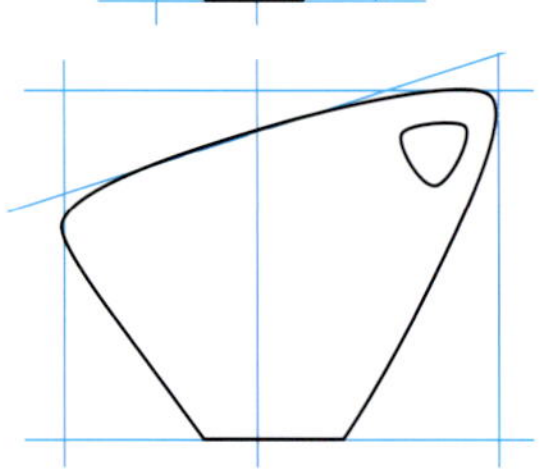

A third variation on the basic shape is to make the form much wider at the base and to build in a single hole. All four forms can be built in varying dimensions, with single or multiple holes to suit your taste.

KEY

Pulling, lifting and supporting movements

Pushing, shaping and reinforcing movements

Begin by rolling out a thick coil as described on page 24. It should be 4–5 cm in diameter so that when flattened it is at least 5 cm wide and 13 mm thick. Flatten the coil on a sheet of plastic, as described on page 24. Put the coil to one side and cover it with a sheet of plastic. Roll and flatten at least six more coils in the same way. Start making the base of the sculpture by curving one of the coils into a leaf shape on a wooden bat. The shape should be no more than 20 cm long and 12.5 cm wide, and should have a slight outward flare from the base to the top of the coil.

Once you have formed the basic leaf shape, reinforce the ends with a coil of soft clay. This is important because all the coils will be joined at this position on the sculpture, and it is a point at which the overall shape can be readily maintained. Blend the reinforcing coil in well but don't worry too much about neatening it. The beauty of sculptural work is that it can take a relatively rough finish. This should not compromise the quality of construction, however – remember to support the form on the outside as the reinforcing coil is blended into place.

Do not score and slip the coils when making the sculpture, as the clay should be soft enough to manipulate. This is important because the form is altered at several points during the building; clay that is too hard will make detail very difficult to achieve. With this in mind, lift the second coil in one hand to form a loop, holding each end of the coil between separate fingers. This will divide the coil into two without breaking it. Fit the looped end of the coil onto a pointed end of the leaf, securing it in place with the other hand. Ease the rest of the coil into position to fit the shape.

Cut through each end of the coil diagonally and over the pointed end of the previous coil so the shapes continue naturally when joined together. Be careful to avoid the fingers of your other hand as you cut through each section. Blend the cut ends together well and reinforce the inside of the join with another coil of soft clay. Work back around the coil using the fingers and thumb of one hand to make sure it is well secured onto the first coil.

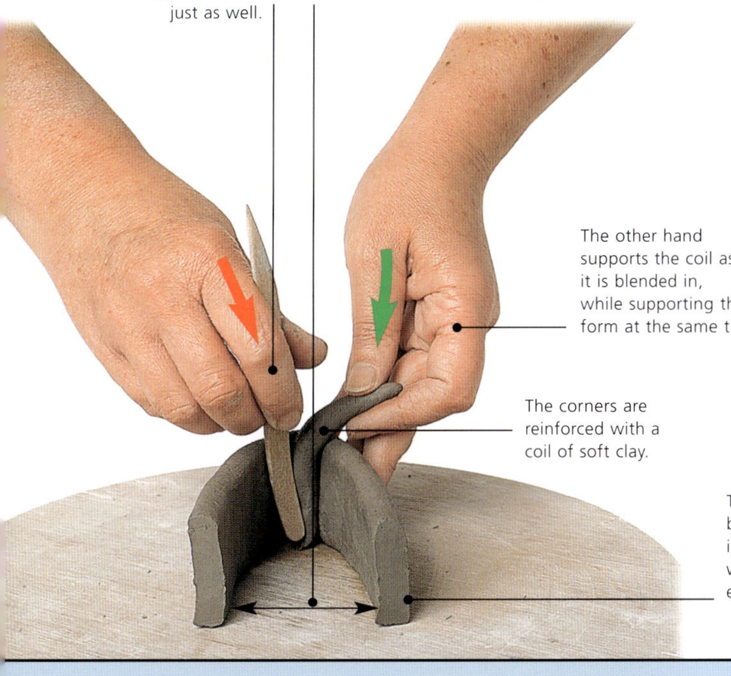

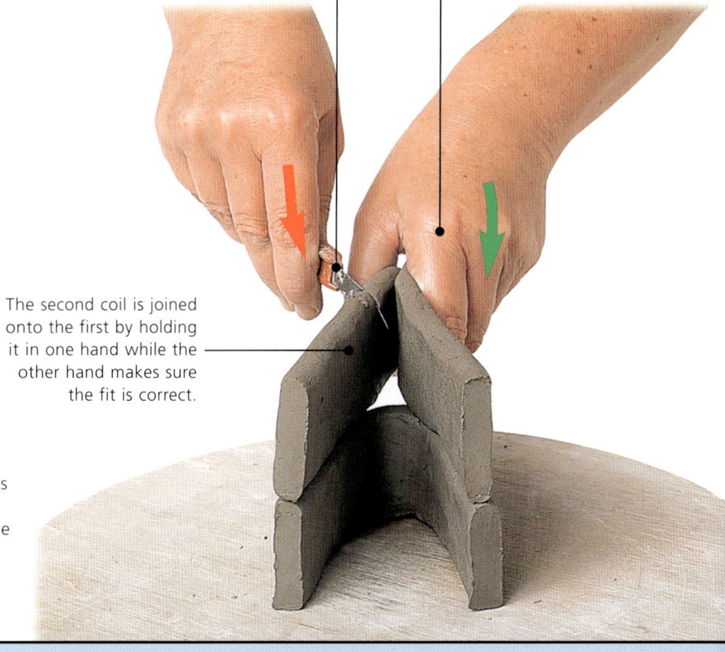

Roll a thin coil of soft clay and use it to reinforce the join of flattened coils on both the inside and outside of the form. Blend the coil in with a finger at first, working it thoroughly into the join. Next, blend the clay even more with a wooden modelling tool, removing any excess in the process. Make sure you complete this process thoroughly because this is where the form is most likely to crack during the drying or firing process.

After you have blended in the reinforcing join, roughly refine the surface by scraping away any lumps and bumps with a metal kidney. This is important, more to maintain an even thickness in the clay wall than to make a smooth surface. Keeping the surface relatively neat at this stage, however, allows you to see the outline shape more clearly and to make adjustments if necessary. Repeat the refining process on the inside.

At a point roughly two-thirds along the upper rim of the form, gently ease the walls together to divide the leaf shape into two as shown. Use both hands, with the fingers easing the outer walls together in a pinching action and the thumbs maintaining the shape. Once the rough shape has been formed, pinch a small area of the two walls together thoroughly between finger and thumb. If the walls don't stick together readily, score and slip each side and try again.

Run a soft reinforcing coil under and around the pinched area carefully, making sure you blend it in well. Take care not to force the pinched section apart again at this stage. It will probably only be possible to use a finger to blend this coil in. If you find it too unwieldy to reinforce the section from above, you can turn the form over carefully and work from the inside. Take care not to distort the shape as it is turned over.

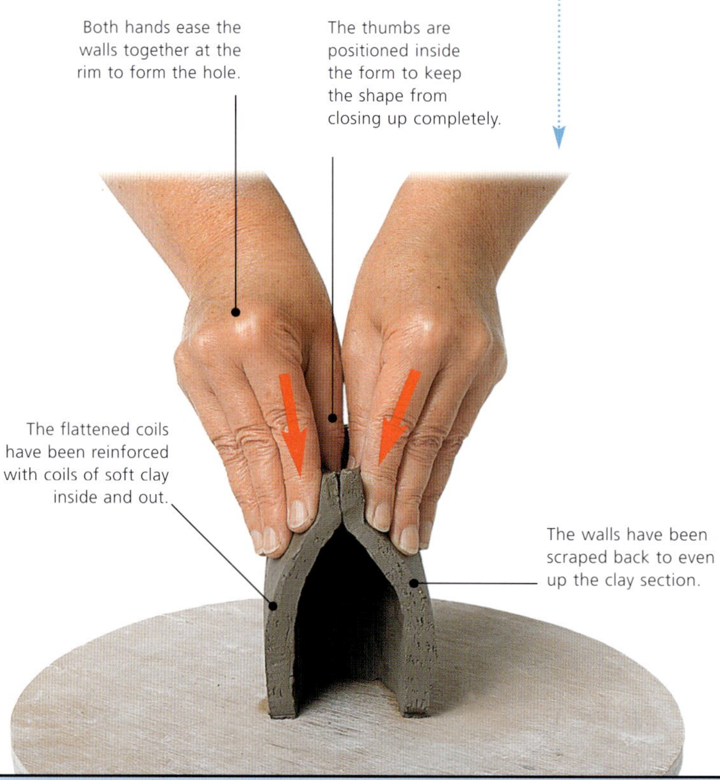

Join the next coil onto the newly shaped double leaf rim of the form using the same technique as before. At the point where the two walls are pinched together, begin to flare the coil out again at the upper rim. Reinforce all the joins inside and out, then roughly scrape back the surface again to redefine the shape. Continue the pinched section into the subsequent coil but try to maintain the outward flare at the upper rim.

Use another coil of soft clay to reinforce the area around the second, upper half of the pinched area. You can do this completely from above this time. Make sure the coil is well worked in around the section without trapping air between the two surfaces. The form may need to be firmed up a little at this stage because of the weight involved when building with thicker coils. Use a hairdryer, keeping it moving over the surface continuously to avoid over drying any one area too much.

Using a wooden tool or craft knife, carefully cut out a hole slightly smaller than the pinched area of the wall. It is better to cut a small hole and to open it up gradually than to cut too much away only to find that the wall is too thin. Once the hole has been cut out, work around it gradually with a modelling tool to refine the shape, removing any excess clay in the process. This also reinforces the surrounding area, which is potentially vulnerable, so take the time to make sure this process is carried out properly.

Build up the form by one more coil, keeping the slight outward flare at the sides. The leaf shape should have elongated by about 10 cm by this stage. Paddle the side edges from time to time to define the outline. Ease the walls together again carefully to form the double leaf shape about 5 cm above the first hole. Pinch out a section to form a hole the same size as before, reinforcing it in the same way, then add the next coil and reinforce around the upper half. Cut out the second hole in the same way as the first, making sure the two shapes are roughly the same size.

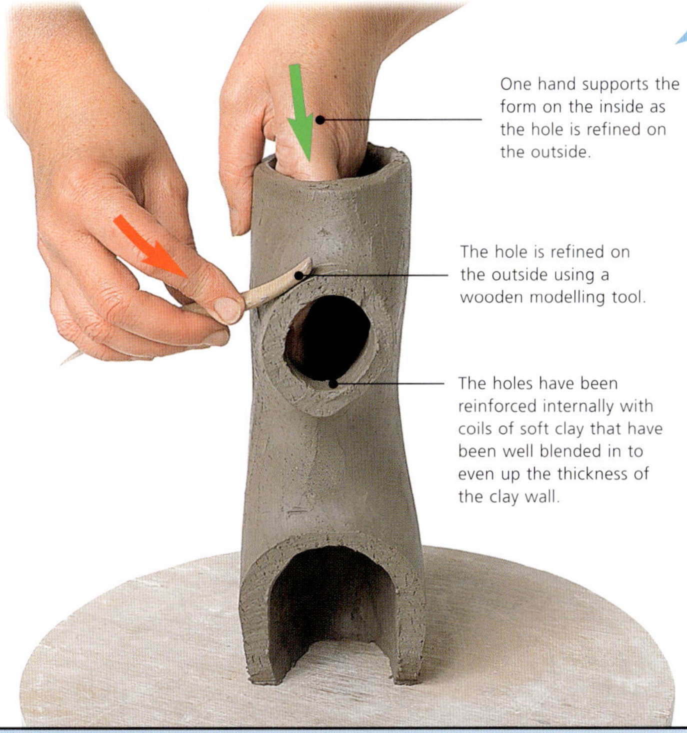

Join a final coil to the form, reinforcing and finishing it off as before. Use both hands to ease the upper rims together carefully, but don't join them together completely. The form's outline should be symmetrical at this point, flaring neatly outward from the base. To change the shape, stand the sculpture on a turntable so that it can be viewed from both sides, then mark a line from one upper corner across and down to a point roughly 5 cm lower on the opposite side edge.

13

Using a craft or potter's knife, carefully cut off the top section of the sculpture to correspond with the marked line. Support the form with one hand as the sections are cut away. Once both sides have been cut, ease the rims together again to check the shape. You may find that more clay needs to be removed to give the form the correct visual balance. If this is the case, refine the edge further by shaving away small amounts of clay at a time using a rasp blade rather than a knife, which risks taking too much off.

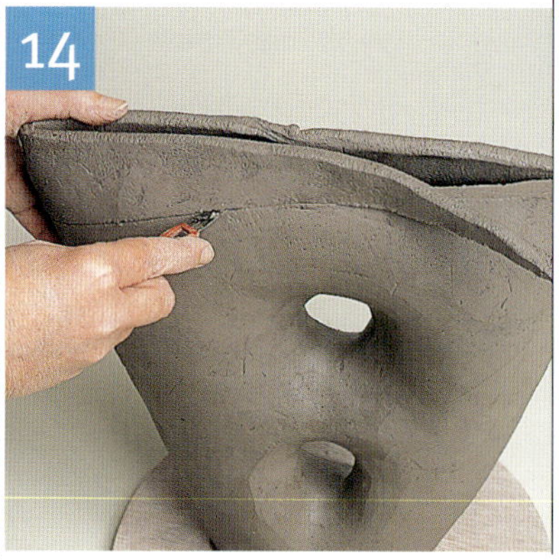

14

Once the correct outline for the upper edge has been cut to shape, score and slip a 13-mm area inside each side of the rim walls; then gently but firmly join them together. Pinch a small area over, and in line with, the two holes, but don't cut it out just yet. Paddle the upper edge with a wooden spatula to define the outline and reinforce the join. Refine the edge further by scraping away any excess clay with a metal kidney.

15

To complete the detail in the sculpture, cut out a semicircle from the rim where the walls have been pinched together. Once the section has been cut away, pinch the clay back together to make sure the join is firm, and neaten the area using a wooden modelling tool as before. Finally, work over the sculpture's entire surface with a kidney to remove any lumps and bumps, and paddle the side and upper edges to form straight lines.

16

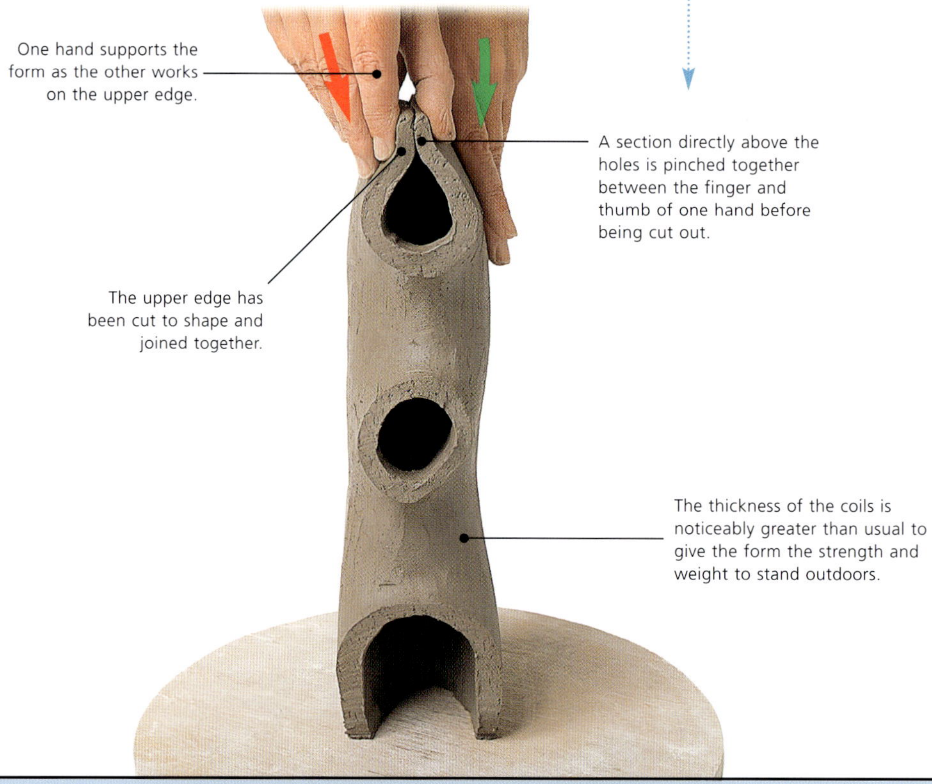

The building of the sculpture is now complete and ready to be decorated in your preferred style. The sculpture should need very little surface decoration because the form is visually strong and too much decoration would detract from this. In this example, the surface was simply textured with a forked tool and channel lines were carved to radiate out from the holes. Three forms were made in varying sizes to work together as one in visual terms.

The finished sculptures work very well in groups of three, although they would look equally good as individual pieces positioned creatively in the garden. The sculptures were fired to 1,260°C after a thick wash of red iron oxide was applied to the surface. It is always better to keep the surface decoration of work like this as simple as possible so that it does not jar with its environment. The sculptures are reminiscent of ancient standing stones and should therefore look as though they belong outdoors – and as though they have been there for a long time.

CHAPTER TWO

Pinching

Pinching is probably the earliest method used by humans to shape clay because it is an instinctive way of handling the material. This is demonstrated in ancient examples of ritualistic vessels, figurines and animal forms. Pinching is usually the first technique taught to beginners to help them develop a feel for clay, but the results of early attempts can be disappointing because the walls tear and crack easily. In fact, pinching needs practice, but once mastered, it offers the potential for wonderful creative expression. It is a contemplative way of working, which may be unsuitable for some potters, but it is worth taking time to discover the pleasing effects that it can achieve.

Pinching a simple bowl form

Beginners are advised to start pinching with a grogged clay because of its strength and ability to hold a shape without cracking. As you gain experience you will be able to progress to clays with finer particles, such as stoneware or porcelain, but a good understanding of how clay behaves is required first. The clay used in this project is a half-and-half mixture of porcelain and a white-firing clay with a grogged stoneware body, which is a good compromise because it combines grogged and smooth clay.

It may take several attempts to perfect the art of pinching. It is important not to become demoralized by early failure but to keep trying, because you will learn something with each attempt.

1

Begin by wedging a lump of clay weighing approximately 225 g – or large enough to sit comfortably in the palm of the hand without feeling too heavy. Roll the clay between the palms of both hands to create a smooth round ball. Use this size ball to begin with because a little clay pinches out a long way, and more would be unwieldy. Small balls will enable you to develop your understanding of the clay and the technique, and you can build up to larger sizes as you gain experience.

2

Holding the ball of clay firmly in the palm of one hand, make a hole by pressing the thumb of the other hand through the centre until some pressure can be felt in the palm holding the ball. Press to within 13 mm of the bottom of the ball, to allow for thinning at a later stage. Take care not to push through the bottom of the ball. Make sure that the thumb is as centred as possible; the pinching process is much easier if you start from a relatively even wall section.

3

Beginning from the bottom of the ball, start to pinch out the wall between finger and thumb in small, close, and even movements, working methodically around the shape. Support the form continuously in the palm of the hand. This maintains a rounded base until you are ready to shape the form at a later stage. Don't try to pinch the wall too thin at this point. Proceed in stages, pinching the ball to an even thickness, then pinching a second or even a third time. Try to keep control of the shape by pinching inside the ball, leaving the rim fuller and relatively closed until ready to form the final shape. This helps to prevent the rim from cracking, tearing and flaring out too quickly.

4

Having pinched out the wall several times to achieve an even thickness, pinch out the rim, so that the form appears to flare from the base. Apart from a small amount of refinement, the clay wall should now be no thicker than 6 mm. Pinch the rim as level as possible, but do not be concerned if it undulates a little – that is an integral feature of many pinched bowls. The action of pinching usually dries the clay quickly, especially if you have hot hands. If the bowl seems floppy, however, use a hairdryer to firm the clay a little, until it can be handled more readily. Don't overdo the drying because some refinements to the shape are still to be made, and the clay needs some flexibility for this.

Turn the bowl over. Holding it in one hand, paddle the outer wall with a wooden spatula to shape a small circular base. Work around the bowl, paddling in small, even strokes to develop the shape. Don't hit it too hard or you could distort the form. A small base on a flared bowl looks elegant, but it is important to achieve the correct proportions. Too small a base will be unstable and will make the bowl look top-heavy. Too large a base will cause the bowl to appear dumpy and bottom-heavy.

The action of paddling the outside wall will also refine it considerably. To refine the inner wall, carefully scrape away any unevenness with a metal kidney. Holding the kidney at an angle, scrape the wall from the base up towards the rim, exercising extreme care because the wall will be delicate. Support the bowl in the other hand, turning it as the surface is refined, so that the kidney on the inside is always working against the most supported part of the wall. If the bowl was pinched evenly, very little clay will need to be scraped away. The action serves primarily to smooth the surface.

Set the bowl on a wooden bat, then roughly roll a coil of clay about 13 mm thick and 10 cm long. This can be done between the palms or on the work surface in the usual way. Starting at one end, pinch the coil flat along its length until it is slightly thicker than the wall of the bowl. Pinch the coil in stages, working down one side first, then the other, until the correct thickness is achieved. Pinch the coil until it is long enough to fit around the rim of the bowl with a small overlap. With the bowl still sitting on the bat, fit the coil in place just inside the rim, so that there is about a 6-mm overlap. Pinch the coil and bowl wall together gently with one hand as the other supports the rest of the coil. The aim is to keep the coil in place until it is completely fitted around the rim. It will be blended in more thoroughly at the next stage. Cross the ends of the coil over one another and cut through both diagonally. Blend the joints together carefully, making sure no air is trapped between them.

Holding the bowl at an angle in the palm of the hand, blend the outer wall upwards onto the coil, using the thumb of the other hand while supporting the inner wall with the fingers. Blend the two surfaces thoroughly, working around the bowl several times. It does not matter if the shape distorts a little in the process of blending – this can be corrected later. It is much more important to make sure that the joint is secure; if not, it could split in the firing.

Once the outer wall is blended onto the coil, repeat the process on the inside, this time blending the coil down onto the wall of the bowl. Again, support the bowl in one hand while blending with the thumb of the other, this time using the fingers for extra support on the outer wall. The shape of the bowl can appear a little ungainly at the completion of this stage, but the purpose of the slightly thicker coil is to allow for additional pinching once it is secured in place, thus regaining the flared shape.

Return the bowl to the bat and, working on a turntable, if possible, begin to pinch out the coil so that the outline shape flares neatly outwards, in line with the lower section. Both hands can be used to pinch at this stage because it is not necessary to support the bowl in the hand. Pinch around the coil several times until it is the same thickness as the rest of the bowl. Keep the rim as level as possible, but don't be concerned if there is some unevenness – it can be accentuated to form a feature of the finished bowl.

After pinching the coil to the same thickness as the lower part of the bowl, refine the surface with a metal kidney, scraping away any tiny bumps that remain. If the coil was pinched well, it should not be necessary to remove too much clay in the refining process. Support the outer wall of the bowl with one hand as the inner surface is refined, but don't apply too much pressure, which could distort the bowl's thin wall. When all of the excess clay is scraped away, work back over the surface, using the side of the kidney to smooth any scratch marks.

If you find that the shape does become distorted, remove a V-shaped section of clay from the wall at the relevant point. Cut the V diagonally, so that when the wall is fitted back together, the sections overlap neatly. Hold the bowl securely with one hand as the section is cut out, to avoid additional distortion. This procedure can be repeated as often as necessary to modify the bowl's shape. The same method can also be used to create decorative details or to alter the design radically.

Variation

Other details could be added to the form – for example, a foot ring to give it some lift. This is made by pinching out a coil as for the rim, then fixing it onto the base using the same technique of overlapping the ends, cutting through both diagonally, and sealing the joint. The position needs to be scored and slipped before attaching the ring, and the joint is reinforced with tiny soft coils of clay, blended in well. The area around the ring must be smoothed with a kidney and dried with a hairdryer until it can hold the weight of the bowl. Any adjustments to height can be made using a rasp blade to remove excess clay, then a rubber kidney to soften the edge.

After removal of the V section, rejoin the wall, using both hands, so that the sections overlap. It should not be necessary to score and slip the joint if the clay is still malleable, but always do so if in doubt. Pinch the overlapped sections together carefully, being sure to ease out any air that may be trapped. Hold the wall with one hand to keep it in place, and use the other to pinch the clay. Once the clay is properly pinched back together, there should be no evidence that the wall was ever cut. Smooth the joint inside with a kidney, as before, carefully supporting the outer wall in the process.

If necessary, repeat the process of cutting and rejoining until the desired shape is achieved. Now, carefully turn the bowl on its side, supporting the weight with one hand inside. Refine the outer joint in the same way as the inner one, removing any excess clay in the process. When the joint is smooth and secure, start to thin out the rim of the bowl using a kidney. Proceed with great care at this stage because the clay wall becomes fragile as it thins, but a delicate rim is an appealing feature.

Stand the bowl on the bat and, using both hands, soften the rim by pinching the edge very finely between the fingers and thumbs. This action will almost certainly result in a wavy rim, but that should look organic and attractive. If you are dissatisfied with the rim, level it carefully with a rasp blade to remove the jagged edge, then soften it with a rubber kidney. Something of the nature of pinching is lost when a piece is finished in this way, however, so persevere with the natural edge, if possible.

Finely smooth the surface of the bowl, using a rubber kidney. Hold the bowl carefully in one hand as you work on the outer surface. Don't be tempted to place the bowl upside down on the bat to do this, because the rim is too delicate and the pressure would almost certainly break it. Aim to achieve as smooth a surface as possible to give the bowl a good outline shape. Rest the bowl in the palm of the hand to repeat the smoothing process on the inside. The finished bowl is a simple form, with a rim that is more uneven on one side than the other. This is turned into a feature by the addition of a small pierced design, made with a hole cutter. The wall must be carefully supported during cutting because it is now very fragile. Don't overdo the design – a delicate pattern in a limited area will add interesting detail without detracting from the rest of the form. The finished bowl is then ready to be decorated in your own style.

One hand holds the wall as the other pinches the overlap together.

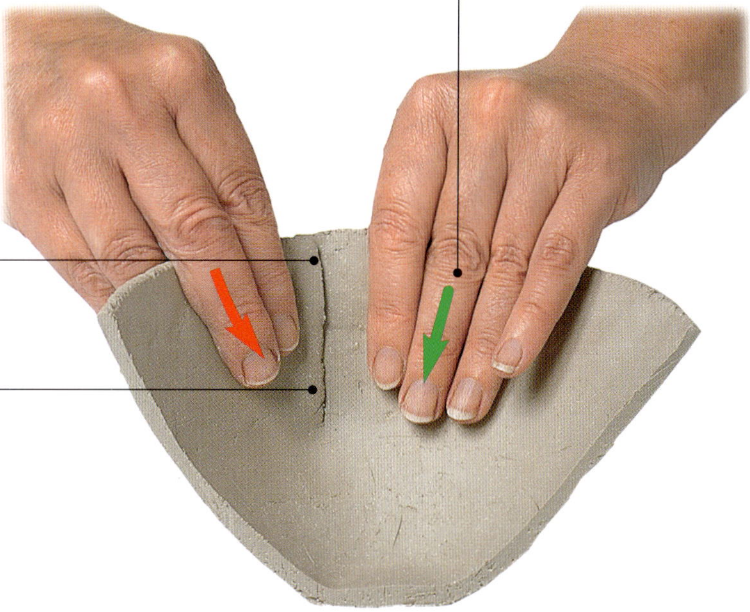

The wall is eased back together so that the cut sections overlap.

A V-shaped section was cut from the wall of the bowl to correct the shape.

Joining two pinched bowls to make a simple pebble

Joining two sections demands that both halves are pinched to the same size. This may seem a daunting task for the beginner, but once you master the art of pinching one form, practice will allow you to pinch another to the same size. In some ways it is easier to pinch out bowls for joining because the walls do not need to be thinned out so much. The secret is to control the size and shape of the rim; then fitting the sections together is much easier. Start on a small scale so that the work can be easily handled, and build up to larger projects as you gain experience.

The clay used for this project is a body with a coarse grog and wide firing range, suitable for pinching and other handbuilding techniques.

1

Using the method described in the previous section, form two equal-sized balls of clay, each weighing under 115 g. It is important that the balls are the same size, so that when they are pinched out they will fit together accurately. Make a hole through the centre of the first ball with your thumb, as before. This can be trickier with a smaller ball of clay – if your thumb seems too large for the task, use a different finger. Hold the ball securely in the opposite hand as the hole is made.

2

Pinch out the clay wall gently but firmly until a small cup shape is formed. Keep the rim as level as possible to avoid adjustments when fitting the two halves together. The shape should remain completely rounded, with a wall about 3 mm thick when fully pinched. Try to develop a rhythm when pinching, which will help you to make an identical shape when repeating the process for the second half.

3

When pinching smaller balls of clay, you can turn the form around in your hand and work with it upside down, so that your thumb is pinching on the outside wall instead of the inside. This is especially useful to even up the clay section at the bottom of the form. If any part of the wall seems too thin, reinforce it with a small piece of soft clay, pinching and smoothing it over the thin area on the inside of the form. Be careful not to trap air in the reinforced area because this could cause explosions in the firing. Pinch the second cup until it exactly matches the first by checking the fit of the two halves regularly during the process. When the second half is almost the same size as the first, pinch the rim a fraction at a time until the sizes are identical.

4

Score and slip the rims of both cups, using a toothbrush and a little water. Apply a toothbrushing action to produce a generous amount of slip and a well-scored surface. It is important to have enough slip on each rim for the two surfaces to adhere well, but be aware that too much water will make the rims floppy.

5

Holding a pinched cup in each hand, ease the two together to make a good fit. Apply gentle but firm pressure and twist each half very slightly to push out any air that may be trapped in the joint. Allow a few minutes to make sure that the two halves are securely fixed, and keep applying gentle pressure until you are certain. When the sections are joined, the form will resemble a dinosaur egg.

Tips for success

- When the walls of the pinched form begin to feel floppy, firm them up a little using a hairdryer. Don't overdry the clay, however, because hard clay is almost impossible to pinch and is more likely to crack.
- If you need a break before the shape is complete, rest it, rim down, on a sheet of thin plastic to prevent the rim from additional drying.
- In addition to pinching the clay, stroke it into shape. This usually happens instinctively as a response to smoothing the clay.

Put the egg aside and roll a thin, soft coil of clay. Wind the coil around the egg to cover the joint, then blend the coil in carefully, using a wooden modelling tool. Support the two ends of the egg so that the halves are firmly together during blending, because pressure on the joint could force it apart. When the coil is blended in, work over the area with a metal kidney to remove any surplus clay and smooth the surface. Take the time to do a good job with this part of the construction because joints are always vulnerable if not well reinforced.

Paddle the surface of the egg with a wooden spatula to round off the shape. Apply gentle pressure and work around the egg rhythmically, supporting it in one hand throughout. The air inside the egg forms a vacuum, preventing distortion of the shape at this stage. The paddling helps reinforce and seal the joint, smoothing the surface in the process. If any tiny cracks appear on the surface, blend them over carefully, drawing the clay from each side. The shape of the egg cannot be altered until some air is released from inside. Holding the egg in the palm of the hand, make a hole in one end with a potter's pin. The hole must be small, or the air will escape too quickly and the egg will collapse. Handle the shape very carefully after piercing the hole, because it can easily be distorted at this stage.

Start to model the pebble shape, using a metal kidney. Hold the form in one hand with the hole pointing towards your body and draw the kidney over the surface firmly from one end to the other, pushing out the air in the process. Turn the shape around in your hand and work in different directions to give the pebble some soft edges and angles. It will be necessary to work over the surface several times to achieve a satisfactory result. If the form shows signs of collapse, reinflate it by blowing gently into the hole until the shape returns; then plug the hole with soft clay and firm the entire shape up a little, using a hairdryer.

Reinsert the hole into what is now a pebble shape, and paddle the surface with a wooden spatula to refine some of the angles. When the form is correct, refill the hole with some soft clay to enable the pebble to hold this shape until it is firmer. It is still possible to paddle the surface after plugging the hole, to define the edges and angles a little more. Aim to make the pebble at least three-sided to give the form interest.

Finally, work over the surface of the pebble with a rubber kidney to smooth it off completely and seal any hairline cracks that were caused by the paddling. Thoroughly smoothing the surface in this way prepares the clay for its final treatment, whether slip decoration and burnishing, or glazing. Allow the pebble to dry to the leather-hard stage, then pierce a final hole in a discreet part of the form to allow the escape of air during firing. Failure to do this will almost certainly cause the pebble to explode. The finished pebble is ready to be decorated. You can do this by covering the surface in several layers of decorating slip, then burnishing it with a spoon. After bisque firing, the pebble could be polished with beeswax, or it could be smoke-fired before polishing, using a resist to create patterned rings.

This form combines the techniques described in the first two sections of this chapter but demonstrates how to pinch in a slightly different way and then model the form into a particular shape.

Modelling a clay pod

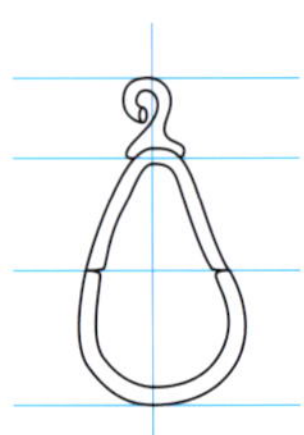

The possibilities for shaping these forms are endless and each one will be different from the next. The simplest shape to begin with is the pear, a form that can be altered by releasing air from the inside.

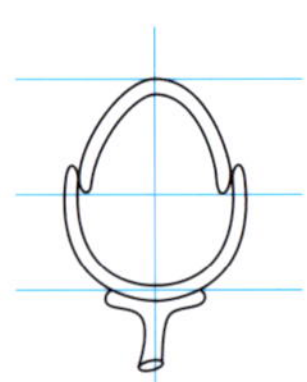

As an alternative to joining the two halves exactly together, one half can be made slightly larger than the other, then joined over the other half to form an overlapping detail that looks rather like an acorn.

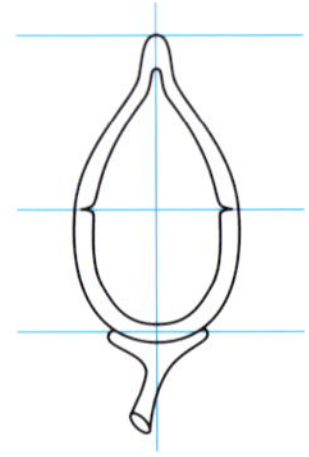

A simple rounded and unmodelled shape always makes a good, easy surface to decorate. Fruit shapes such as lemons or plums are pleasing to the eye and easy to make in multiples.

Once the two pinched halves are joined securely, the shape can be dramatically altered with the release of some air. In this model, the pod has been paddled into the shape of a seed head with a wide, flattened surface tapering to the stem.

The form need not reproduce the appearance of a real pod or seed head, but these shapes are a good creative starting point, so observe the form and proportion of a few natural pod shapes before letting your imagination take over. From then on, the choice of forms is endless.

The clay used in this project is a a body with a coarse grog and a wide firing range, which is good for pinching.

It is important to remember to put a hole in the form when it is leather-hard to allow for the release of air during firing.

A curled coil stem is added to one end of the form to make it look more realistic and finished.

The upper half of the form is paddled into a cone to create a basic pear shape. This acts to refine the surface and seal the join as well as form the shape.

The join is reinforced and completely sealed on the outside of the pod, but it cannot be blended in on the inside because the form is closed.

The walls are pinched to an even thickness throughout the form, then the surface is scraped back to smooth it.

KEY

Pulling, lifting and supporting movements

Pushing, shaping and reinforcing movements

Weigh two small balls of clay, no more than 115 g each. Pinch one ball into a rounded cup shape, using the method described on page 64. Begin to pinch the second ball by pushing the thumb into the centre; then replace the thumb with the forefinger and pinch the shape around the fingertip to form a soft point. This involves stroking or easing the clay over the end of the finger, using the thumb on the outside – a pinching/pulling movement. Pinch the rest of the ball out from the point to form a conical shape.

If the shape becomes thin or distorted in areas, cut a line through the relevant section of wall, then overlap each side and gently pinch them back together again, taking care not to trap air in the overlap. Blend the joint until there is no trace of it. It may be necessary to cut and rejoin in this way to make the two halves the same size. The process can be repeated as many times as needed, but with experience, few if any adjustments will be required.

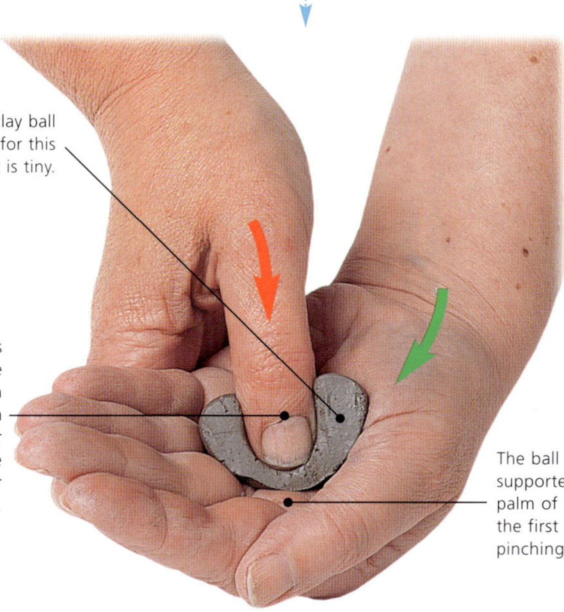

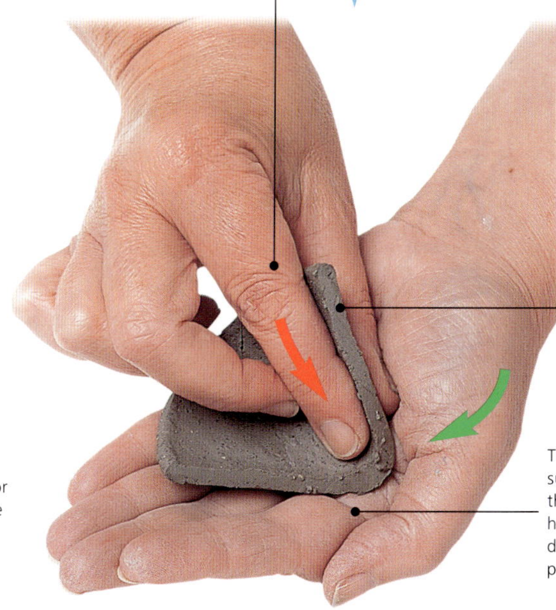

Pinch the two halves to between 3 and 6-mm thickness, measure them against each other to check the fit, then score and slip the rims thoroughly using a toothbrush and a little water. Join the two halves, applying a slight twist to adhere the surfaces well and force out any air that was trapped between them. Take the time to make sure the two sections are securely bonded. The form should look roughly lemon-shaped at this stage.

Using a coil of soft clay, reinforce the joint, following the method described in the technique section (see page 88). After blending the coil in well, remove any surplus clay with the modelling tool. Be careful not to re-expose the joint by removing too much clay. Finish this stage by paddling the surface of the form with a wooden spatula to refine the shape and bond the sections completely. Remember that the shape cannot be altered until air is released from the inside, so paddling will not distort the form at this stage.

Smooth and refine the surface of the pod, first using a metal kidney to scrape away any remaining tiny lumps. Work over the surface carefully, using the kidney on its side to compact the clay as much as to remove it, so that there is no evidence of the joint. When the pod is lump-free, complete the smoothing process by working over the surface with a rubber kidney. Firm the pod up a little using a hairdryer, so that it won't deflate completely when a hole is made in it for modelling.

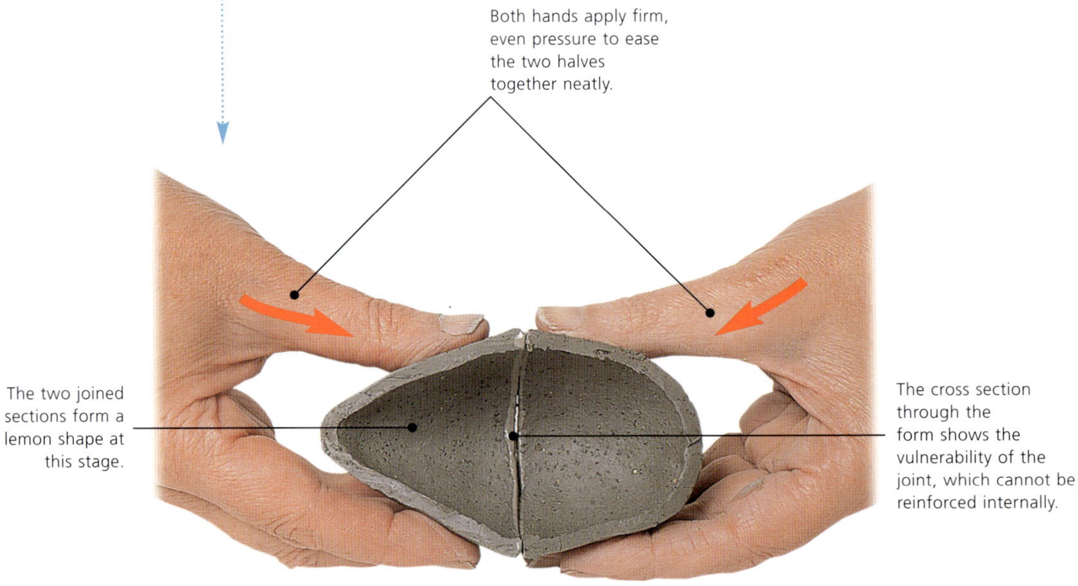

Using a potter's needle, make a hole in the pointed end of the pod. Then tap the rounded end of the pod gently on a wooden bat until the form sits securely. Hold the pod in place on the bat and paddle the shape using a wooden spatula to form three equal sides, flaring from the point down to the wider base. It may be necessary to reopen the hole several times during the course of paddling because the action pushes the clay together and closes the upper space of the pod as the shape is defined.

Lift the pod from the bat and hold it in your hand on one side, with the pointed end away from your body. Using your forefinger and thumb, model a groove down the centre of the two exposed sides of the pod, working from the point down to where the base begins to round off. Turn the shape over in your hand and model another groove down the centre of the third side. Aim to make each groove equal in depth, so that the proportions of the pod look balanced.

Fill up the hole in the point of the pod with some soft clay. Firm the shape up a little, if necessary, using the hairdryer. Sometimes, modelling the shape of the pod with the fingers and thumb in this way creates an uneven surface, which may or may not enhance the form, depending on your chosen decorative finish. If the surface needs to be smooth, use a metal kidney to ease out any irregularities. Then finish off with a rubber kidney, as before.

Tips for success

- Cut your fingernails – pinching clay is impossible with long nails.
- Use freshly wedged clay so that the outer surface does not have time to dry out.
- Grogged clay is good for beginners because it holds its shape more readily than finely particled clays.
- If the rim begins to crack, stroke the clay from either side over it to seal it up again.

Roll a short coil of clay, about 5 cm long and 13 mm thick, between the palms of your hands. Model the coil to form the shape of a stalk. Flatten one end by tapping it on the work surface, then twist the other end so that it curves over in a quirky shape. When you like the shape, dry the clay with the hairdryer until it is as firm as the body of the pod. Score and slip the pointed end of the pod and the flattened end of the stalk using a toothbrush and a little water.

Holding the pod in one hand, ease the stalk over the pointed end, pushing out any trapped air in the process. Check that the stalk is completely fixed onto the pod; then continue to model the shape by pinching three indentations at the base of the stalk where it sits on the main body. These indentations should correspond with the grooves in the pod walls. Using a damp sponge or paintbrush, wipe away any slip that oozed from the point where the stalk was joined. Do not use a lot of water; it will spoil the surface of the pod by exposing the grog in the clay.

Taking great care not to knock the stalk, turn the pod over and, holding it in one hand, pierce a series of holes in the base using a hole cutter. Start the piercing in the centre of the base and radiate out in a pattern that complements the shape of the pod. Do not cut the holes too close together because this can distort and weaken the clay wall – and even break it. Instead, make a few holes, then build up the pattern with a potter's pin or pointed wooden modelling tool to give the impression of a pierced surface. The pod is finished and ready to decorate in your style.

9

10

11

This pod has been formed and shaped using the same technique as above, but extra detail has been added in the form of small squashed balls of clay extending around the body from the stem. As an added detail, the balls have been stamped with a pointed wooden tool.

This pod has been formed to look like an acorn. Instead of joining the pinched sections together, one was made slightly larger than the other to fit just over the rim of the other (see page 66). Sections joined in this way cannot be reinforced with coils of clay without spoiling the form's natural look. The lower half of the pod was textured with a pointed wooden tool.

In this example, the pod has been modelled into three distinct sections. Extra coils have been joined along the raised parts of the body extending from the stem, and then long holes have been cut out of the body between them.

Before bisque firing, the pods were coated in several layers of slip and then burnished using polished pebbles and spoons. After bisque firing, paper resist pattern was applied and the surface covered in clay slurry. Once the slurry had dried, the pods were smoke-fired in newspaper several times. The slurry was subsequently removed to reveal the pattern absorbed into the surface. A final beeswax polish imparts a wonderfully tactile surface to these forms.

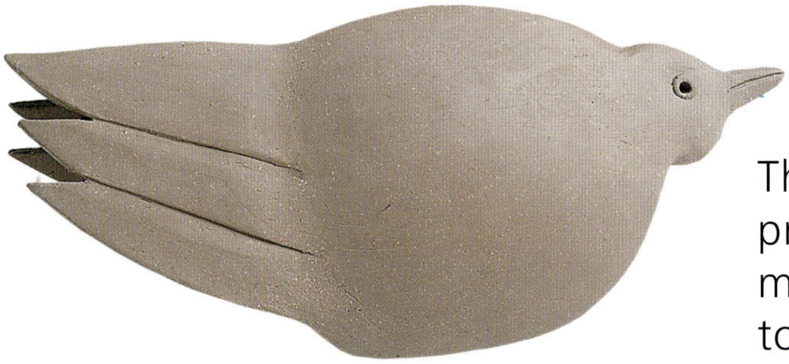

This project builds on the previous one by adding more pinched sections to the basic form.

Modelling a clay bird

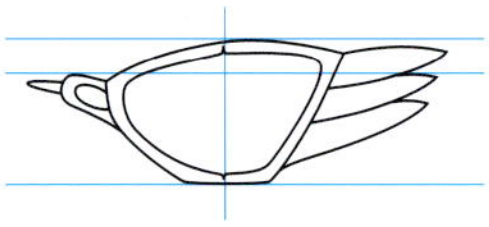

The basic shape of the bird places the head pointing directly forward and the tail feathers extending back in line with the body. A different character of bird can be created by altering the length of the beak and feathers or by positioning these at different angles to the body.

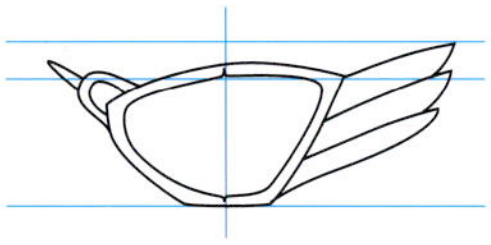

Here, the head has been raised so that part of it is positioned above the body's top line. The tail feathers have also been raised a little. You can do this by either cutting the tail section down to the appropriate shape before joining it to the body or by fixing the original sections onto the body at a different angle.

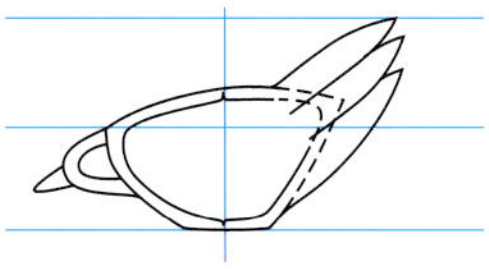

This version of the bird places the head pointing down. The tail feathers are positioned at an even jauntier angle to give quite a different character to the bird.

This version of the bird appears almost quirky, but in fact shows a pose struck by many birds. A model like this reflects the essence of a bird instead of a more traditional interpretation of what it should look like.

It also incorporates slabbed feather sections and some basic carved detail. The clay used for this project is a mixture of a white-firing clay with a grogged stoneware body for strength, and porcelain, to refine and whiten the body. This mixture has a wide firing capability, allowing the potter to smoke or Raku-fire the finished work, or to glaze and fire up to stoneware temperatures.

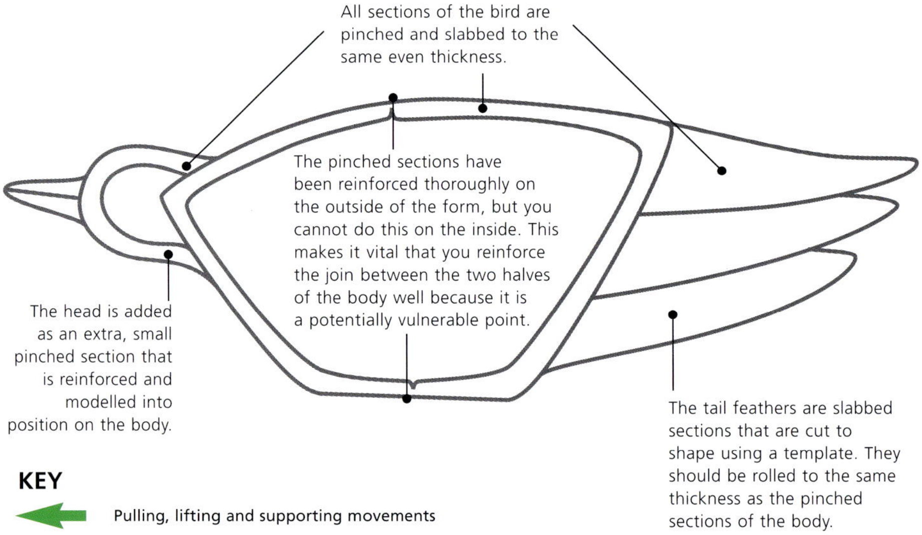

KEY

Pulling, lifting and supporting movements

Pushing, shaping and reinforcing movements

Following the method described on page 64, weigh two 225-g balls of clay, then pinch and join them to form an egg shape. Pierce a hole in one end of the 'egg' and, using a wooden spatula, paddle the walls into a body with five sides in the following way. First paddle the base, which must be no more than 5 cm wide and 6.5–7.5 cm long. Next, paddle the side walls, narrowing up from the base to form a backbone ridge across the top. The final two ends are somewhat V-shaped, with the head slightly lower than the tail. When the shape is formed, fill the hole with soft clay and smooth the body with a metal kidney.

Put the body to one side on a sheet of thin plastic. Pinch out the shape of the bird's head from a tiny ball of clay. Begin by making the ball cup-shaped, in the usual way; then paddle the walls to make a ridge that will follow the line of the bird's back. Allow the head to rest on a finger when paddling the ridge. When the head is the right shape, hold it against the body at various angles to find the best position. While the head is against the body, mark the spot where it will be attached by lightly scoring around the head with a knife. Remove the head, then score and slip both the marked position on the body and the rim of the head.

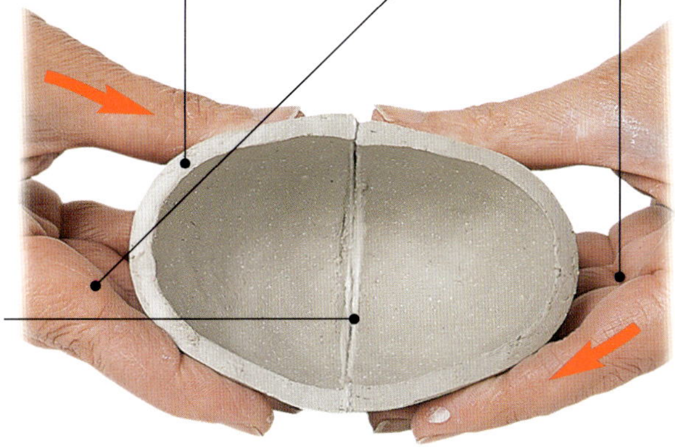

The clay wall shows that each half was pinched to the same thickness for an accurate fit.

Each hand holds a section in place, twisting the rims together very slightly to make them adhere.

In cross section, the joined halves show the approximate size of the body before shaping.

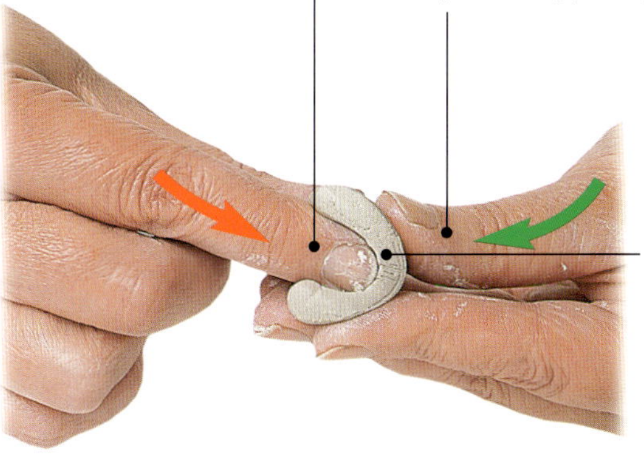

The head is pinched from a tiny ball of clay, using a finger on the inside.

Because the clay ball is so small, it is held in the fingers of the opposite hand (instead of the palm) during pinching.

Pinching such a small ball of clay may require practice.

Fit the head onto the body, keeping the ridges in line. Roll a thin, soft coil of clay and secure it around the joint; then blend it into both the head and the body using a modelling tool. Neaten the joint with a metal kidney, then smooth the area over with a rubber kidney. At the point where the head attaches to the body along the line of the back ridge, use a thumb to form a slight dip to accentuate the difference between the two parts. Support the underside of the head while the top is modelled, and hold the body securely on the bat to prevent distorting the shape.

At this stage, the emerging body could be modelled into any number of creatures, but the addition of a beak transforms the body into a bird. Model a small amount of clay into a beak shape. Check the beak against the head for its size and position in relation to the body. When the correct position is finally established and marked, score and slip the beak and the head, then fix the beak into place. Use a minute coil of soft clay to cover the joint of beak to head, and blend it in well with a wooden modelling tool. Smooth around the area with extreme care, using a finger.

Firm up the head and body a little, using a hairdryer, to prevent any distortion when handling. Take care not to overdry the beak – because it is thin, it will dry faster than the rest of the body. Using a wooden tool or potter's pin, score a line along each side of the beak to make it look more realistic. Hold each side in place with a finger as the line is scored to prevent dislodging the beak. Now roll two minute balls of clay for the eyes, and use a little slip to fix them in place on either side of the head. Flatten the eyes slightly; then use a modelling tool or pencil to create a hollow in the centre of each one.

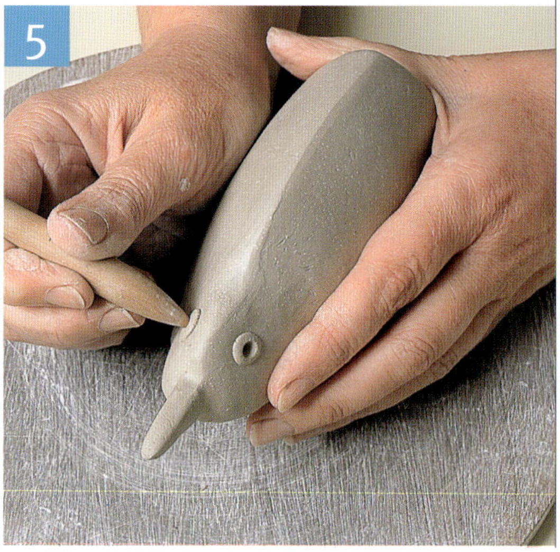

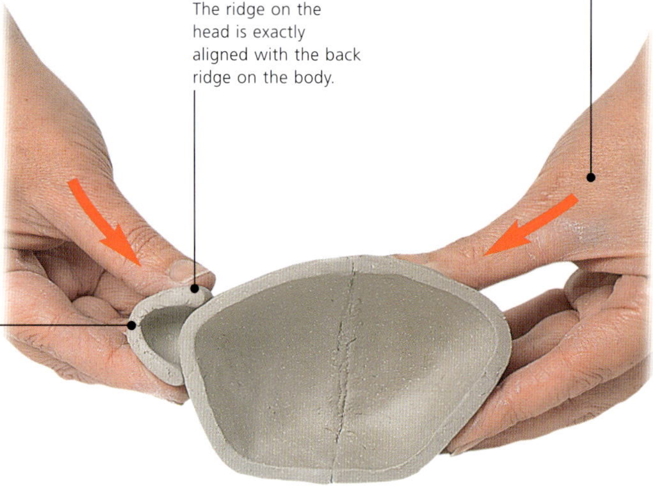

The head is positioned partly over the back and front sections of the body at a slight angle.

The ridge on the head is exactly aligned with the back ridge on the body.

One hand holds the body securely in place as the other hand fixes the head into position.

Set the bird aside. Roll out a slab of clay about 3 mm thick, following the method described in the slabbing section (see page 86). Leave the slab to become almost leather-hard. Meanwhile, on a sheet of paper, draw a template for the wing feathers, checking that the proportions are accurate for the size of the body; then cut the two wing pieces out. Position the templates on the slab and cut carefully around the shapes with a potter's knife.

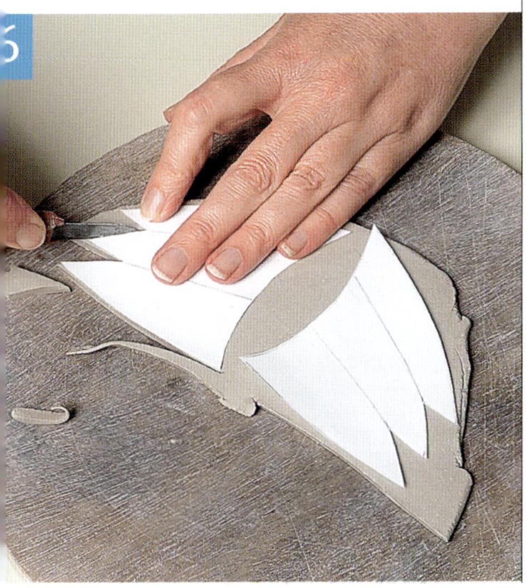

The wing sections will join at the top to continue the line of the back, so mitre both the feather sections along the shorter, upper edge by holding the knife at an acute angle. Keep the point on the work surface and cut the clay, taking care to avoid the fingers that are holding the slab in place on the bat. Repeat the process along the edges that join the feathers to the body. Check that the mitred edges fit correctly where they join along the top edge. Beware of mitring both sections identically. They must be cut as a mirror image in order to fit together.

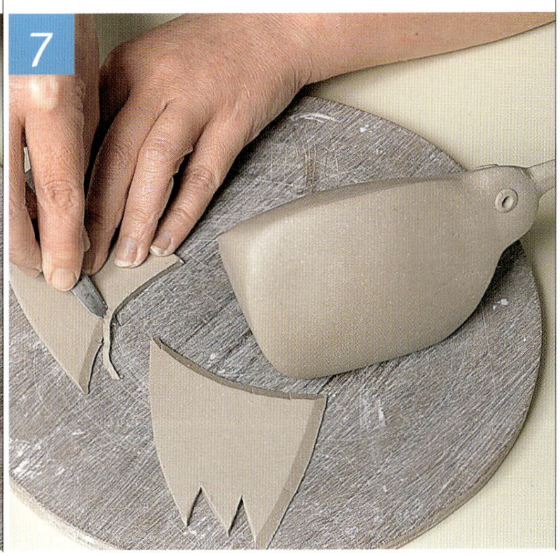

Hold the wing sections against the body and mark the position, remembering that the slabs must fit together at the top. Score and slip the marked positions and the mitred edges of the feathers; then fix them in place on the body, gently squeezing out any excess slip and trapped air in the process. Use both hands for this task: one to hold the body on the bat, using a finger to secure the mitred edge onto the body, and the other to hold the feathers in place. Pinch the upper ridge edges together, again squeezing out any excess slip and air. Run a finger along the joint to soften the edge in keeping with the rest of the back line.

Tips for success

- Look through illustrated bird books for inspiration.
- Do not attempt to make the bird too realistic – aim for a general impression.
- Use minimal detail – simplicity is the key to success.
- Make sure the base is sufficiently balanced to support the form when details are added.
- Allow the work to dry slowly under loose plastic to prevent cracking caused by the extremities drying more quickly than the rest of the form.

Reinforce the joints on the outside of the body with a thin coil of soft clay. Blend the coil in well, using a wooden modelling tool, then smooth over the area with a metal kidney. The feathers should appear to grow naturally from the body, so take time to make sure they are well fixed and blended, removing any unsightly ridges along the joint and finally smoothing over the area with a rubber kidney.

Turn the bird over, taking care not to knock the beak; then, holding it securely in your hand, reinforce the underside joints with a soft coil of clay. Ease the coil into place with a finger, being careful not to part the joints. Use a wooden tool to blend the coil into the awkward angles under the feathers. Scrape away any surplus clay with the same tool, then smooth over the joints with a finger.

Using a small plastic rib or modelling tool, score two lines from the body along the tail to mark the space between the feathers. Carve the clay from underneath each line to make a slight groove. Each feather should appear to overlap the one below. Be sure to support the feathers on the underside while you carve the details, to prevent the slabs from distorting. The carving action may scratch the surface a little, so work the rib back over the groove to compact and smooth the clay to match the rest of the body while keeping the feather line clearly defined.

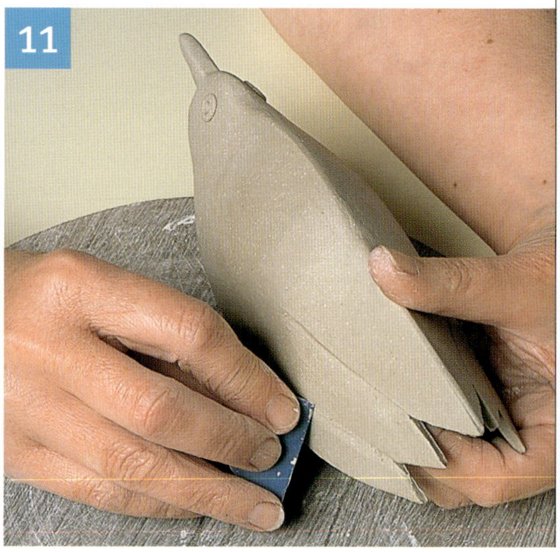

Each of these wing samples has been textured and stamped, using a variety of wooden tools to show how each bird can be changed subtly using the simplest details.

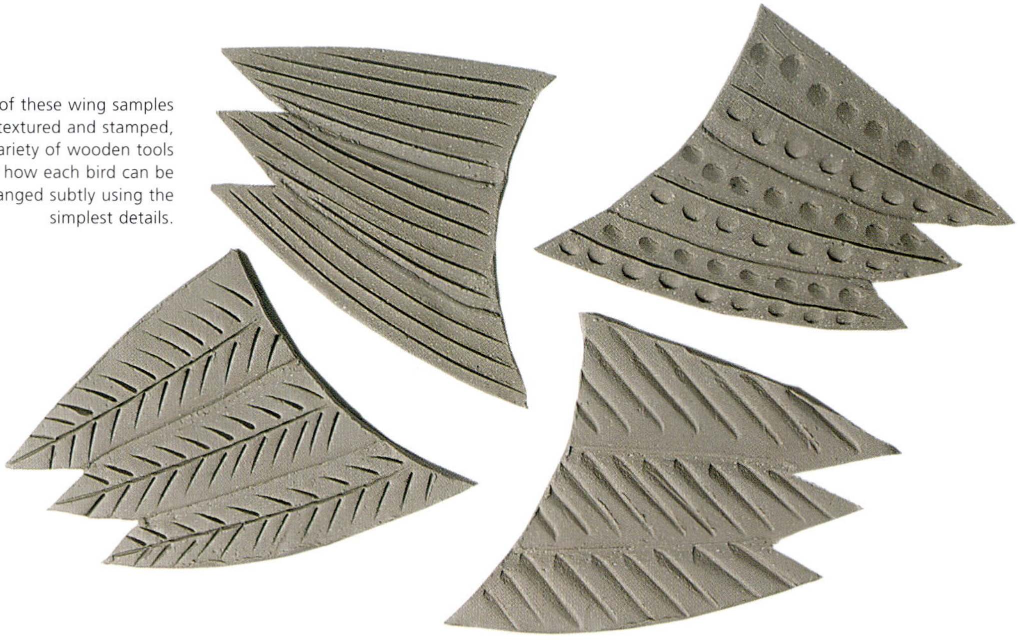

Finally, pierce a hole in each eye with a potter's pin to allow the release of air from the head during firing. Also make a discreet hole in the main body because this is a separate cavity. It is important to remember that all pinched additions must be pierced separately, unless there is a hole between the addition and the main part, because trapped air can cause explosions. Other carved and modelled details can be introduced at this stage, such as wings. The bird is now ready to decorate in your chosen style.

2

Before bisque firing, the birds were burnished in order to compact and refine the clay surface. A simple paper resist line pattern was applied to suggest feathers along the wing sections; then the birds were coated in a grogged clay slurry. Once the slurry had dried, the birds were smoke fired in sawdust for several hours. The distinctive marbled effect on the surface is created when the slurry coating cracks, allowing the smoke into the body of the bird. A final polish with beeswax seals the surface and gives the bird forms an attractive sheen.

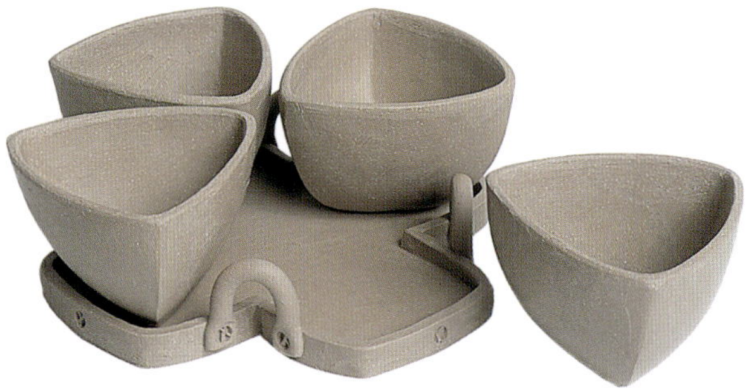

This project expands on the technique of pinching a simple bowl by altering the shape after it has been formed.

Bowl set

The bowls are shown in plan view to show how they fit together on the tray. The design for the tray is adapted from a basic circle which, for accuracy, is measured after the bowls have been pinched and fitted together.

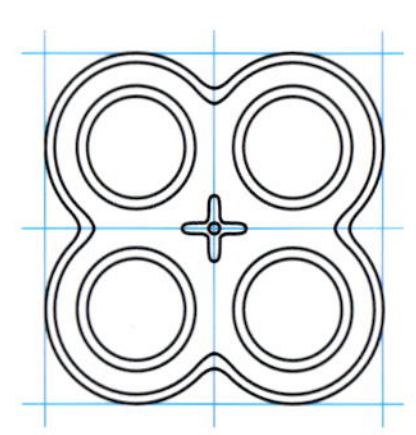

An alternative is to pinch four round bowls and to measure and cut the tray section to match the shape of their combined outline. A handle extending upward from the centre could replace the handles created for the tray in the design above.

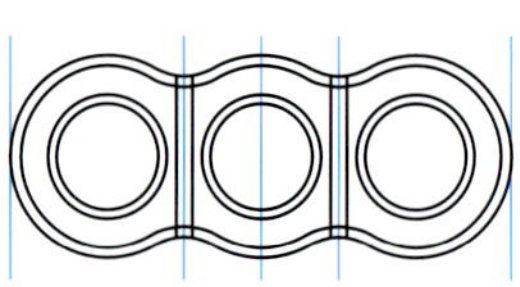

The set of bowls need not be based on multiples of four. In this example, a long tray is designed from three circles placed side by side to form a line. The bowls are rounded and each of two handles positioned on either side of the central bowl. The handles are slightly higher than the bowls.

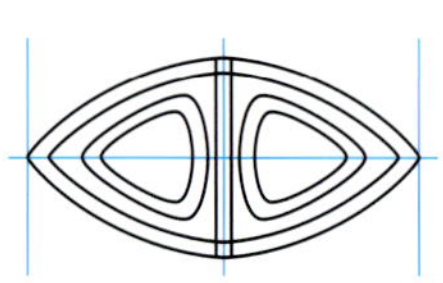

Here, the triangular bowls of the first design are arranged in a set of two on a leaf-shaped tray. A single central handle extending from side to side between the two bowls completes the design.

Some practice may be required to pinch four identical bowls in this way, but the process can be made easier by weighing the clay balls before pinching them. The clay used in this project is white-firing stoneware, which provides a good surface for under-glaze decoration, but any clay can be used together with a white decorating-slip painted over the surface for the same effect.

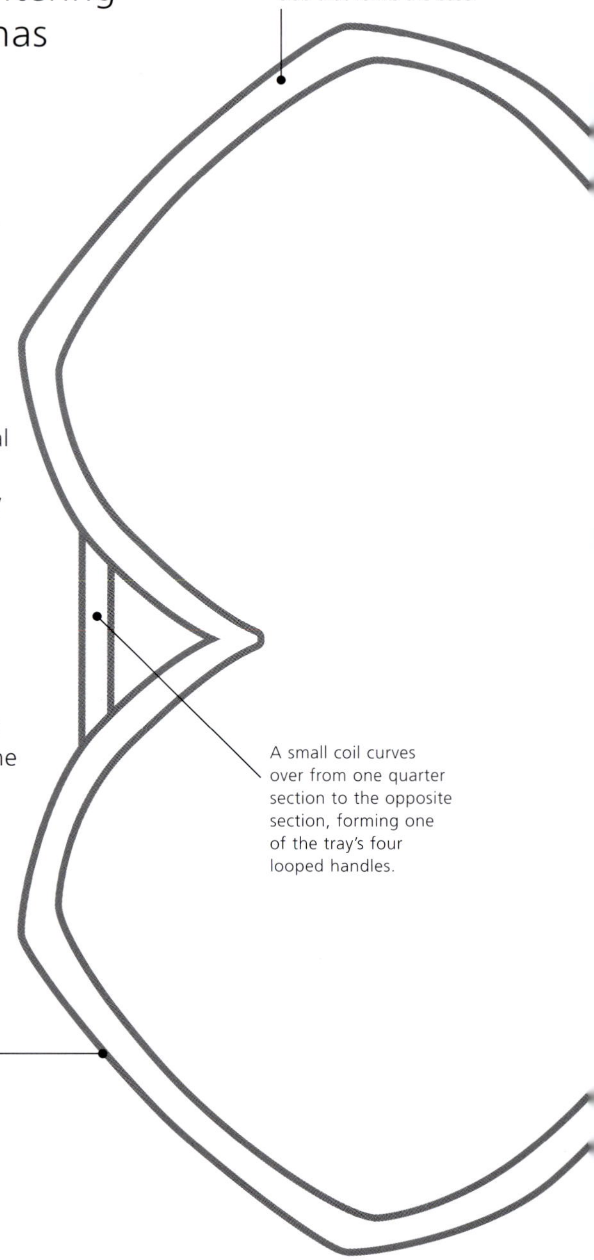

KEY

Pulling, lifting and supporting movements

Pushing, shaping and reinforcing movements

The size of each pinched bowl is determined by the weight of clay used to make it. You can decide the weight required for the bowls of your chosen design by roughly pinching out a ball of clay to the required size then weighing it. Once the weight of one ball has been determined, three more can be weighed to replicate it. Alternatively, you can simply take four balls of equal weight and base the size of the bowl set on that.

Holding a ball of clay in one hand, pinch out the shape using the technique shown on page 60. The clay wall should be pinched out as thinly as possible to form a rounded cup shape. Firm up the clay with a hairdryer to allow the pot to hold its shape, while retaining enough malleability in the clay to allow the shape to be manipulated later.

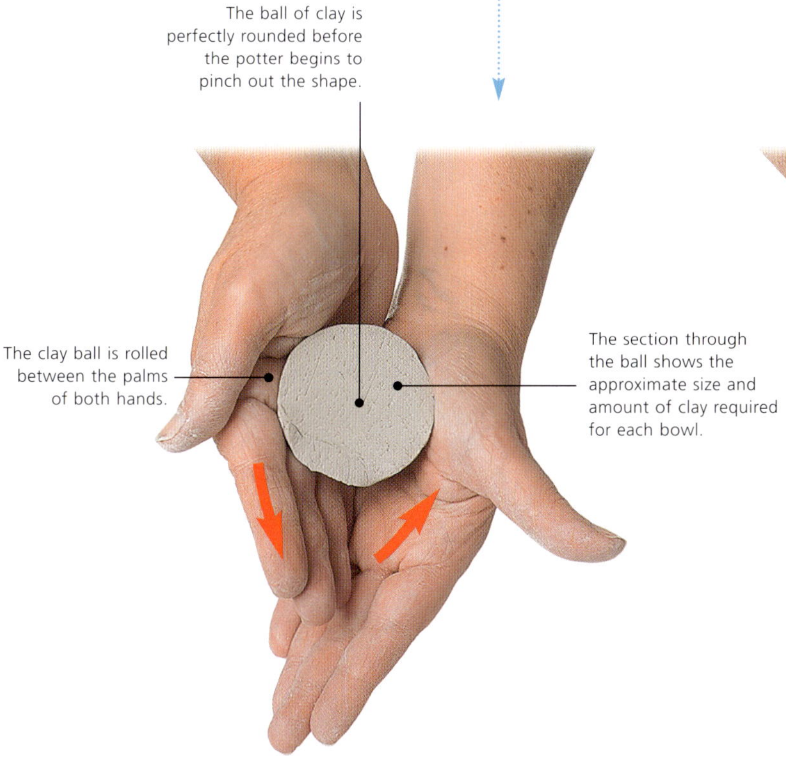

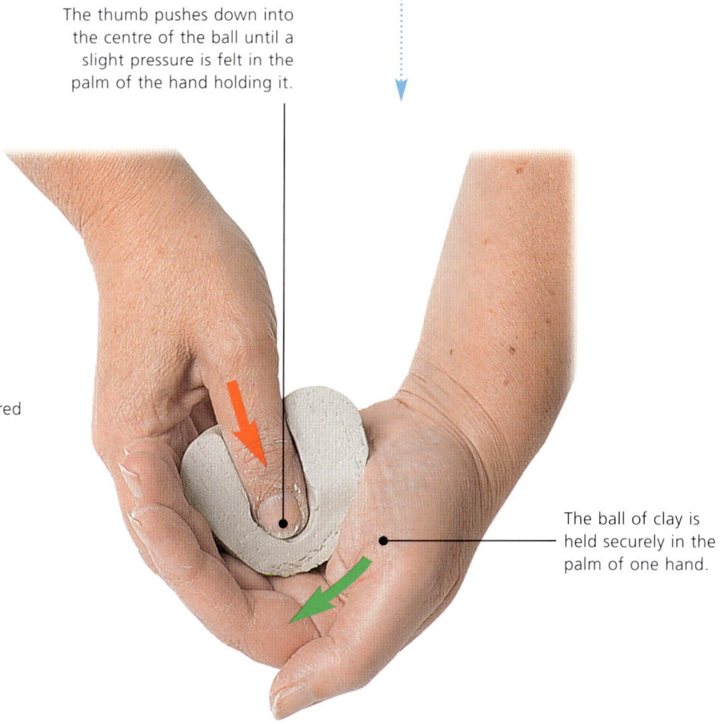

Pinch out the remaining three balls of clay to match the first as closely as possible. Don't worry too much about slight variations in height because these can be adjusted later – it is the general size and circumference of each cup that is most important. Measure the rims of the cups against one another to make sure the circumferences are equal. Place the cups on thin plastic to prevent the bases from drying out too much before the shapes are altered.

Turn one of the cups over onto a bat; then, using a wooden spatula, carefully paddle three equal sides to the form, narrowing the shape in from the rim to form a small triangular base. Support the bowl firmly with one hand as the shape is altered. You may need to paddle each side several times to get the correct shape. Once the base has been formed, turn the bowl the right way up to make sure the bowl is level.

Turn the bowl upside down again on the bat and carefully refine the surface using a metal kidney. Define and sharpen the edges using the kidney, then soften them back by running a finger over them. Work over the external surface with a rubber kidney to smooth it off completely. Firm the clay to a leather-hard state using a hairdryer so that the shape does not distort when the inside is refined.

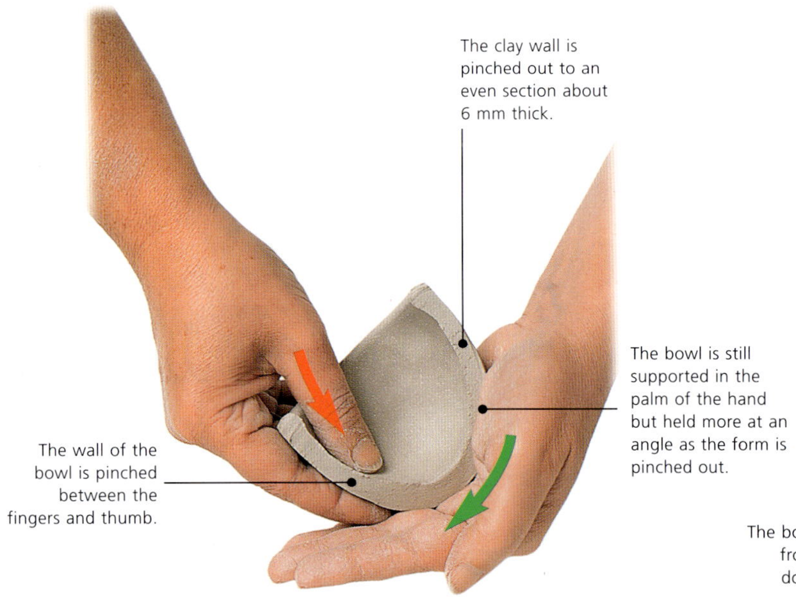

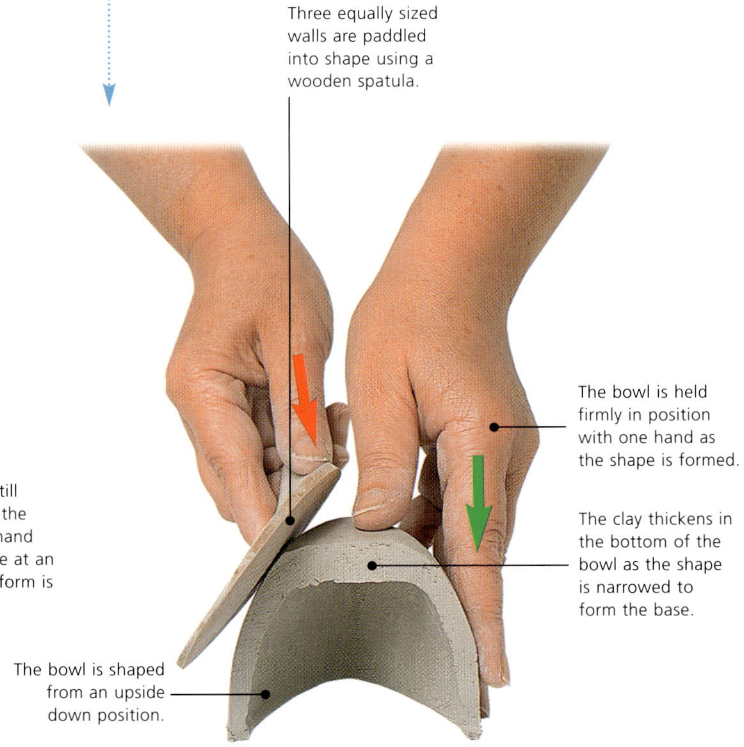

Turn the bowl back over and refine the inner surface by scraping away any irregularities in the thickness of the clay wall. This will be tricky because the bowl is quite small, so use the smallest scraping tool available (page 9). Because the clay was narrowed and compressed in the process of forming the base, you will need to scrape away quite a bit from this area. Aim to thin the wall to the same thickness as the rest of the bowl. It may help to hold the bowl in one hand as the clay is scraped out, but be careful not to distort the shape; otherwise, hold the bowl firmly on the bat to complete the task.

Level the rim of the bowl using a rasp blade. Try to remove as little clay as possible, but small cracks are common around the rims of pinched pots, so be sure to rasp just below these if you see any. Place the bowl upside down on the bat at regular intervals to make sure the sides of the bowl are level. Shave away tiny bits of clay at a time from the rim to avoid taking off too much.

Hold the bowl firmly on the bat the right way up and refine the rim by running a metal kidney along the outer edge to round it off slightly. Repeat the process on the inner edge, and then finish off using a rubber kidney to smooth the clay. The first bowl is now complete. Wrap it in soft plastic to prevent it from drying out further, and make the remaining three bowls in the same way. Measure each successive bowl against the first to maintain the correct shape and height, and wrap each one up when complete to prevent further drying.

7

8

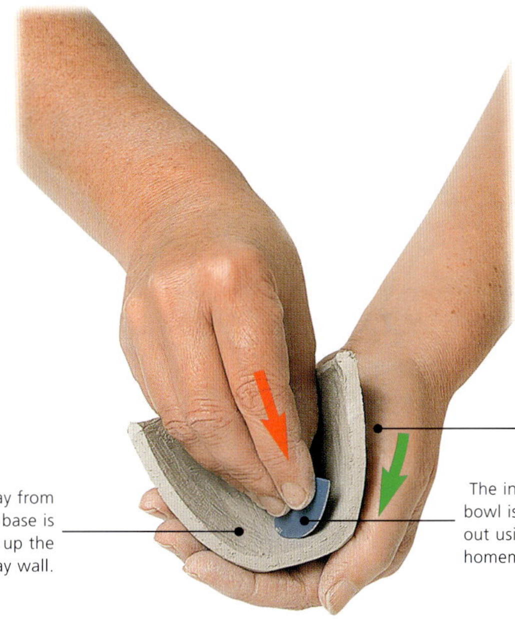

The excess clay from the narrowed base is removed to even up the section of clay wall.

The bowl is again held in the palm of the hand for the inside to be neatened up.

The inside of the bowl is scraped out using a small homemade tool.

Roll out a large slab of clay using roller guides no thicker than 6 mm and allow it to dry almost leather-hard. There needs to be some flexibility in the clay to allow the rim strips to be curved into place on the tray.While the slab is firming up, prepare a paper template for the tray by adapting the outline shape on the introductory page to the project. Lay the template on the clay slab and cut out the shape carefully with a craft knife. In addition, cut four 13-mm strips long enough to fit around each quarter section of the tray's rim.

Carefully transfer the base template for the tray to a wooden bat. Position one of the rim strips around a quarter section of the base, then cut it to size, mitring each end to fit the next strip. Remove the strip; then measure and cut the remaining three to the same size. Score and slip around the edge of one quarter section and the edge of the rim strip, then fit it onto the base carefully, taking care not to trap any air in the join. Continue to fit the second strip around the edge in the same way, paying particular attention to the mitre join.

When the final rim strip has been joined to the base, neaten up all the joins inside and out using a small rib tool or similar. Remove all the excess slip that has been squeezed out from the joins and smooth the surface back where possible. Soften the edges of the rim slightly by running a finger and thumb around it. Finish off the rim by stamping a tiny decorative detail into the outside edge in a central position on each quarter of the tray.

Tips for success

- When weighing the clay for the bowls, remember that a little clay pinches out a long way, so practise with different weights first to find the best one for you.
- Homemade tools are very useful for reaching difficult places because they can be tailored to specific requirements. Make some of your own, such as the examples in the Tools section (page 9), before starting the project; you'll be amazed how much they can help you.

Roll a small round coil to about a 6-mm diameter and cut it into four 5-cm lengths. Curve one of the coils around to fit between the quarter sections on the tray and mark the position where it will be joined. Place the coil handle on a bat and curve the remaining three coils to match it. Firm them all up a little with a hairdryer so that they will hold their shape. Join the handles to the base, scoring and slipping the surfaces beforehand. As a finishing detail, stamp the same decorative detail used on the sides into the end of each handle where it fits onto the base. The bowl set is now finished and ready to be decorated in your preferred style.

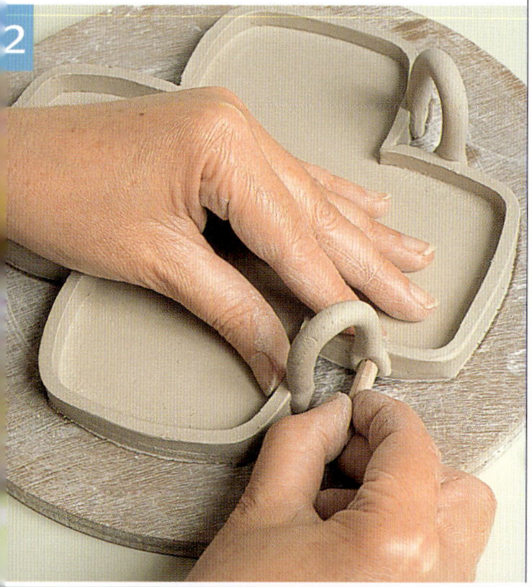

Dry the set slowly under loose plastic with the bowls in position to prevent the tray from warping. The bowls can be fired to bisque in place on the tray to help keep it flat, but the same is not possible for glaze firing. If the tray remains flat through the drying and bisque-firing processes, it should not distort at the glaze firing stage. The bowls in this project have been decorated with a single under-glaze leaf design on each of their three sides. The leaf is also repeated on the tray, and the same under-glaze colours are sponged lightly around the rim of each bowl to define them. The set was then glazed in stoneware transparent before firing to 1,260°C in an electric kiln.

CHAPTER THREE

Slabbing

Slabbing is a versatile technique, allowing the potter to build forms from either soft or hard clay. It can be challenging, however, because it is more prone to problems than other methods. For this reason, the beginner is advised to pay close attention to detail – especially the uniform thickness of slabs – and to aim for a high standard of finish. Historically, slabbing was widely used to make tableware, boxes, sarcophagi and roof tiles and other architectural features. The tiles that adorn the walls and floors of many ancient buildings were made by this method, and tiled surfaces are just as popular today.

In their soft form, clay slabs are flexible, allowing considerable manipulation of the material. Hard slabs, by contrast, call for precision and close attention to detail during construction. A huge range of forms can be built by slabbing, and extensive surface decoration can be applied at all stages of the making and firing. The techniques and projects in this section are basic, but they will provide you with all the information you need to progress to making a multitude of exciting forms.

Using firm slabs to make a lidded box

This section introduces the technique of building forms with firm slabs of clay. Making a box may seem basic at this stage, but it requires an understanding of the capabilities of the clay, some attention to detail, and accurate measuring and cutting to make the box well. Once in possession of these skills, you could successfully build a slabbed form to any dimension. Stoneware clay is used for this box, but the same principles of construction could be applied to earthenware.

Thoroughly wedge a block of clay weighing about 900 g and form it into an approximately square shape to make rolling easier. Position the block on a sheet of plastic and place a roller guide no thicker than 6 mm on either side of it. Using the length of a rolling pin, beat the clay to reduce the size of the block and force out any trapped air. Use evenly weighted strokes and work systematically from one side of the block to the other. This helps the slab to remain a manageable shape. If the block seems too bulky to roll after the first beating, turn it over and through 90 degrees, and beat it again in the same way, to regain a roughly square shape.

Begin to roll the block, starting from the middle and pushing the clay away from the body and back again. Check that the roller guides are still in position on either side of the clay so that the ends of the rolling pin can rest on them to gauge the final thickness of the slab. Do not try to roll the slab in one manoeuvre because this will distort the shape and cause stresses in the clay. Aim to keep an even pressure on the rolling pin and roll until a natural resistance to move any farther is felt in the slab. This indicates that the slab must be turned before rolling again.

To turn the slab over, lift it on the sheet of plastic and turn it over carefully onto the opposite hand before peeling the plastic off the back. Turn the slab over, rotate it 90 degrees, and position it back on the plastic sheet so that it will be rolled in the opposite direction next time, thereby maintaining the shape as far as possible. Rolling on plastic in this way reduces moisture loss from the clay at a time when it must be soft for easy rolling. It also makes the slab much easier to handle because it can be moved about on the sheets. Always remember, however, to peel the plastic from the clay and not the clay from the plastic, to avoid ripping or distorting the slab.

Roll the slab again until the rolling pin glides over the clay and the guides without meeting any resistance. If small air bubbles appear on the surface during rolling, pierce them with a potter's pin and then roll the slab again. Repeat the process as many times as necessary to remove all bubbles. When the slab is bubble-free and rolled out to the correct thickness, refine the surface with a rubber kidney. Use a light touch to avoid causing gouge marks.

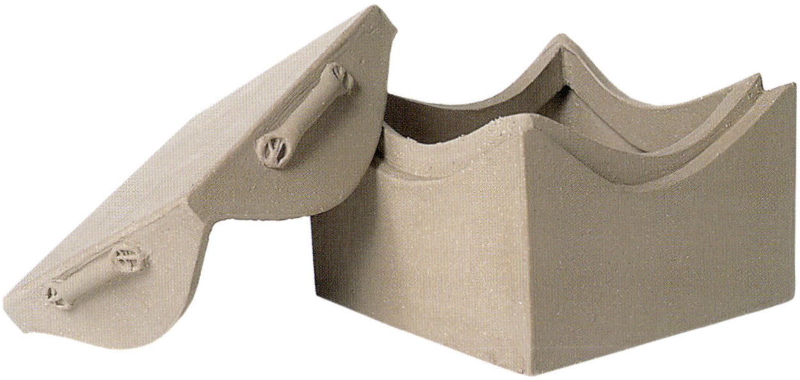

Lift the slab on the sheet of plastic and turn it over onto an absorbent board. The board used here is a fireproofing board, obtained as a remnant from a building supplier. Some potters roll the clay directly on such a board. This causes the clay to dry as it is rolled, and the slabs are instantly ready to use. It can be difficult to get the clay sufficiently thin in this way, however, and if the potter does not roll quickly enough, the surface often has hairline cracks. Beginners are advised, therefore, to roll on plastic sheets before transferring the slab to the board.

To stiffen the slab quickly to the correct stage for cutting, dry the surface with a hairdryer. The board will absorb moisture readily, so turn the slab over several times during the process. Dry the slab to the leather-hard stage, where it still has a small amount of flexibility but will basically maintain its shape when held upright. Transfer the slab to a sheet of soft plastic to prevent additional drying before use. Alternatively, the slab can be left to dry naturally on the board. Remember to turn it over from time to time for even drying.

Cut out a cardboard template for each section of the box: two 12.5-cm squares to form the base and lid, and four sections measuring 12.5 cm wide and 10 cm high for the walls. Place the templates on the slab as economically as possible. Wrap the spare clay in plastic to keep it moist for later use on the box rim. When cutting the sections of clay, use a ruler along the edge of the template for extra support and to make a sharper cut. Always cut away from your body and fingers wherever possible.

Remove any unneeded pieces of slab so that all the sections are ready for the next stage. Position a ruler 6 mm inside the edge of one section. Holding a knife so that the tip rests on the board and the blade on the ruler, cut a mitred edge, starting from the left and working toward the middle, then cut from the right back to the same point. Cutting the mitre in this way prevents the corner edges from breaking off. Mitre *every* edge of every section in the same way. Transfer all of the sections, except the base, to a sheet of plastic, and place the base section on a bat.

Using a toothbrush and water, score and slip one mitred edge of the base section and one long edge of a side section. Ease the sections together, checking that both are accurately aligned and that the joint is well sealed. Hold the base section in place on the board with one hand and tap a wooden block or ruler against the side base to secure the joint. Because the slabs are firm, the side should not need to be supported during this procedure.

Continue to score and slip the base edge next to the previous one, and the edge of the side section that was attached. Score and slip the corresponding edges of another side section and fix it into place as before. Check that the panels align and that the two corner edges close together well. Some of the slip is squeezed out as the sections are eased together, but this is a good indication that trapped air is also being removed.

Holding the wall of the box with one hand, paddle the corner joints using a wooden spatula to make sure of a good fit and to squeeze out any remaining air. It may seem to the beginner that the need to eliminate air from the clay is too often emphasised, but this is essential to avoid trapped air causing the clay to explode during the firing process. In a slabbed form, air is most often trapped in the joints, where splits frequently occur, so take time to make sure that the edges are thoroughly fixed together.

Reinforcing the joints with coils of clay can be done at any stage, but it is usually easier to do this as each section is added. Roll thin, soft coils and ease them along each joint, using a finger. Don't apply too much pressure because this will force the joints open again, but it is important to work the coil completely into the angle (again, to avoid trapping air in the seam). If possible, support the outside edge corresponding to the point where the coil is being applied on the inside.

When the coil is securely in place, neaten the seam with a round-ended modelling tool to remove the bulk, leaving only a small amount to soften the angles. Support all outer joints as you work on the inside, especially the corners, because these can be vulnerable to splitting. There should be no evidence of the reinforced joints when the box is complete – it ruins the appeal if the lid is lifted to reveal a messy interior. It is important always to give as much consideration to the inside as to the outside of a form.

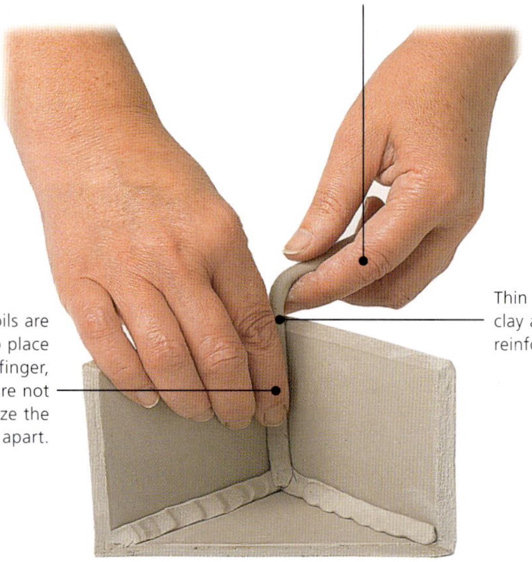

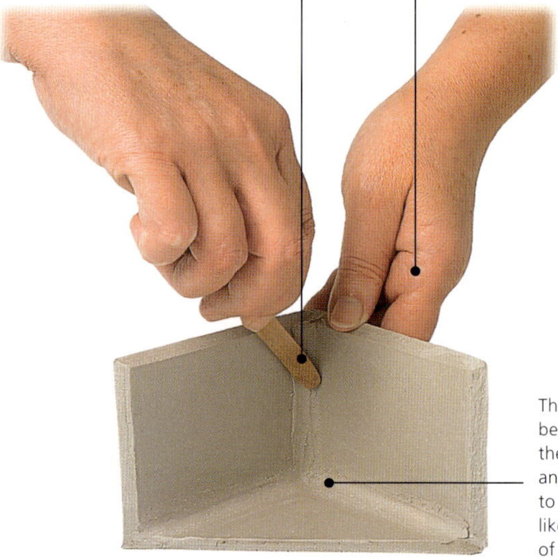

Continue to add the remaining side sections to the box, reinforcing each joint as it is fixed into place. If you cut out each section accurately, the box should fit together perfectly and the mitred edges ensure that the original dimensions remain unaltered. When the last side is fixed in place, paddle each corner again, using a wooden spatula. Smooth over each side of the box with a metal scraping tool, used on its side instead of its edge, paying close attention to the corners. If this proves too difficult, use a rubber kidney instead.

The box must be turned over at this stage to complete and neaten the base, but often the base is fixed to the bat as a result of slipping the edges. It can be released by carefully running a metal kidney around and underneath the outer edge, but take care not to gouge the base slab in the process of doing this. Rotating the bat on a turntable can help to accomplish the manoeuvre more smoothly.

When the base is released, turn the box over and use a metal scraper to smooth the surface, remove any slip from the edges, and make sure the joints are well sealed. If the joints appear to gape in places, push a few bristles of a wet toothbrush into the gap to moisten it, then join it back carefully, checking that it is absolutely secure before continuing. Apply the paddle to both sides of the rejoined edge to sharpen and reinforce the base.

Turn the box back over onto a cleaned bat. Score and slip all of the remaining mitred edges on the box and the final section. Carefully fix the lid section into place on the box, sealing it completely. This may seem illogical, but the reason will become clear later. The lid should fit into place perfectly. Pinch the seams together gently, supporting the box with fingers on each side to prevent the shape from distorting as each edge is secured. This final section is perhaps the trickiest part of the technique, so take time to do it correctly. Never rush any part of the process when slabbing – attention to detail is more important.

Finish securing the lid by paddling all the edges carefully with a wooden spatula. Hold the box in place on the opposite side when paddling to prevent altering the shape. It is also important not to mark the surface with the edge of the spatula because ridges can be hard to remove later. Finish by smoothing over the surface with a metal kidney or scraper. The inner joints can only be reinforced when the box is opened up again at a later stage. Meanwhile, the lid section is slightly more vulnerable than the rest of the box, so handle it with extra care.

Tips for success

- When mitring edges of slabs, position the ruler along the edge at a distance equal to the slab's thickness. For example, if the slab is 5 mm thick, the ruler should be positioned 5 mm from the edge.
- Save leftover sections of slabs to make smaller boxes or simple slabbed vases. Remember to keep them well wrapped up in thin plastic until you are ready to use them.
- Slabs that may have dried out too much for construction can be softened up a little by layering them on damp (not wet) sheets of cloth for half an hour or so. It may help to cover them in thin plastic as well.
- Have several clean bats available to transfer the work to at regular intervals. This avoids bits of clay and scrapings getting stuck to the slab walls and spoiling the surface.

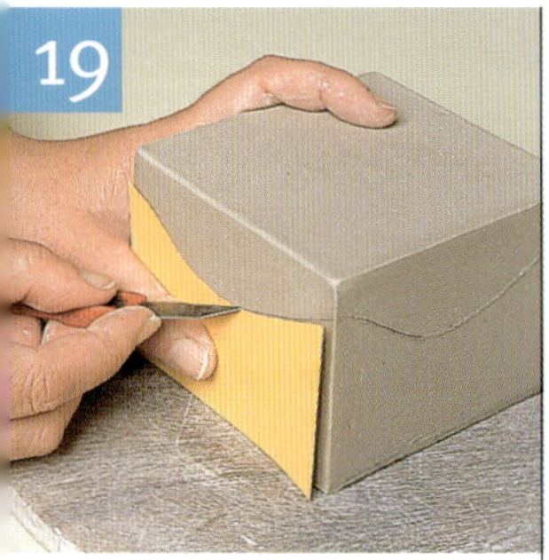

19

Draw a curved line on one of the side section templates, about two-thirds of the way up. The line should measure 25 mm down from the lid equally at each corner, but it can be random between these points. It is important, however, not to draw a line that incorporates undercuts, which would make it impossible to remove the lid. Cut the template in two along the line; then, holding the lower half of the template against the side of the box, carefully score along the curved edge of the cardboard with a knife or pointed tool to mark the position for the lid. Repeat the process on the remaining three sides, aligning the template in the same way each time.

20

Turn the box onto its side and use a craft knife to cut carefully along the scored line. Try to keep the knife pointing directly downward as the line is cut, and be especially cautious at the corners where there is a risk of cutting through to the next side at a point that does not coincide with the line. Using the tip of the knife will help, but it may be necessary to make several small cuts at the corners instead of one. Cut around all four sides in the same way, to form the lid.

21

When the lid is cut away from the base, lift it off carefully. If some areas snag, don't force the lid off; instead, cut gently through the clay with the knife. Do not attempt to alter the cut surface in any way after the two sections are separated, or the lid will not fit back into place accurately. That is why it is essential to cut the lid as cleanly as possible.

22

The lid section can now be reinforced with a coil of soft clay. Run the clay around the seams with a finger, and remove the excess with a modelling tool. Blend the coil in well so that it is unobtrusive. It is important not to make this reinforcement too bulky, because a locating rim to be fixed inside the box will extend into the lid to hold it in place when closed, and too much clay around the lid seams would prevent the lid from sitting squarely on the base.

23

After reinforcing the lid, soften all of the cut lines *very slightly* by carefully running them between finger and thumb. This action serves primarily to remove any fragments of clay or slip that may be stuck to the surface. Do not squeeze the rims because that would alter the fit of the lid – although the clay should now be firm enough to make this almost impossible. Check that the lid fits neatly back into place before proceeding because the walls can become slightly distorted during handling. If this has happened, ease the walls out very gently to align them with the base. Make sure you don't ease them out too much as this could force the corner joints apart.

This box demonstrates how different styles of openings can be cut to separate the base from the lid. In this example, the opening is designed around the stamped decoration, which was added after the sections of the box had been cut out. The same decoration is repeated around each side of the box and a variation stamped onto the lid.

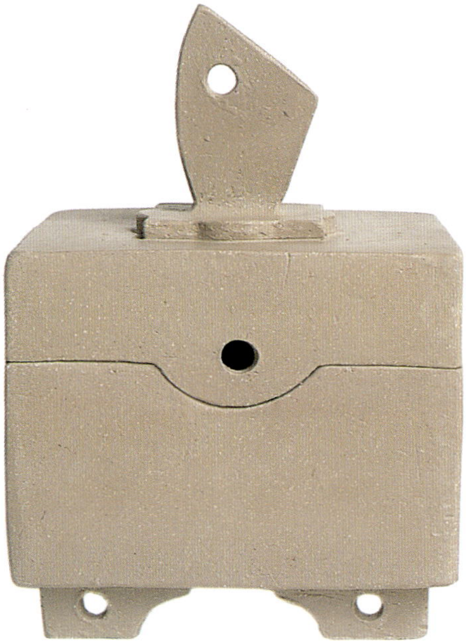

This design features a theme of pierced holes at various points on the box. The holes on each of the four sides mark the point where the lid is cut – the lid is cut from a straight line on each side of the box that dips into a central semicircle. A slabbed handle has been fitted onto the lid, and pierced to match the sides and feet.

Using the slab pieces left over when the main parts were cut out and the cardboard template that marked the lid position, cut out four strips of clay about 13-mm deep that correspond with the rolling line of the lid. These sections will be slightly too wide to fit inside the box, so cut each one carefully down to size by measuring it against the inner wall. When the size is correct, mitre each 13-mm side in the same way as for the main part of the box. Score and slip 6 mm inside the rim of the base of the box, along with the mitred edges and back of the strip to be fixed into place. Ease the locating rim section into place, allowing 6 mm to protrude above the box edge. The strip should align exactly with the rolling edge.

As each locating strip is fixed into place, remove the excess slip that is squeezed out around the edges, using a small scraping tool with a pointed angle. Hold the strip in place as the slip is removed, but take great care not to scrape any clay from the original cut rim. Continue to fix the remaining sections into place, removing the excess slip in the process. Reinforce the tiny mitred corners and smooth them off neatly. Test the fit of the lid again. If it is difficult to locate properly, scrape away some clay from the locating rim. It may take several attempts to fit the lid comfortably, but persevere by scraping away small amounts of clay and retesting until it works.

When the lid fits properly, turn the box over onto a clean bat. From the remaining clay scraps, cut four neat squares of clay to form the feet. Using a patterned texturing tool or the end of a screw or nail, make a small decorative mark in the centre of each square. Sit the squares on the base of the box and mark their position. Score and slip the marked areas on the base of the box and the underside of each square and then fix them into place, wiping away any slip that squeezes out around the edges.

Roll a thin, even coil of clay and cut it into four 25-mm lengths. Position a section of coil on one side of the lid, just below the top, and mark the point with a tool. Score and slip the marked area on the lid and one side of a section of coil and fix it into place – without squashing it down too much. Repeat the process on the remaining three sides of the box lid. The coils are a decorative feature but they also make it easier to lift the lid safely. Alternatively, a handle could be fitted to the top.

As a final detail, stamp each end of the coils with the tool used to decorate the foot squares. Hold the lid in place as the coils are stamped to prevent distorting the inner locating rim. After stamping, run a finger around each end to soften and round it off, in keeping with the shape of the stamp. Finally, using a metal or rubber kidney, scrape away any pieces of clay or slip that remain on the surface of the box. The completed box is ready to be finished in your chosen style.

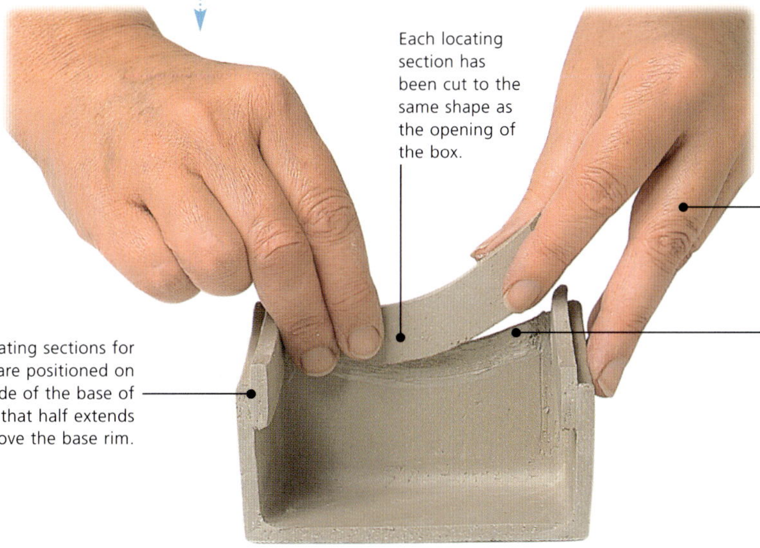

Building a vessel with soft slabs

Constructing a form with soft slabs of clay calls for a little more dexterity than using firm slabs. It also requires a greater understanding of the behaviour of clay. This simple form is nevertheless within the capabilities of the beginner, provided he or she follows the guidelines carefully. The soft slabbing method is also a good starting point for other projects and lends itself especially to simple figurative work.

In this project, the clay slab is shaped around a tube. A piece of the cardboard tubing used for rolls of fabric or a section of plastic drainpipe from a building supply centre can be cut to size for this purpose. The clay is a white stoneware that includes some grog for strength, but any clay would be suitable – with the exception of porcelain, which is difficult to manage on this scale.

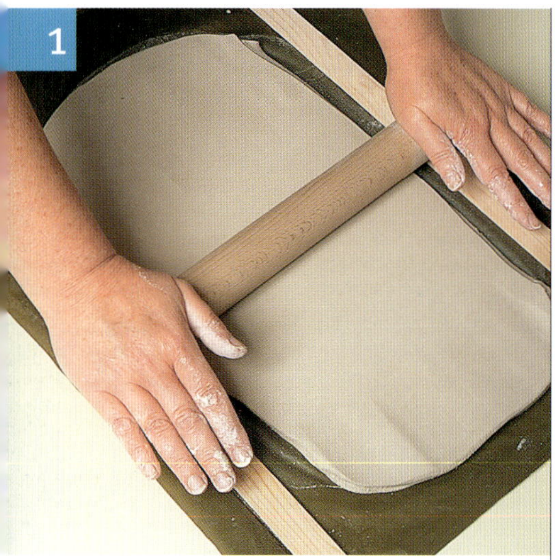

1

Prepare a block of clay weighing about 900 g by wedging it well to remove air and excess moisture. Measure the circumference of the tube to be used by wrapping an A4 sheet of paper around it widthways. If the sheet is not large enough, extend it by taping another sheet to the end until the required length is achieved. Add an extra 25 mm to allow for adjustments when the clay is wrapped around the tube. Roll out the clay using the method described on page 86, checking that the slab is large enough to fit the paper template.

2

When the slab is the required size, place the paper template over it and carefully cut out the shape, using a roller guide along each edge as additional support for the knife. Remove all of the surplus clay from around the edges, taking care not to rip or distort the main slab as you peel it away. Gently smooth over the surface of the slab with a metal or rubber kidney, again without altering the shape. Finally, pierce any visible air bubbles using a potter's pin and smooth the area afterwards.

3

Leave the slab in position on the sheet of plastic, then texture the surface using a selection of stamping tools and found objects that make interesting marks in clay. Here, a bisque-fired clay stamp made from a button and a selection of wooden stamps adapted from old pieces of batten are used, in conjunction with a fragment of ancient coral, but almost any small item can be effective. Experiment on scraps of clay before making your choice. The pattern can be built up randomly or ordered, as here, where simple repeats are created across the sheet.

When the basic structure of the design is established, the spaces between can be filled. The coral provides a simple texture to set off the more controlled pattern. Do not overwork the design. Choose a few patterns and textures that harmonise well and repeat them. However randomly this is done, it always looks better than filling the slab with an abundance of patterns and textures.

Put the decorated slab to one side and roll out a smaller slab of clay for the base and rim. Transfer this slab to an absorbent board to firm up a little, remembering to turn it over from time to time so that it dries evenly. When the slab is leather-hard, transfer it to a sheet of plastic to prevent additional drying. Meanwhile, prepare the tubular template by wrapping it in a couple of sheets of newspaper. It is important to do this neatly because lumpy paper can mark the clay and distort the inner wall of the vessel. Secure the paper by stuffing the excess into the ends of the tube.

Turn the textured slab over onto a clean sheet of old fabric so that the patterned surface is on the cloth, then peel the plastic from the back. This method of removal is essential to keep the shape intact. Peeling the slab off the plastic could distort and will probably tear it, ruining all of your creative work!

Position the tube on the clay so that the bottom of the tube is in line with the bottom edge of the slab. Very carefully roll the clay around the tube, holding it in place the entire time and making sure that it rolls in line with the bottom edge. The clay should fit the tube exactly and not be floppy. If you feel that the fit is unsatisfactory, unroll the clay and start over. Some potters find it easier to roll the slab with the help of the fabric to keep a tight fit.

When the clay is wrapped around the tube completely, there should be a 13–25 mm overlap. Holding a ruler across the point where both ends meet, cut a wide mitre through both sections of the overlap. This is a little tricky and may require the help of another person to hold the tube while you cut through. The slab may part as the ends are cut, but this is not critical because the slab needs to be reopened to score and slip the edges before joining.

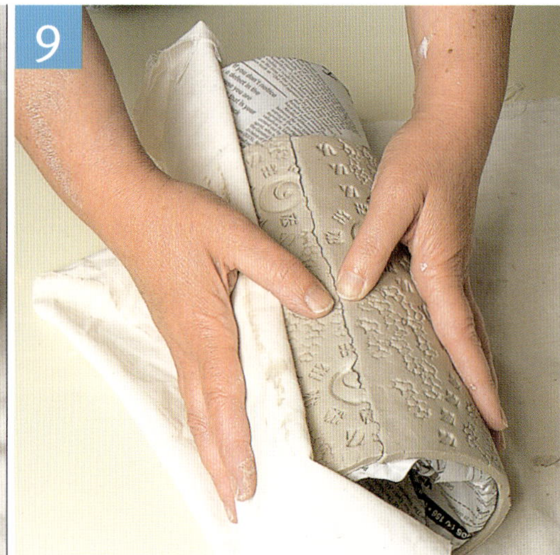

Unroll the slab back onto the fabric sheet. Score and slip each mitred end thoroughly, using a toothbrush and water or some slip made from the same clay body. Using the cloth, roll the slab back around the tube as tightly as before, making sure that the mitred edges overlap. Holding the slab in place with both hands, use the thumbs to seal the joint firmly, working up and down the length of it several times. Try not to squash the surrounding texture too much, but if a little damage occurs, it can be remedied.

This sample demonstrates how simple patterns can be cut into a blocks of wood for stamping onto clay. Each side of this block has a different pattern carved into it.

Anything can make a mark in clay. This is demonstrated here with a piece of weathered rock.

Once the joint is secured, work back over the area with the texture stamps to complete the patterning and fill the gaps. Provided the original design was fairly simple, this is easily done. Try to line the stamps up in the same way as before, then fill in the gaps to complete the cover up. Stand the cylinder upright on a wooden bat. If the clay seems very wet, firm it up a little using a hairdryer. Rotating the cylinder slowly on a turntable while this is done helps to promote even drying. The clay must be dried to the point where it can stand without sagging when the tube is removed but retain sufficient flexibility for the shape to be altered. This can be difficult for the beginner, but an understanding of the nature of clay comes with practice, so persevere to get it right.

When the clay is firm enough to hold its shape, the tube can be removed from the centre. Unplug the newspaper from the inside of the tube and then lift the tube out, leaving the paper behind in the clay cylinder. (The paper wrapping is vital to the removal of the tube because without it the cardboard would absorb moisture from the clay and stick to it; the clay would eventually shrink and crack as it dried, and only then could the tube be released.) If the clay holds its shape well after the tube is removed, the newspaper can also be carefully taken out. If in doubt, continue to dry the clay with the paper inside until it reaches the correct stage for removal.

Holding the cylinder between both hands, gently squeeze it into an oval shape. The point where the two ends were joined should be midway along one of the straight sides of the oval and not at the rounded end, where it would be more likely to crack in the firing. When you are satisfied with the shape, dry the form again, this time to the leather-hard stage. It may be necessary to hold the vessel in place while it is dried in order to maintain the new shape.

Old Asian printing blocks make excellent stamps for clay and are available in numerous sizes and shapes from many stores, galleries and museums. The blocks are carved from wood, and some have excellent repeats for large slabs of clay.

Shells make wonderful marks in clay and can be used on their own to wonderful effect or combined with other stamp patterns to create intriguing designs.

Position the oval on a section of the slab that was prepared earlier, allowing a 6-mm margin all around the base. Score the position of the oval onto the slab. Set the oval aside, then cut out the base, including the 6-mm allowance around the scored line. The extended base is necessary to reinforce the joint on the outside, because your hand will not fit inside the form to reinforce it in the usual way. Cut out the base as neatly as possible.

Turn the oval vessel over and score and slip the base rim using a toothbrush and water. Work up a generous amount of slip as you score. Score and slip the oval base slab in the same way, inside the scored outline. Fit the two sections together, taking care to match the body evenly to the scored outline on the base. Hold the body in place on the base for a few seconds, applying firm pressure until the two surfaces adhere well.

To secure the fit of body to base, lift the form carefully off the bat, then tap it back down onto the surface several times. Lift the vessel only 25 mm or so to do this, and tap the form squarely on the bat to prevent the base from slipping out of place. Hold the body lightly to avoid distorting the shape.

Roll a coil of soft clay. Using a finger, reinforce the joint by blending the coil around the extended base section. When the coil is in place, blend it carefully into the wall, using a wooden modelling tool with a rounded end. Try not to disturb the texture pattern too much, but make sure that the coil is thoroughly fixed to both the base and the wall. Finish off by running a finger around the edge again to soften it and remove any surplus snags of clay. Turn the form over and repeat this procedure around the underside edge to improve the appearance of the base.

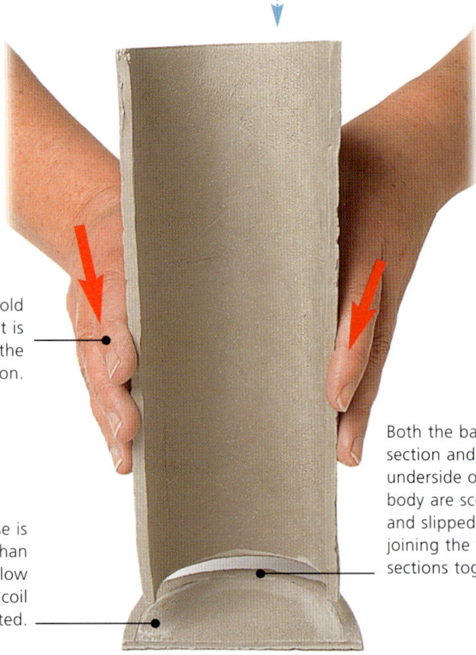

Both hands hold the body as it is fitted onto the base section.

The base is slightly larger than the body to allow a reinforcing coil to be fitted.

Both the base section and the underside of the body are scored and slipped before joining the two sections together.

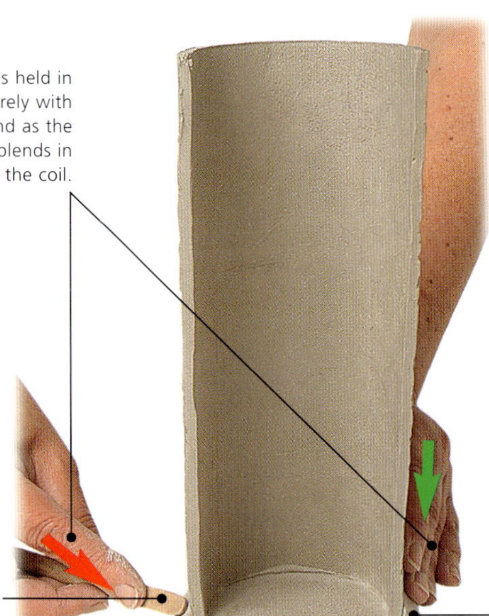

The form is held in place securely with one hand as the other blends in the coil.

The coil is carefully blended onto the base and wall of the form using a wooden tool.

A reinforcing coil is fitted around the base on the outside of the form because the inside is too difficult to reach.

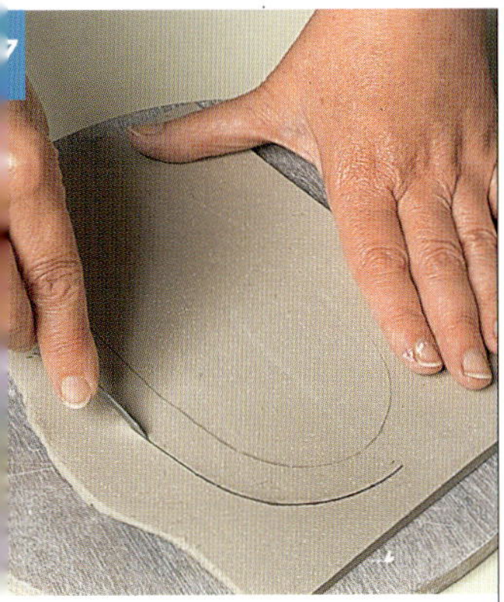

Transfer the remaining slab that was prepared earlier to the bat. Turn the vessel upside down and position it on the slab with a margin of at least 13 mm all the way round. Score the position of the vessel on the slab using a knife or modelling tool. Remove the vessel and cut out the shape carefully, 13 mm wider than the scored line. Then cut out a centre oval in the same way, 13 mm in from the scored line. This will allow plenty of clay to make adjustments later.

18

Score and slip the slab oval inside the marked line, using a toothbrush and water. Brush the surface well to create plenty of slip. Score and slip the rim of the vessel in the same way, then fix it in place on the slab, making sure that it sits within the marked line. As with the base, lift the form and tap it back on the bat a few times to secure the two sections together. Remember to do this squarely to prevent the slab from slipping out of place. Reinforce the underside of the rim in the same way as the base, using a soft coil of clay and blending it in well.

19

When the rim is secured to the body, turn the form over and return it to the bat. Using a craft knife, carefully cut the excess clay from the centre of the oval back to the wall of the main body. Then blend the joint with a wooden tool or metal kidney, finishing off with a rubber kidney to smooth the surface thoroughly. The reason the inner rim is cut to size at this stage is that the shape can often be altered a little as the outside is reinforced, and this allows the excess clay to remedy the problem.

20

Finish the rim by carefully smoothing away the sharp edges with a metal kidney. Support the form with the other hand to prevent the shape from distorting. Work around the rim slowly, rounding off the cut edge above and below. This makes the rim look softer and more appealing. Badly finished details are the first to be noticed, so it is worth taking time to complete this task properly. If the rim is too wide for the form to look balanced, shave it down carefully using a rasp blade, then finish it off as above with a kidney.

Making a decorated window box with large slabbing

This technique involves the preparation of larger slabs of clay that would be difficult to roll from one block, so a slightly different method is used. Apart from this, and the obvious differences in handling the slabs, the technique is similar to that used for the firm slab box (page 86). The decorative sprigs are made by the method demonstrated in Moulding (page 132), and the Coiling chapter (page 24) shows how to make the flattened coils for the rim. A stoneware clay with some grog for strength was chosen to make the box frostproof for outdoor use.

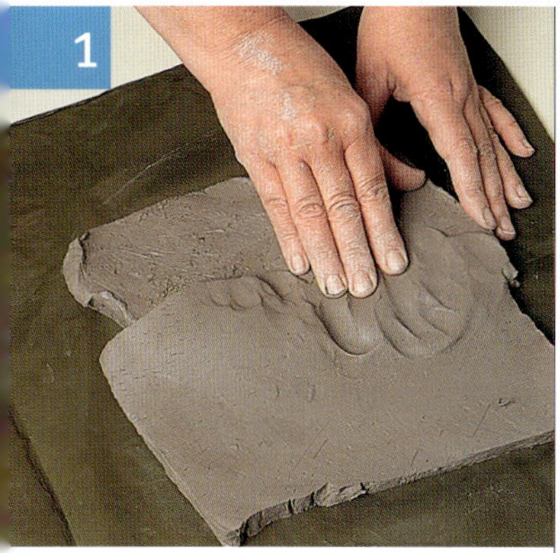

Wedge about 12.5 kg of clay to remove all air and excess moisture. This will probably be too much clay, but it will not be wasted, and it is better to prepare too much than too little! Form the clay into a square or oblong shape to make cutting easier. Using a cutting wire, slice off several slabs of clay about 25 mm thick and place three of them on a sheet of plastic so that the ends overlap to make a long slab. Blend the slabs together roughly with your fingers, then turn them over and repeat the process on the underside.

Because the slabs are large, they need to be slightly thicker to hold their shape for construction, so use 10-mm thick roller guides on either side of the clay and roll the slab, starting from the middle. It may be easier to roll one half of the slab away from your body first, then turn the sheet around to roll the second half. Do not force the clay too much. Roll until the clay seems to resist, then lift the plastic sheet and turn the slab over onto the opposite hand. Peel the plastic off the back of the slab, then reposition the slab on the sheet and roll again until the pin glides easily over the guides.

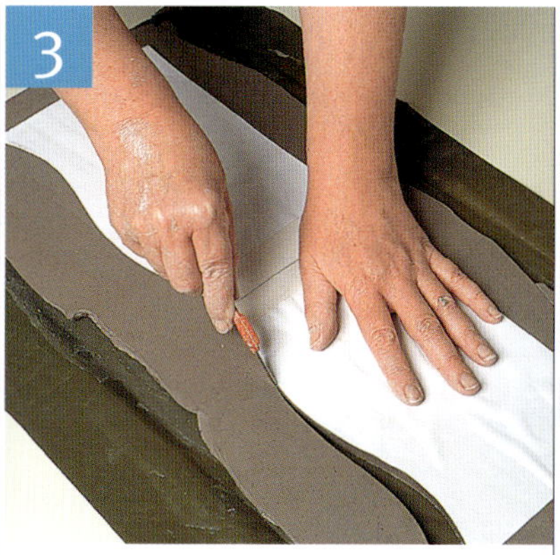

Roll four more slabs of the same size, then begin to dry them on an absorbent board, turning them over from time to time. Meanwhile, prepare the paper or cardboard templates for each section of the box. The base should measure 15 cm wide and 45 cm long, or as long as needed for the box to fit the window space. The long sides are equal in length and measure 15 cm deep at the highest points (the corners and the centre). The wavy top was drawn by making a template the same size as the base, folding it in half, then drawing in the line, so that the dips were formed between the highest points. That way, when the line is cut, the shape is exact along the length. Two end sections measure 15 x 15 cm, with a dip between the corner points to match the sides. Position each template on the clay slabs and cut them out, using a roller guide as extra support along the straight lines.

Using the method described in the section on building with firm slabs (page 86), mitre the edges of the slabs in the following way: all four sides of the base slab; three edges of the side panels (not the rolling edge); three sides of each end panel (again, not the rolling edge). You will need to place the ruler a distance from the edge that is roughly equal to the slab's thickness in order to cut the mitres for the edges so that they fit together neatly. Remember to cut from one side to the middle, then cut back from the opposite side to the central point, to avoid breaking off the corners.

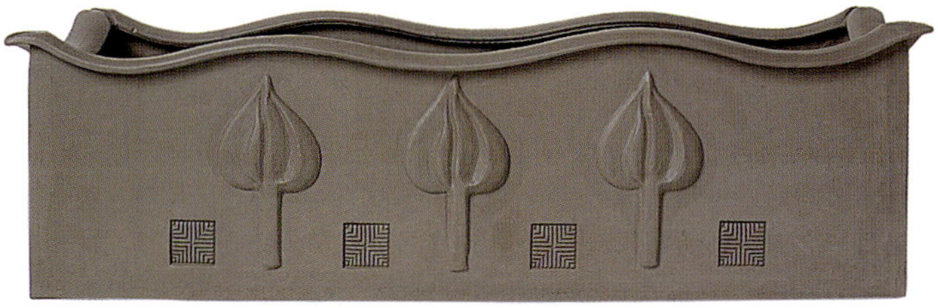

Tips for success

- Check that you have enough wedged clay for the size of the project before rolling it out.
- Roll all the sections at the same time so that they can dry out evenly. Warping and cracking will occur if all of the panels are not dried to the same level before construction.
- Roll the slabs to an even thickness using the roller guides – discrepancies will cause the form to warp and crack.

After mitring all of the sections, score and slip one end of the base panel, using a toothbrush and enough water to build up a generous amount of slip. Score and slip the lower mitred edge of the end panel in the same way, then fit it into place on the base, checking that it is properly aligned. Hold the end section in position for a few seconds until it can support itself. The clay should be at the leather-hard stage for construction, so it should hold its shape well without extra support when each section is added, allowing you to move on to the next stage with ease.

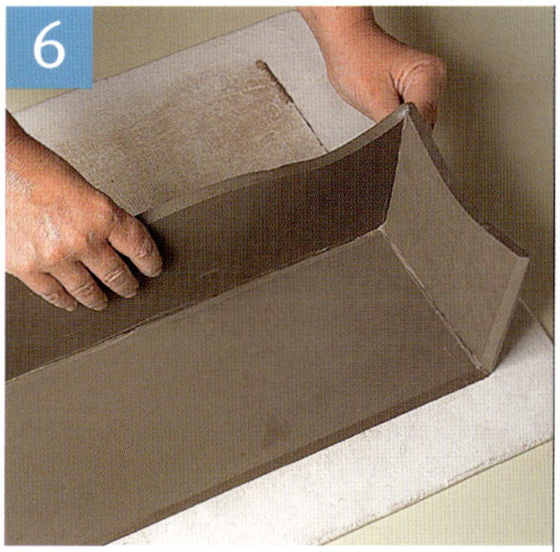

Score and slip a side panel along the bottom edge and up the side that will fit to the end section. Score and slip the relevant edge of the end panel already in place. Fit the side section into position, checking that the corner fits neatly with the end section. When the two sections are in place on the base, use a block of wood or a ruler against the outer wall at the base to ease the sections together more. It is difficult to turn the box over at this stage to deal with the joint on the underside, but this can be done later.

Roll a soft coil of clay and reinforce the joints made so far by easing the coil into place with a finger. Blend the coil into the sides with a modelling tool, removing any surplus in the process. It is just as important to reinforce this box well as it is the smaller one – more so if it is to be used outside. And for a potter to feel proud of a piece of work, it is essential to make it to the very best of his or her ability, inside and out!

Continue to join the remaining sides to the box, being sure to align all of the corners and levels correctly. Reinforce all of the joints in the same way; then smooth the inner and outer surfaces of the box with a metal scraping tool, paying close attention to the corners. At this stage the box can be turned over carefully to neaten the underside. Check that the base joints are good by using a wooden spatula to tap them together. Smooth the joints over first with a metal kidney and then with a rubber kidney to soften the edges. Turn the box back over onto a clean board.

The next stage is to make the sprigs for the side decoration. Press a small strip of clay into a sprig mould (page 132), making sure that it fills the space completely. Set the mould on the workbench and remove the excess clay by dragging a roller guide over the surface towards your body, with your thumbs supporting one end of the mould. The guides should sit flat on the plaster. Do this in small stages to avoid dragging the sprig out prematurely. It may take several attempts to achieve the correct technique because the clay starts to dry as soon as is placed in the mould and releases easily because the amount is so tiny. When the sprig has thin extensions, as in this case, extra care must also be taken to avoid breaking these sections off. A little practice is the best way to get the procedure right.

After clearing the excess clay from the surface of the mould, score the clay surface in a crosshatch action, using a pointed tool or knife. To remove the sprig, form a small ball of soft clay, gently squeeze it onto the clay in the mould, then lift the sprig out and place it on a plastic sheet to prevent additional drying. Repeat the process to make as many sprigs as required to decorate the sides of the box – in this case, eight (three for each long side, and one for each end).

Measure the position for the sprigs so that each will be equally spaced on the sides of the box. Hold a sprig at each measured point to mark the outline shape. Score and slip the marked position and the back of the sprig using water and a toothbrush, then fix the sprig into place, taking care to squeeze out any air and excess slip. Wipe around the sprig with a paintbrush or barely damp sponge to remove the slip that oozed around the edges; but don't overdo this because it will wipe away the details in the sprig. Repeat the process until all the sprigs are in position around the box.

To complete the side decoration, a wooden stamp is used to make a formal pattern between each sprig. It can be difficult to stamp the clay at this stage because it is fairly firm, but it can be done by placing a block of wood inside the box against the section of wall being stamped. The block must be held firmly in place. Alternatively, the clay can be stamped when cutting the sections out. This means planning the design in advance and measuring each detail with care. The stamps are not essential to the design, however, and can be omitted.

Tips for success

- Have a selection of roller guides of different thicknesses for various needs. Make sure they are long enough, and always keep them in pairs.
- Equip yourself with a long, straight rolling pin for larger projects.
- Eliminate air bubbles under the surface by piercing them with a pin as soon as you notice them, to avoid explosions in the firing.

Roll a thick coil of clay and flatten it, using the method described in the coiling chapter (page 24). The coil must be slightly longer than the side of the box – in this case, about 51 cm long. Position a 25-mm wide roller guide over the coil and roll it backwards and forwards to round off the coil, giving it a domed shape. Cut off the clay that is squeezed out by the roller guide at each side of the coil, and run a finger over the edges to soften them. Make two more flattened coils in the same way. Position one of the coils along the edge of a long side of the box, allowing a little overlap at each end. The coil should rest on the edge, overlapping slightly inside and out. Cut both ends on the diagonal, so that when the side sections of coil are cut and added, the joint will form a right angle. Remove the coil, score and slip the underside and the relevant rim on the box, and fix the coil back into position, making sure that it adheres thoroughly.

Cut one of the remaining coils in half and measure it against an end section. Angle each end in the same way as for the previous section, checking that the cut end fits well with the one already in place. Score and slip the coil again, along with the end rim and the two angled ends of the coil to be joined. Fix the coil section into place carefully, making sure that the ends fit together neatly. Fit the remaining two coils in place in the same way. Spend a little time checking that the coils are entirely secure. As an extra precaution, a soft coil of clay can be used to reinforce the rim on the underside of the overlap on the inside of the box. Blend this in well, so that it is not apparent from the outside.

As a final detail on the corners of the box and to help secure the ends, stamp a groove along the angle of the joint, using the side of the roller guide. Do not make the groove too deep but just enough to compress the clay. Use a different stamp to seal the corners, if you prefer, or omit this detail entirely. It is a decorative feature that is not essential to the construction of the form but rather a matter of personal choice.

Turn the box over very carefully onto a clean board, taking care not to knock the corners. Roll and flatten two more coils of clay the length of the box, and finish them off in the same way as those for the rim. Mark the position of each coil along the length of the base, 13 mm in from each side and within about 25 mm of each end. Score and slip the marked strips and the underside of each coil and fix them into place, making sure that they are stuck down securely. Using a wooden modelling tool, remove any slip that squeezed from the sides of the coils. Firm the coils to the same level as the rest of the box, using a hairdryer. This will prevent them from flattening out when the box is turned back over. When the coils are firm enough, set the box upright.

The end of each coil was cut on the diagonal, so that each corner forms a right angle when the ends are fixed together.

The interior of the box was completely reinforced and finished off neatly.

One hand holds the coil in place at a corner while the rest of the coil is lined up correctly on the rim.

The coil is positioned so that it protrudes an equal amount inside and out.

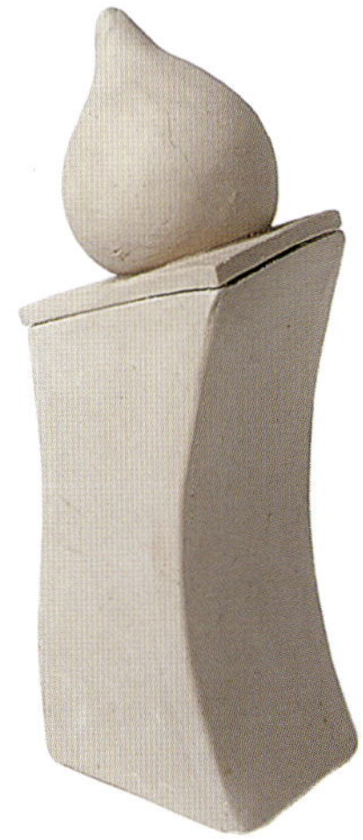

This project is slightly more advanced than the others in the book because it involves the use of a clay that is renowned for its sensitivity.

Porcelain boxes

The first of the boxes has three sides and curves up from the base, which will allow the next box to fit neatly into the outward curve. The porcelain slab is rolled very thin to make this box, as the latter is quite small – if the clay were thicker, the delicacy of the shape would be lost. The onion or minaret on the box's lid is pinched to the same thickness as the body sections and is positioned at a slight angle, as shown.

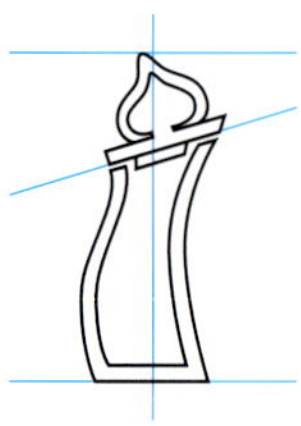

The shape of the second box is designed to fit into that of the first. This box has four sides, again curving up from the base. The lid is slabbed and follows the curves of the body, although it should be possible to turn it around so that it curves in the opposite direction.

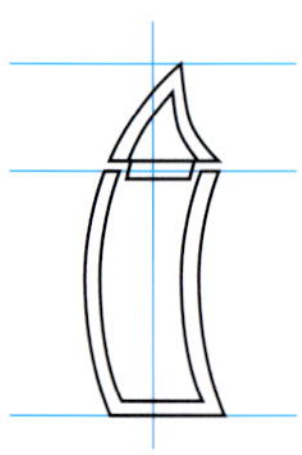

The third box is also four-sided and curves into the second box on one side. The opposite side curves in a different way to balance the form and add interest. The onion or minaret is positioned squarely on top of the lid and tear-shaped sections are carved out of its body to allow in some light.

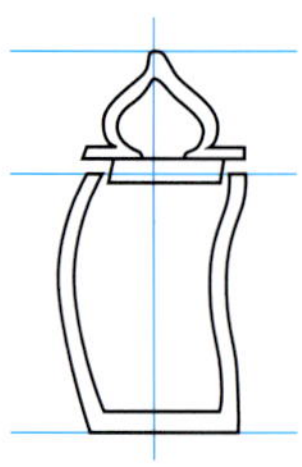

The fourth box in the series has not been included in the finished photograph (see page 107), but shows once again how the forms can be built to fit together like a jigsaw puzzle by curving one side into the shape of the previous box.

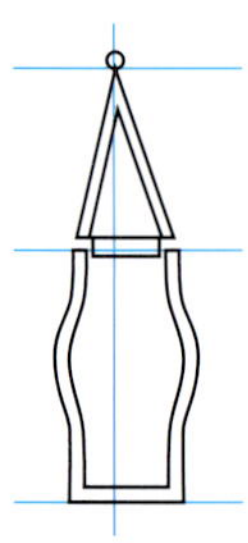

Porcelain is uniquely susceptible to the way in which it is handled. For this project the clay needs to be leather-hard before being cut because in its plastic state it would stretch and distort when lifted. The slabs are also much thinner than any used before, so construction calls for a delicate touch.

Two of the boxes have tiny pinched onion domes on the lids. These can be made in advance, ready to fix in place when the lid is completed. It is also advisable to pinch several domes to give some choice of size – and in case of accidents!

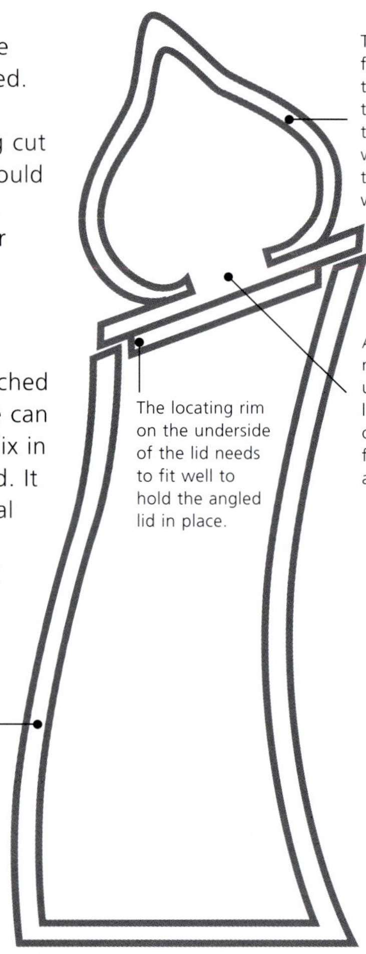

KEY

Pulling, lifting and supporting movements

Pushing, shaping and reinforcing movements

Roll a slab of porcelain on a sheet of clean cloth, thinning it out gradually by turning it over regularly and rolling in different directions to reduce stress in the clay. Roll separate slabs, each one large enough for all the sections of the individual box, using a clean, dry cloth for each. The rolling pin must be immaculately clean. Use the thinnest roller guides possible, or roll to the thickness of those available, then carefully continue without them. Put the slabs on absorbent boards to dry out. Monitor the slabs carefully, turning them over frequently. When they are leather-hard, transfer them to plastic sheets and cover them to prevent additional drying.

While the slabs are firming up, prepare the cardboard templates, using the dimensions shown in the diagram or following your own design. Cut a template for each separate section of the box. If cutting templates for all of the boxes at the same time, keep the correct sections together by numbering and naming each one. Make one box at a time. Unwrap a slab of clay and transfer it to a clean bat; then position all of the template parts as economically as possible on the surface. Cut each section out carefully, using a ruler as extra support along straight lines. Wrap the remainder of the slab in plastic because it will be needed later.

The box being constructed here is triangular, so it has only three walls. Using the technique described in the section on building with firm slabs (page 87), mitre the base and sides of each body section, leaving the upper edge unmitred. Use a ruler, where possible, for extra support, but this will not be possible along the wavy sides of the sections, which you will need to cut freehand. The triangular base section should be mitred on all three sides. It is vital to cut the mitre from each end to the middle to avoid breaking off the corners of the sections. This rule applies more to porcelain than to any other clay, although it is a good practice for all mitred edges.

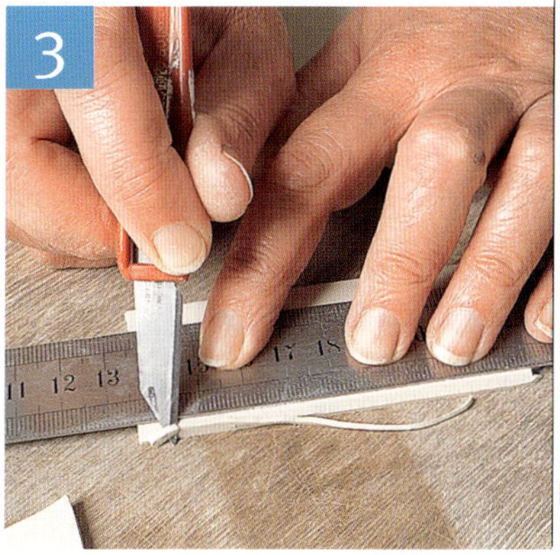

This photograph shows how thin the porcelain slab needs to be for this project. It also demonstrates how firm the slabs are. This can be misleading, however, because there is still some flexibility in each section, and this is essential for the construction of the box. Working a clay to a stage where it is both firm and flexible can seem difficult at first, especially as porcelain moves quickly from one state to the other – flexible one moment, rigid and unusable the next. Practice will help in understanding how to handle the clay, and you should work as quickly as possible to prepare and construct the parts – without compromising the quality of the workmanship.

Templates for three-sided box

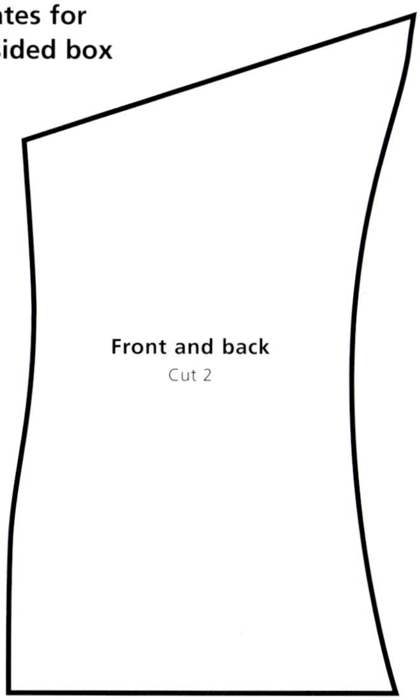

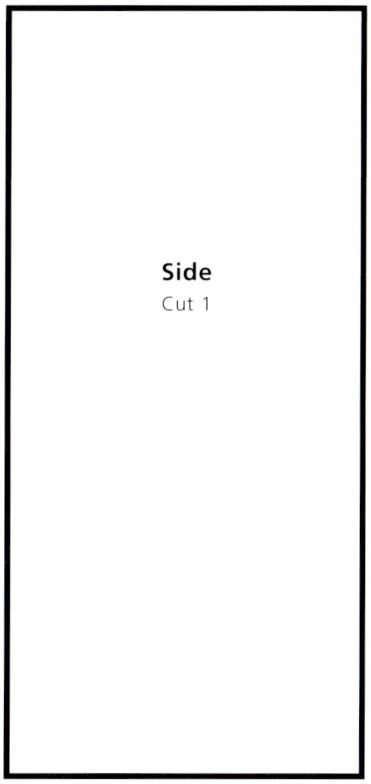

All the templates on pages 102–107 are shown at actual size. The onion dome box is pinched to size as described on page 106.

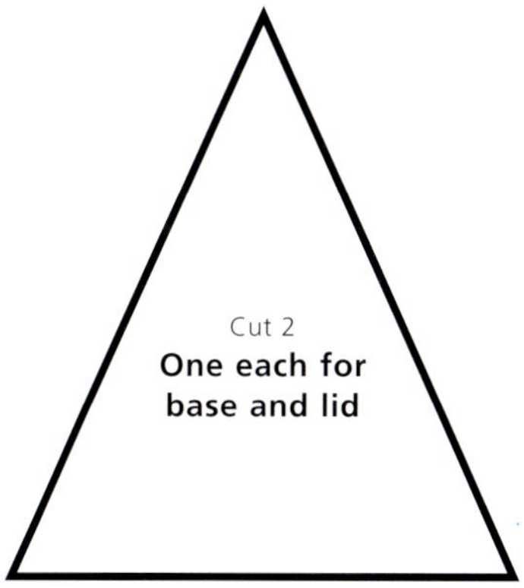

Mitring the curved edges of the side panels of the box is slightly more difficult because it cannot be done with the aid of a supporting ruler. Carefully hold the panel in place on the bat and cut the mitre freehand around the curve from each side to the centre. Use the tip of a clean, sharp craft knife and rest the hand that is cutting on the hand that is holding the section on the bat, to keep it steady. Try to keep the angle of the mitre the same as for the straight edges. Practise first on some leftover scraps of slab, if necessary.

To prevent the sections from drying any more before construction, place them on a sheet of plastic and cover them loosely. In the meantime, prepare some slip by grinding down a few scraps of dried porcelain using a pestle and mortar or the end of a rolling pin and a dish. The finer the porcelain, the quicker and easier it will be to make it into slip. Wear a mask for this task, which can release particles of dust. When the clay is a dustlike consistency, add some water a little at a time and mix it thoroughly until the slip is the consistency of whipping cream.

A toothbrush would ruin the delicate edges of the porcelain sections, so use a piece of fine hacksaw blade to score the mitred edges. All mitres can be scored in advance like this, making construction much faster. Use the blade in a crosshatch action, but be cautious at corners to avoid breaking them off. Hold the sections in one hand to score the edges, but take care not to distort the shape in the process.

With all the relevant parts in position on the bat, apply a liberal amount of the slip to one side of the triangular base section and the base edge of one of the side panels, using a small soft paintbrush. It is better to use too much slip than too little because the excess can be wiped away easily after the sections are joined, but check that the slip does not contain any hard lumps of clay.

Tips for success

- When working with porcelain, it is essential to keep the work area and all of your tools and materials spotlessly clean to avoid contamination.
- Many of the problems encountered in joining porcelain slabs result from the clay's high shrinkage rate and fast drying. All the slabs must be of equal dampness or dryness, and the finished work must be dried out very slowly.
- Discrepancies in thickness cause great stresses in porcelain. Rolling out and cutting sections accurately will help avoid warping.
- Roll out several extra slabs of clay and store them between sheets of plastic to be used in case of mishaps.
- Always fire boxes with the lids in position, even at the highest temperatures. This applies especially to porcelain because of the higher potential level of shrinkage and warping.

Templates for small four-sided box

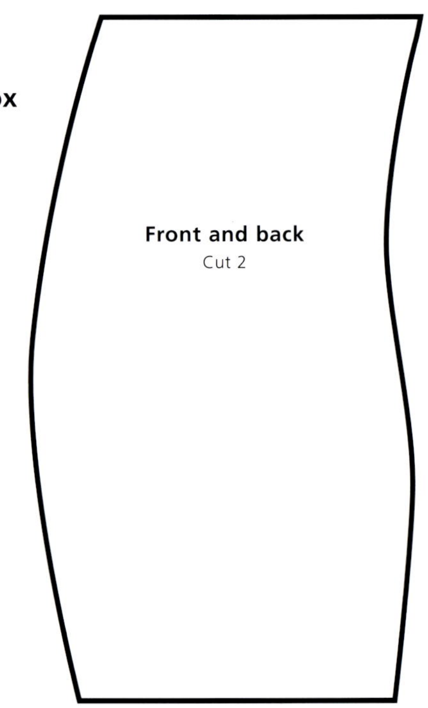

Fit the side section onto the base and hold it in place for a second or two until the joint is sealed. To check that the sections are well joined, turn the side panel so that it lies flat on the board and the base is standing up. Gently tap a ruler or block of wood against the joint as it sits on the board. Tap again with the side the right way up.

Score and slip the next side panel of the box and the corresponding side on the base section. Ease the section into place, making sure that all the levels align. Gently pinch the front joint together, taking care not to distort the shape. Use the block of wood again to tap the base gently together. With a barely damp sponge, wipe away any slip that oozed onto the outside of the box. Run a metal kidney along each side of the curved joint at the front of the box to seal it more securely.

Before joining the third side to the box, scrape any slip from the inside using a sharp-ended tool, such as a scalpel or craft knife. This is a good opportunity to check that the joints are well sealed. If the seams look questionable, ease the sections apart very gently and apply some more slip, then rejoin them in the same way as before. It is essential to join the sections securely, because the boxes are too tiny and delicate to be reinforced on the inside, as in other techniques.

Slip the three sides of the remaining section and the base and sides of the sections already joined. Ease the panel into place, curving it gently to the shape of the side walls. This is when it becomes apparent why the clay needs to retain some flexibility. Pinch the edges together gently, as at the front, wiping away any oozing slip as it appears. Turn the box over and check that the base is properly located to the body, scraping and wiping away any slip in the process. Using the metal tool, neaten the joints on the inside, as before.

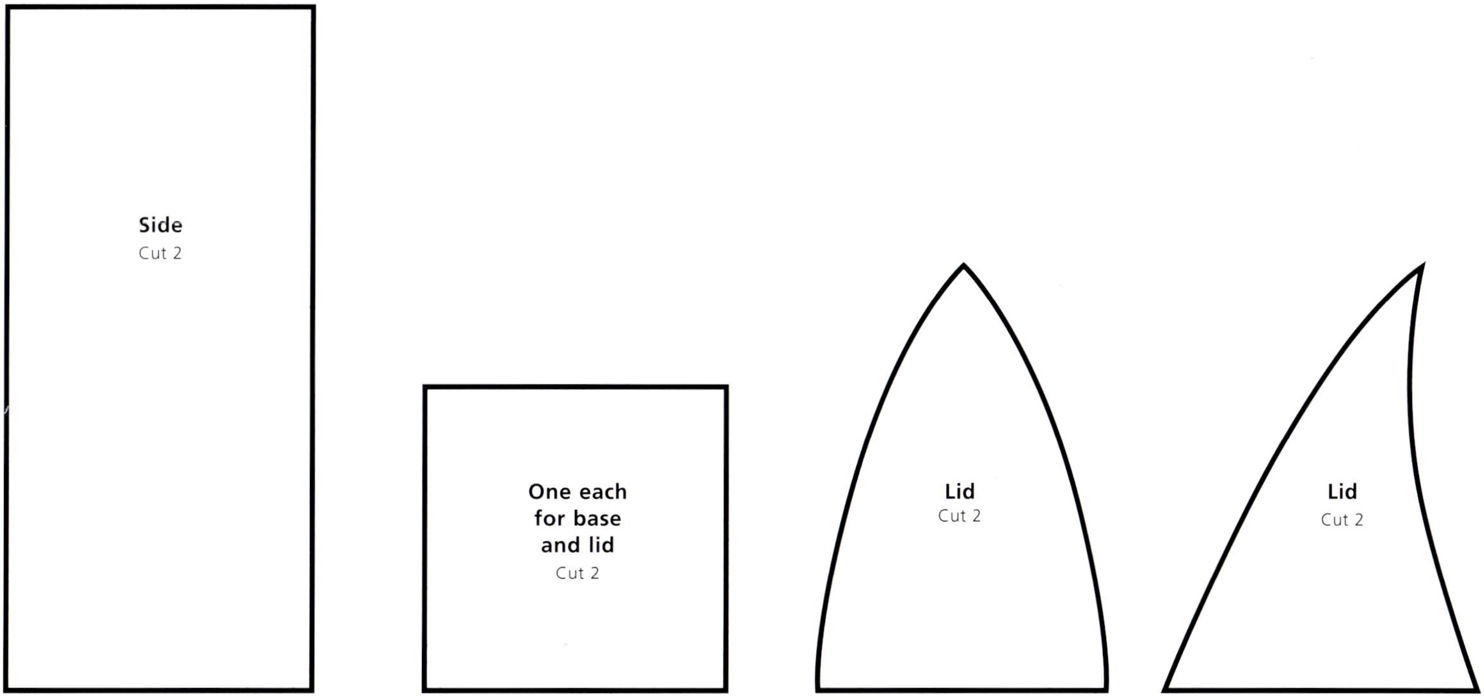

These 2 sections fit together and are then fixed onto the square lid section.

Now that the main part of the box is constructed, sharpen the angles by scraping them back gently with a plastic scraping tool. This helps to seal the joints more firmly, improves the appearance of the form and removes any fragments of clay that may be stuck to the surface. Hold the box on the board, where possible, to scrape the sides, but do not apply too much pressure, which would strain the joints. For difficult areas, scrape while holding the box in your hand.

To make the lid, unwrap the spare slab you prepared earlier, and cut another triangle the same size as the lid. Carefully reduce the size of the triangle fractionally along each side so that it is smaller on all sides by the same thickness as the wall of the box and will just fit inside it. Cut out a smaller triangle from the centre to avoid air being trapped between the two surfaces when joined. Mark the position of the second triangle over the first, then score and slip both surfaces to be joined and fix together. Wipe away any excess slip and neaten the surface with a plastic scraping tool. Check the fit of the lid on the box and make any adjustments by scraping the inner triangle back where necessary.

This part of the box – the onion dome – can be made before constructing the body, as suggested initially, because it must be dried to the same level as the rest of the clay before being attached. However, if you choose to make the onion dome after constructing the body, it can be dried with a hairdryer. To make the onion dome, form a tiny amount of porcelain into a ball the size of a large marble. Using the forefinger or smallest finger possible, pinch out an onion shape with a little point on the top. Try to pinch the shape a little more, using the pinkie and thumb, until you achieve an even clay section, then allow the shape to dry to the leather-hard stage to fit onto the lid.

Using a rasp blade, very carefully shave the underside of the onion to make it level. Score and slip this surface and the top of the box, then fit the onion into place, holding it down for a few seconds to seal the joint. Roll a tiny coil of porcelain and reinforce the joint by running it around the base of the onion where it sits on the lid. Blend the coil in until it is no longer visible. Wipe over the onion with a barely damp sponge to smooth the surface and remove any remaining pieces of clay and slip.

Template for large four-sided box

To finish the lid, pierce a hole through the underside into the onion using a hole cutter, to prevent it from exploding off in the firing. Fit the lid back on the base to check that the shape was not distorted in the handling. If it was, the clay should still be flexible enough to encourage the lid back into shape. Spend a little time checking that the surface is as neat as possible, that there are no clay scrapings stuck to the walls or base, and that the edges were not damaged in handling. The first of these boxes is now complete. Wrap it carefully in soft plastic to dry out slowly while you make its companions. The principles for making all three boxes are exactly the same.

7

Base
(This is slightly larger than the lid to allow for a flare shape at the base of the box.)
Cut 1

After bisque firing, selected areas on the boxes were waxed before a stoneware transparent glaze was applied. The boxes were then fired in an electric kiln to 1,280°C. Precious metal lustres were painted onto both glazed and unglazed areas of the boxes to impart shiny and matte contrasts to the design. Some areas of the boxes were left unlustred to better define the surface decoration. The boxes had a final firing to 750 °C.

This project combines several techniques but mainly uses soft slabbing. You will need a sheet of textured or embossed wallpaper for the cover of the dish.

Butter dish

The simplest shape for this dish locates the lid inside the base dish. Added details in the form of handles and feet can supply much variety to the basic form.

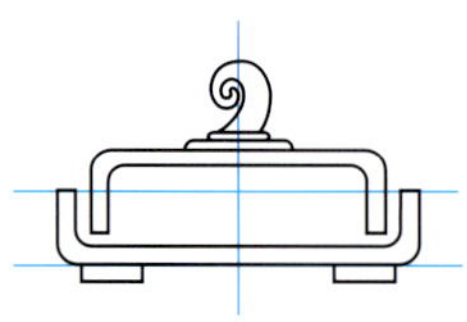

An alternative to the basic shape would be to change the shape of the lid. You must work this out on paper first to create an outline template as a basis from which to cut the slab. The form is also changed by a more solid foot rim.

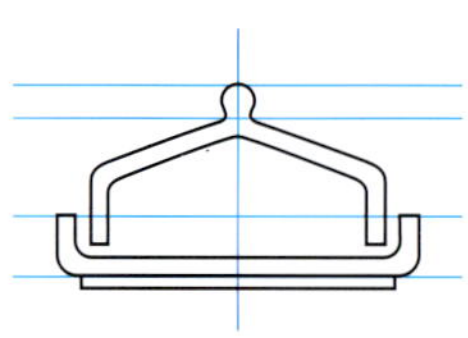

Here the basic shape is altered dramatically by the addition of a curly coil handle and feet, giving the form a whacky appearance.

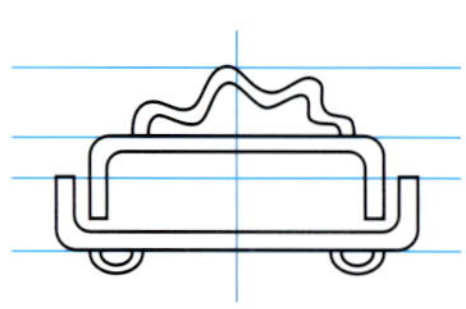

The lines of the basic dish shape are repeated in the shape of the handle and feet in this version, giving the design a modern, stylish look.

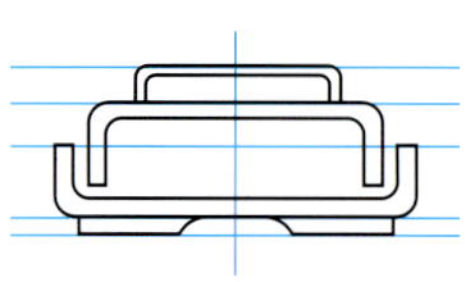

Wallpaper samples can often be obtained from a decorating store, and collecting several patterns will give you a variety of designs to choose from. The paper can be used many times over, so a small piece can last a long time.

All-purpose stoneware clay is used in this project, but earthenware clay would also be suitable and would take a brighter glaze. The shrinkage rate for stoneware is greater than that for earthenware, so this must be taken into consideration when calculating the size of the dish.

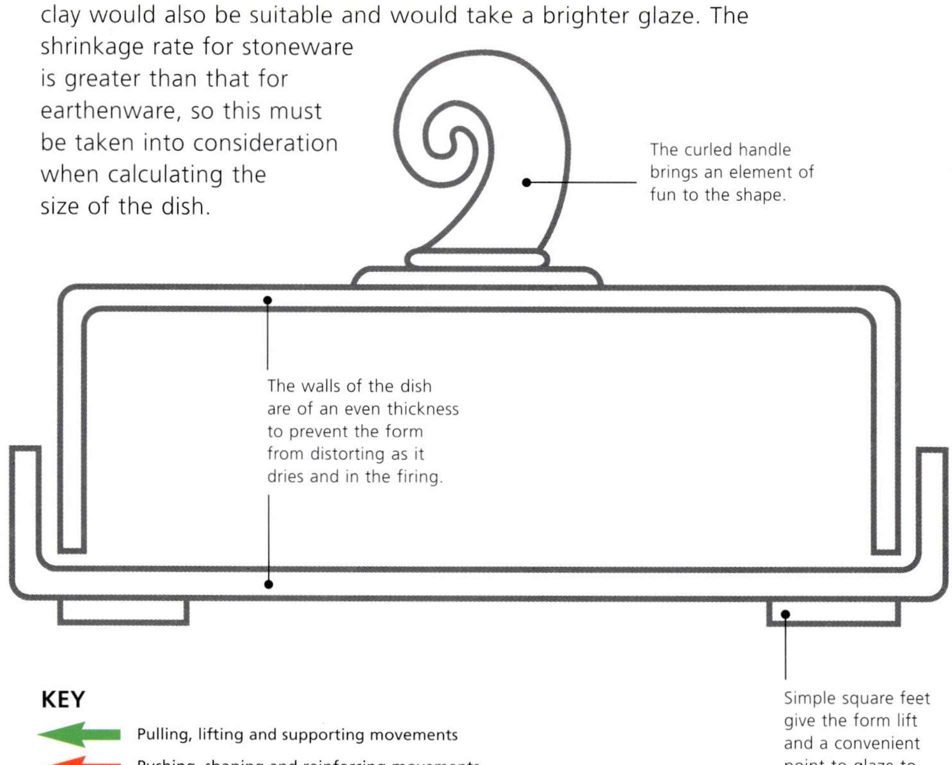

KEY

Pulling, lifting and supporting movements

Pushing, shaping and reinforcing movements

Roll a slab of clay on a sheet of clean cloth or plastic using the method described on page 92. The roller guides should be no more than 6 mm thick. Place a sheet of embossed wallpaper on the rolled slab, pattern side on the clay, and roll the paper over the slab to create a patterned surface. It should be possible to use the roller guides and still impress the clay sufficiently, but if the pattern does not appear deep enough, remove the guides and roll the paper carefully and evenly until it makes a clearer impression. Check by lifting one corner to see the depth of the pattern. If the entire sheet is lifted, it cannot be fitted back into place correctly.

Cut out a paper template using the diagram shown below for the lid as a guide, and place it over the clay while it is still in position on the fabric. Carefully cut around the template with a craft knife, using a ruler for extra support. Always stay safe by cutting away from the fingers holding the ruler. The surplus textured clay will not be needed again in this project but it provides good test material for glazes, so remove it carefully, wrap it in plastic, and put it to one side.

Turn the clay over onto a clean bat, with the pattern underneath. Using a piece of wooden batten to hold the clay down on the board and allow for a neat finish, curve one of the long side flaps upwards gently but firmly, using the fingers of both hands while the thumbs hold the batten. When the clay section is upright, place a ball of clay behind it to stop it from flopping back again, then repeat the procedure with the side section. The clay should be soft enough to accomplish this easily and without the clay cracking as it bends around the wood.

Score and slip the edge of one section and the area just inside and next to the edge in the corresponding section to be joined. This will form what is termed a butt-ended joint; it avoids the need to cut mitres in the adjoining edges. Use a toothbrush and water to score and slip, but be aware that very little water should be necessary because the clay is soft enough. Ease the sections together and hold them in place for a couple of seconds to seal the joint. It is important that these joints are as neat as possible because the clay cannot be adjusted on the patterned side of the slab without spoiling the effect.

1

2

3

4

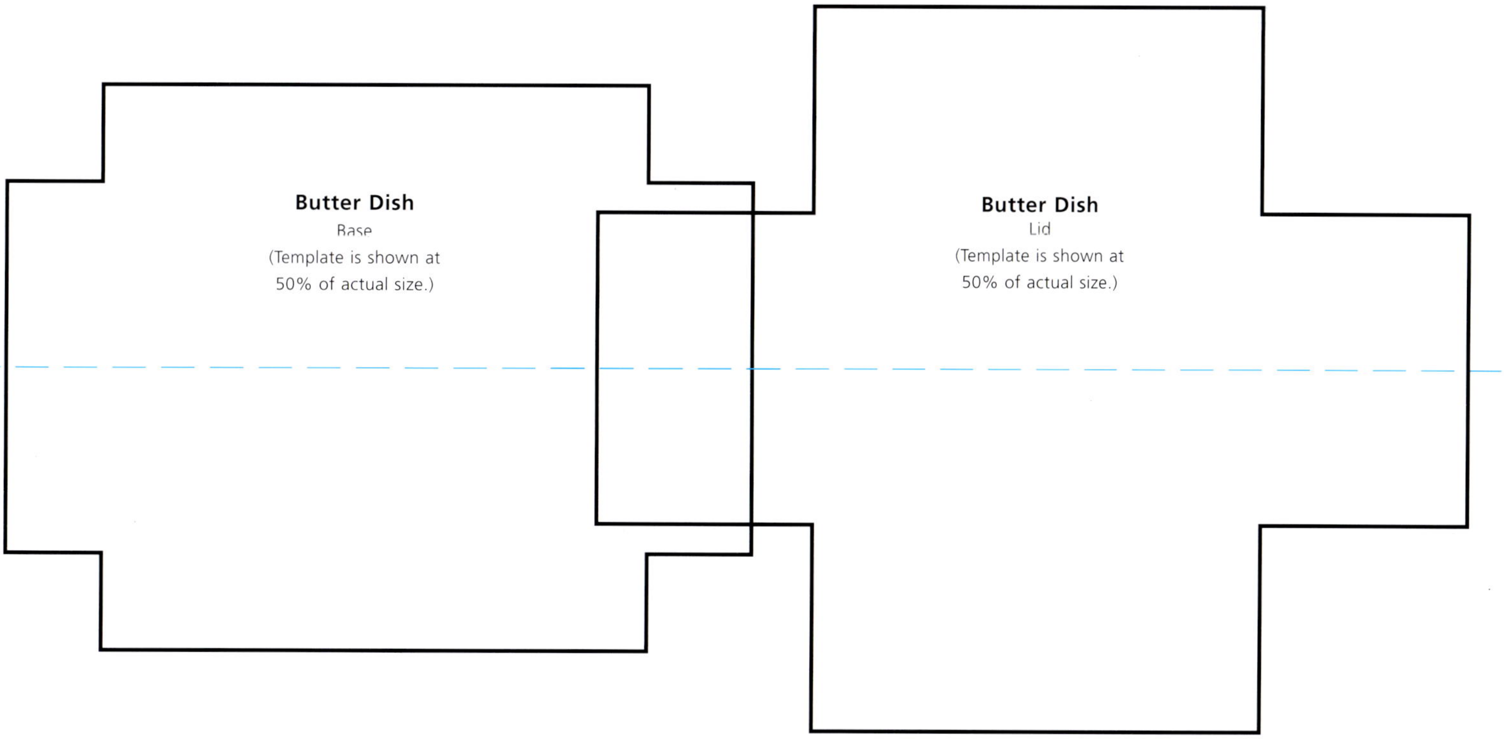

Join the remaining two sides to the two already done, following the same method and using the batten where possible to achieve a straight line in the angle of the curve. Cut a smaller piece of batten (or any implement with a straight blunt edge) to fit inside the lid, in order to angle the final section correctly. Hold the batten in place inside the lid with one hand as the other lifts the final sections into place. Use your entire hand to lift each section to prevent it from distorting or stretching out of shape. This can happen easily with such soft clay!

Butt-join the edges so that they align in the same way at each corner – this makes the lid look neat and well designed. The best way to do this is by lifting the end sections up to butt onto the side sections, as shown in the photograph. Butt-joining normally involves making some adjustment to the size of the slabs after they are fixed into place, but the joints in this project should fit exactly because of the softness of the clay and the shape of the template.

When all of the sides are joined, reinforce each corner with a tiny coil of soft clay. Blend the coils in well, but take care to hold the corners with one hand as each coil is fixed into the angle because the walls will easily distort in the handling. Use a round-ended wooden modelling tool to soften the reinforcement, then run over the area with a finger to smooth the clay.

Put the lid to one side on the bat to allow it to firm up. Meanwhile, roll a second slab of clay using the same-sized roller guides as for the lid. Cut out a second paper template using the diagram on page 109 for the base as a guide, and place it over the slab. Using the roller guide for extra support, cut out the base section and put the spare pieces of slab from around the edges to one side for later use. Lift the slab carefully on the cloth and turn it over onto a clean bat, peeling away the fabric when the slab is in place.

5

6

7

8

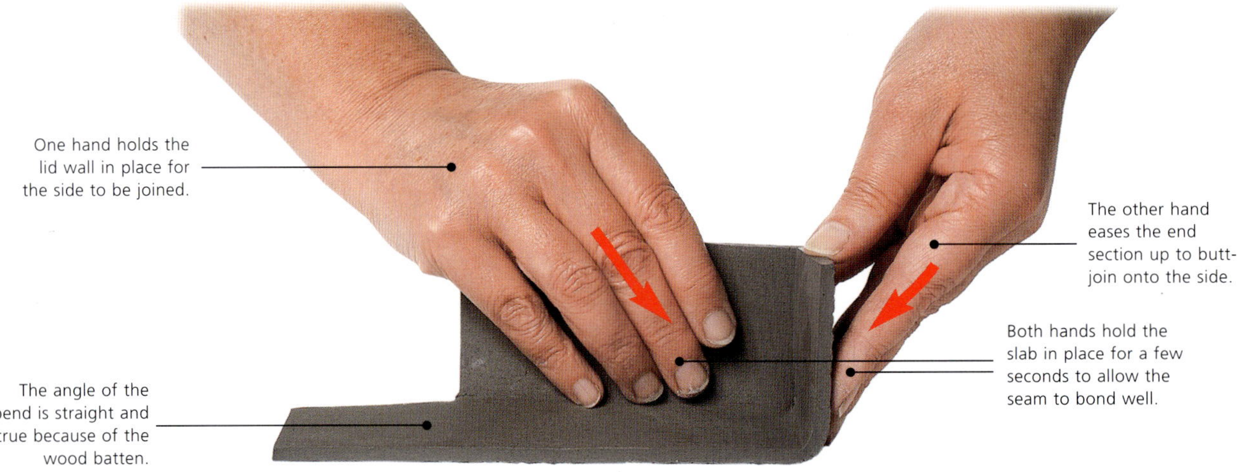

With the cut slab section in place on the bat, mitre each tiny angled corner by placing a ruler fractionally in from each edge, then cutting off a thin sliver of clay. Cut each mitre from the outside edge in to the angle, but take care not to cut into the main part of the slab. Use a sharp-pointed knife for the task – a craft knife is better than a potter's knife because it has a thinner blade. The reason the base is mitred instead of being butt-joined is because of the depth of the walls, which offer less room to manoeuvre in this slab.

Using the piece of wood batten as before, position it along the point where the clay needs to bend. Holding it in place with the thumbs, gently ease the clay wall upright with both hands. Score and slip the mitred edge and the corresponding edge on the wall to be joined, then carefully bend the second wall up to the first and join the seams together. Pinch the seams gently on the outside to make sure that they adhere. Because the clay was curled up, it will be inclined to unroll, so the joints must be very secure to hold the slab in place.

Continue to join all of the walls in the same way. When the last wall is fixed, set the wooden batten on the board and tap it against each wall in a paddling action several times to define the shape and encourage additional sealing of the joints. Hold the base in place as the walls are paddled to prevent it from moving across the board and altering the shape. Round off each joint slightly on the outside by running a finger over the seam. This should not alter the definition of the outline but simply remove any sharpness.

Reinforce each inner corner with a tiny coil of soft clay. Remember to hold the corner in place on the outside as the coil is blended in. Make this reinforcement as minimal as possible to avoid diminishing the space inside the dish, but remember that this part of the dish will be the most visible when the butter is on it, so the finish must be perfect. Use a wooden tool to blend in the coil, and smooth the area again with a finger.

One hand holds the wood batten in line on the surface of the slab, with the thumb helping to ease the clay into position.

The cutout slab lies on the surface to allow the sides to be manipulated into shape while keeping the base completely flat.

The other hand lifts the clay upright, gently easing it around the angle of the wooden strip.

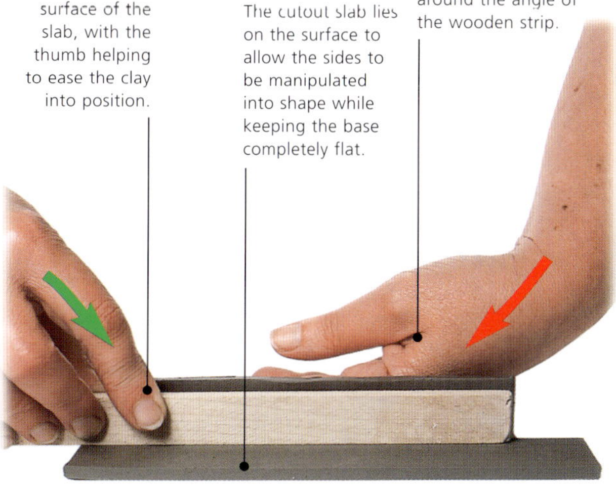

The walls will be paddled slightly to define the shape when all sides are joined.

One hand holds the side wall in place as the corner is joined.

The other hand pinches the joint together on the outside of the base.

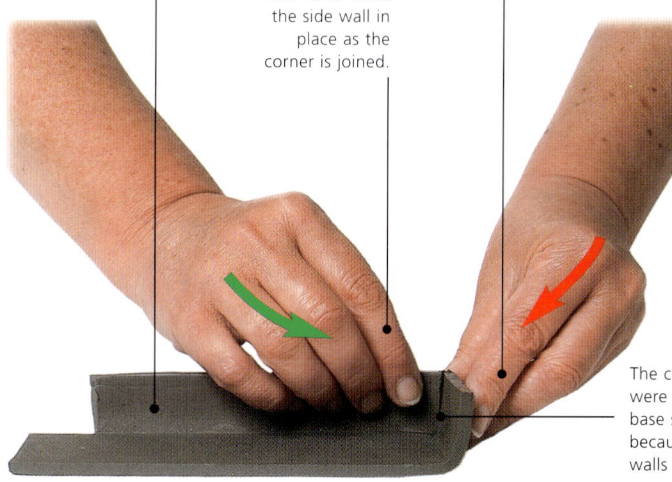

The corner sections were mitred on the base section because the clay walls are so shallow.

Before the feet can be added to the base, the clay must firm up considerably. Either set the base aside to dry slowly or speed it along with the help of a hairdryer. When the clay seems dry enough to support its shape, turn the base over and dry the underside a little more. Provided the clay is dried evenly, it should be possible to reach the leather-hard stage in this way. The danger lies in drying one area more than another, which creates stresses in the clay, so keep the hairdryer moving continually over the surface.

Carefully cut four square sections for the feet from the slab pieces left when the base was cut out. The quickest method is to cut a strip of clay from the slab using a ruler or roller guide. Once the strip has been cut, rotate it 90 degrees, then reposition the ruler crossways over it and cut four equal-sized squares. Set the squares on a clean bat and stamp a pattern into the centre of each one. It is always a joy to turn an object over and find an extra little detail to add interest to the form. Return to the base of the dish and stamp the same pattern once into the middle of each wall. Support the wall on the inside as the pattern is stamped.

Set the squares on the underside of the base to mark their position, then remove them and score and slip the marked areas and the underside of each square before fixing them in place. Use a toothbrush and water to make a generous amount of slip. When all of the feet are in place, wipe around each one with a barely damp sponge to remove any slip that squeezed out, then leave the base in this position for a little while for the clay to firm up where the feet were added.

Roll a coil of clay, about 13 mm thick and 6–7.5 cm long. Thin the coil at one end, then twist this end around to form a curl. Cut the base of the curl so that when it sits on the work table it looks balanced and has a jaunty angle. Leave it on the table to firm up. Meanwhile, cut a small disk of clay from the leftover sections of slab. Make the disk slightly larger than the circumference of the coil's base. Score and slip the base of the coil and the corresponding area on the disk, then fit the two together. Reinforce the base of the curl by adding a coil, but leave it as a decorative detail instead of blending it in. Blend the ends of the decorative coil carefully.

13

14

15

16

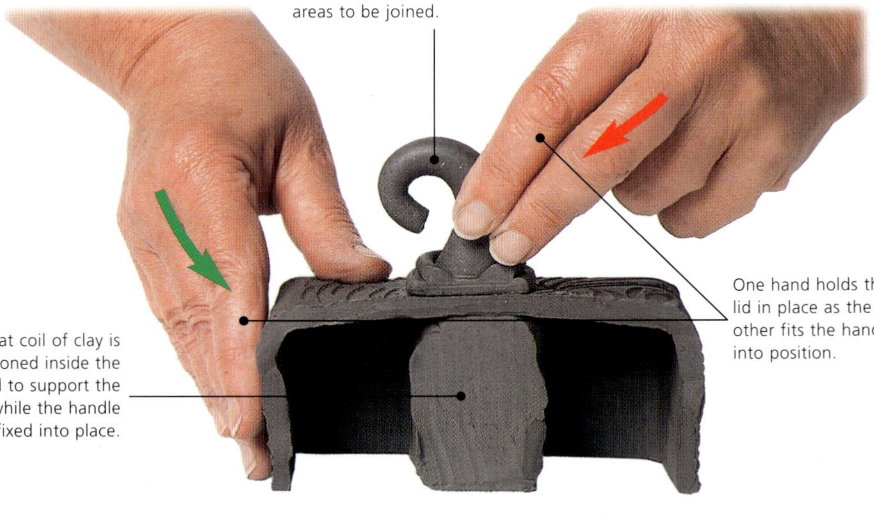

Form a thick rough coil of clay the height of the lid of the dish. Sit this on a bat with the lid over the top so that it cannot be seen but will support the shape for the handle to be fixed in place. Mark the position of the handle in the centre of the lid. Score and slip the marked area and the underside of the disk, then fit the handle in place with the thick coil inside to prevent the shape from altering as the two surfaces are eased together. Wipe away any surplus slip carefully. Remove the supporting coil from inside the shape. Fit the lid inside the base – it should fit comfortably with at least 6 mm to spare all the way around the lid.

7

Once complete, the butter dish should be allowed to dry relatively slowly with the lid in place on the base at all times. The dish should also be fired with the lid in position to keep the shape true. Here it has been glazed in bright earthenware colours. An iron-rich orange glaze nicely pools in the detail of the pattern on the lid while the blue glaze forms a good colour contrast, especially when repeated on the curled handle. A little gold lustre picks up the detail of the stamped pattern on each side of the dish base to complete the design.

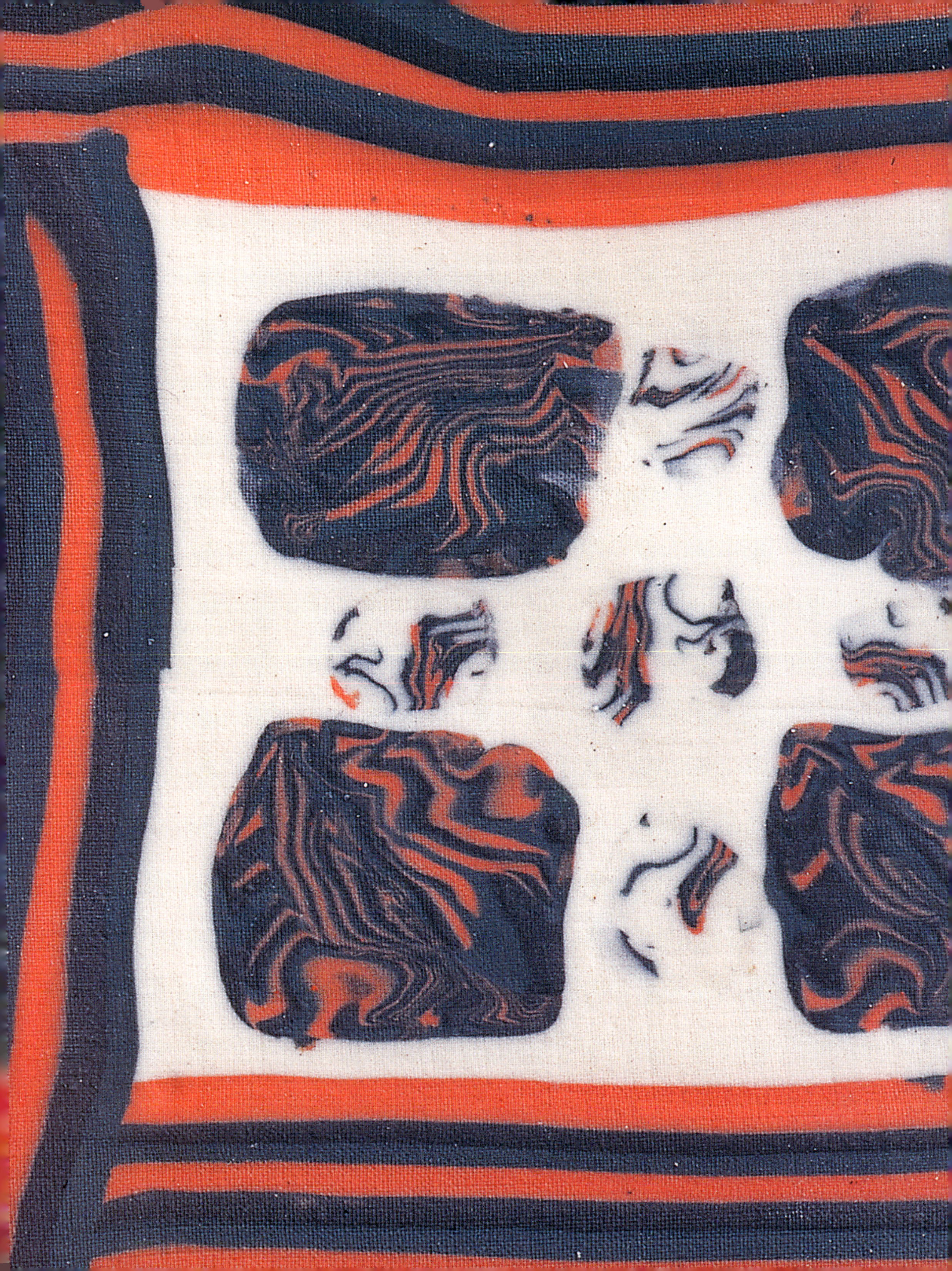

CHAPTER FOUR

Moulding

Most people associate moulds with relatively modern mass-production techniques, but moulds have been used since our earliest ancestors pressed stones into clay to form shapes. Moulds were often made of combustible materials, and the clay was packed against the inner walls before the object was fired to leave a clay form of the moulded shape. Examples of moulds made from fired clay, wood and stone from early civilisations around the world survive today. Nowadays, however, most pottery is made in plaster moulds — including kitchen and tableware, sanitary ware and many items not usually associated with ceramics, such as electrical components.

The mould was long overlooked as a useful tool for the studio potter because of its association with industry, but more recently potters have recognised its value in reproducing a particular shape that can then be decorated individually or in forming a starting point for other work. This section introduces simple mould making and techniques that act as a good basis for the creation of more advanced shapes.

Making a press mould

Press moulds can be made in a confusing variety of ways, but if you prepare everything in advance and follow the simple technique described here, the process should be relatively easy. The model and the walls are made from smooth clay, to minimise the amount of equipment needed. The cheapest clay is chosen because the clay cannot be reused – except for making more moulds. This is because plaster can adhere to the clay and contaminate it, causing an explosion when fired. It is advisable, therefore, to make the mould away from the studio to avoid contaminating other clay. If this is not possible, cover bags of clay and clean up meticulously after the mould is made.

1 Draw the outline of your chosen shape onto a piece of rigid cardboard to make a template. The template must be cut out accurately, allowing about 10 cm on each side of the outline to form a grip when shaping the model. It is important to choose a shape for the press mould that enables the finished ceramic to be released easily. Do not create undercuts in the model or template that would cause the clay to be trapped in the mould. Put the cardboard template aside. On a piece of laminated plastic board, draw a 30-cm square outline for the model, using a marker pen. There should be at least 5 cm to spare around the model to allow the walls to be fitted. Start to fill in the square, packing small balls of soft clay together well to form the shape of the dish.

2 Once the model is formed into a rough shape, paddle the surface with a wooden spatula to compact the clay a little and define the shape. Be aware that you are working upside down, so that the line drawn on the board will form the walls of the dish and the completed model will form the underside. Have the template close by to help you gauge the shape, but the outline is only approximate at this stage. It is not necessary to refine the surface totally in the process of paddling – this will be done later.

3 Position the cardboard template over the model, so that the edges line up with the lines drawn on the board. Hold the template at each side and, starting at the corners, carefully drag it across the surface of the model, keeping it in place against the lines at all times. It will take several attempts to do this accurately, because the template will drag away excess clay in the process and this will create some resistance. Remove the excess clay regularly to make the shaping easier. Work over the surface in one direction several times until the clay model is well shaped. If there are any areas that do not reach up to the level of the template, fill these in with more clay; then work back over the surface in the same way until the shape is exact.

4 Turn the model around and work the template over the surface in the opposite direction, paying particular attention to the corners. It should be much easier to shape the model this way, because the bulk of the clay is already removed. Make sure that the template remains in line with the outline and, as before, work over the surface several times to smooth it off thoroughly and shape the model precisely. Try to drag the template in one smooth action from corner to corner at this secondary stage of the shaping rather than stopping halfway, which often causes a ridge to form and makes it necessary to start over.

5 When you are finished forming the model with the template, refine the upper surface, using a metal scraper held at a flat angle. Take care not to make any marks in the clay or to alter the level of the edges in any way, because although these mistakes may not be immediately apparent in the plaster mould, they will distort the shape of the fired dish. Check for air bubbles under the surface of the clay and burst any that occur with a potter's pin, then smooth back over the area carefully. Even bubbles will manifest themselves in the plaster if they are not removed!

Once the upper surface is smooth, work around the sides in the same way. This can be fairly tricky, so take care – especially at the corners, where the edges can easily be caught with the scraper. When the sides are thoroughly smoothed, run a finger along each edge extremely carefully to gently remove the sharpness of the lines and round them off slightly. Again, take care not to distort the shape. To check that it is still true, remove any dry clay that has accumulated on the template and when it is completely clean, carefully test the shape again and make any necessary adjustments.

Roll out four long slabs of clay, using the technique described in Slabbing (page 86). Each slab must be 5 to 7.5 cm higher than the depth of the model and 7.5 cm longer – 38 mm at each end. It must also be at least 13 mm thick to support the weight of the plaster. Dry the slabs to the point where they will hold their shape and not bend easily (just past leather-hard). Use the slabs to build a wall around the model, allowing at least a 25-mm gap all the way around between the two. The surrounding walls, known as the 'cottle', can be made from any material that will support the weight of the plaster. Pieces of wood or linoleum can be used – or clay, if nothing else is available.

Cut the slab walls to size and butt the ends together to form a square cottle around the model. Support the slabs on the outside with thick coils of soft clay to seal any gaps and hold them in place. Include the joints at the corners where the slabs butt together. Make sure that the coils are blended onto the board and the walls securely to prevent the weight of the plaster from bursting the cottle. It makes a terrible mess if this happens! Check that there are no specks of clay on the board inside the cottle. Remove them carefully if they occur, taking care not to damage the model. The model is now ready to be cast.

Weigh out 5.4 kg of plaster and tip it into a dry plastic bucket or bowl. When using kitchen equipment, it may be necessary to weigh in stages, so keep a record of each amount as it goes into the bowl. In a separate bucket, measure 4.6 litres of water. Lukewarm water causes the plaster to set more quickly, so if you are unused to mixing plaster, cold water will give you longer to achieve the correct result. When making smaller-scale moulds, use the ratio of 675 g of plaster to 570 ml of water.

Always add plaster to water, *never* the other way around. Holding the plaster bowl over the water bucket with one hand, ease all of the plaster into the water with the other hand, taking care to avoid lumps. It is advisable to wear rubber gloves when mixing plaster, because the powder absorbs moisture from the skin. Wear a face mask also if you are concerned about inhaling the powder. When all of the plaster is in the water, it may break the surface and appear to be too much, but simply tap the sides of the bucket and it will soon disappear below the water. Let the mixture stand for about a minute to allow the plaster to absorb the water. If you are using warm water, however, do not let the mixture stand for too long, because it will quickly begin to set. While the mixture is standing, line another bucket or container with a plastic bag and place it next to the plaster bucket.

Stir the mixture gently with your fingers under the surface. Try to avoid creating air bubbles by mixing too vigorously, because this will weaken the mould and leave holes that will affect the surface of the cast piece. As you mix the plaster, gently break up any unabsorbed lumps between your fingers until they are thoroughly blended into the mixture. When the mixture is smooth and lump-free, agitate it gently from side to side with your hand splayed to bring any air bubbles to the surface. Scoop the bubbles off the surface, into the bucket with the plastic liner. This enables the plaster to be disposed of easily and without mess.

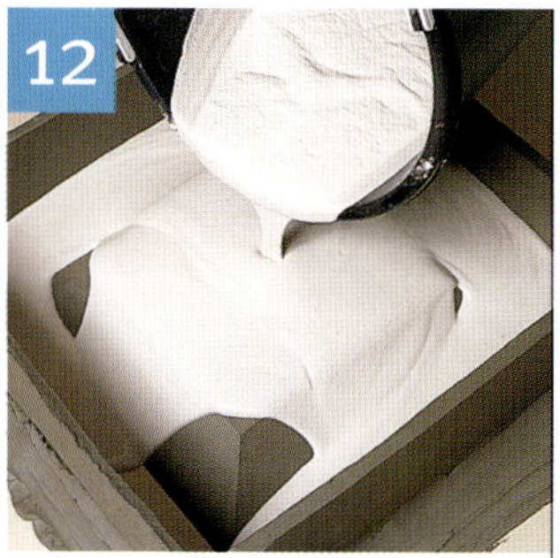

When the mixture starts to thicken to the consistency of cream, it is ready to pour into the cottle. It is important to work quickly once the mixture begins to set. Lift the bucket and pour the mixture slowly and evenly over the model, trying to avoid the creation of air bubbles. The mixture should be liquid enough to fill the container easily, but it is important to cover the model itself first in case there is insufficient plaster to complete the mould at one attempt. This can often happen in the case of a large mould, where the plaster mixture can be too heavy to lift and the mould must be made in two stages. There should be at least a 25-mm thickness at the base of the mould.

When all of the plaster is in the cottle, agitate the surface again with a splayed hand to displace any air bubbles. Alternatively, lift the board slightly and tap it gently on the work surface a few times. This is a useful method for smaller moulds, but if the mould is large, lifting the board can be difficult and can cause the cottle to burst, so it requires great care. Burst any bubbles that rise to the surface – just touching the bubbles with a finger is usually sufficient. The mould is now complete and must be left to harden. Clean the bucket by wiping out as much plaster as possible with newspaper.

If you think the mould is not thick enough at the base, it is possible to add a second layer of plaster. While the plaster in the cottle is still relatively soft, score the surface roughly with a pointed tool or knife. Don't score too deeply if the base layer is very thin because this may scratch through to the model beneath and affect the surface of the mould. The purpose of this exercise is to form a key for the next layer of plaster.

Mix up another bucket of plaster in the same way as before. It is unlikely that the same amount will be needed again, and a rough guide is to mix one-half of the original amount – 2.3 l of water to 2.7 kg of plaster. When the plaster is mixed and the bubbles removed, pour it over the first layer in the cottle, making sure that the mixture fills the corners. Agitate the mixture again to bring any air bubbles to the surface, burst them, and then leave the mould to harden.

Tips for success

- Never wash excess plaster down the sink – it will set in the pipe and cause a blockage that will be impossible to remove.
- Use newspaper to clean out excess plaster from the plaster bucket; then transfer the newspaper to a bag-lined rubbish bin immediately for easy disposal.
- Wipe excess plaster from gloves or hands with newspaper before washing them.
- If the model is still in place in the mould when it is turned right side up after casting, scoop the clay out carefully using fingers rather than tools to avoid damaging or scratching the mould surface.

6

After several minutes, as the plaster hardens, a chemical reaction causes it to begin heating up. When this happens, remove the clay seals and the walls. These can be discarded or stored for reuse when making other moulds. Keep contaminated clay for future mould making in a clearly marked bag to avoid confusing it with other clay.

17

With the cottle removed and the mould still in position upside down on the board, bevel all of the sharp edges using a rasp blade. This prevents the mould from becoming chipped during use. The plaster is still relatively soft at this stage, but bevelling would be much more difficult on a completely dry mould. If the base of the mould is uneven because it was caught by a hand when the plaster began to set, level it with the rasp blade or a metal ruler so that it will sit flat when turned up the right way.

18

When the plaster is cool again, lift the mould carefully off the model. With luck, the mould will slip off, leaving the model in place on the board. It is rarely that easy to release the mould, however, because the plaster and clay form a tight seal. If necessary, to break the seal, push the mould to the edge of the board and slightly beyond it. This provides a grip with which to lift the mould, although you may need someone to hold the board down while you lift.

19

Turn the mould over onto a clean work surface and check that it is level. If it is not, turn it back over and make adjustments, as before. Bevel the outer edge on the upper surface, paying particular attention to the corners, which are especially vulnerable to knocks. These can be rounded off considerably for safety. Neaten all of the other outer surfaces of the mould, using the rasp.

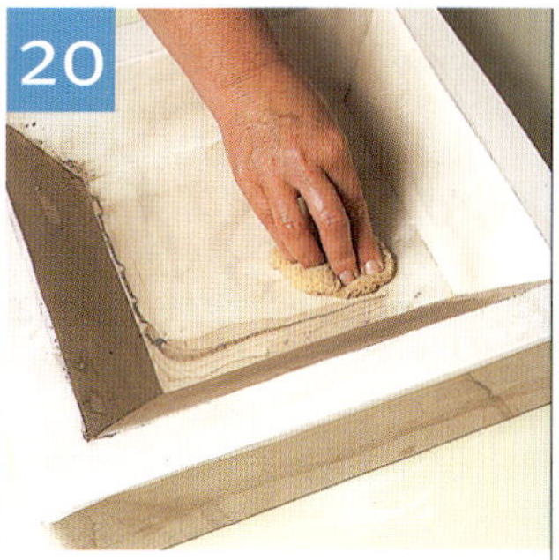

20

When you are finished neatening the outer surfaces and edges of the mould, the inner dish part can be cleaned with a wet sponge. Rinse the sponge regularly to remove surplus clay. Clean the outer surface in the same way to remove all traces of clay, which could contaminate the clay to be used in the mould. This extra attention not only improves the appearance of the mould but could be crucial later. The mould is now complete. Put it in a warm, dry place to dry out fully. The top of the kiln is a good location, but the mould must be raised on stilts to allow air to circulate, because if plaster dries too quickly it can become crumbly. It will take several days for the mould to dry completely, and the bigger the mould, the longer the drying time. The mould made here is fairly large but not beyond the capabilities of the beginner. It would be possible to scale down the size, however, while preserving the same shape. Remember to reduce the amount of plaster mix if the size is reduced.

These molds represent a selection of basic shapes, including (from left to right) a sprig mould for low-relief decoration, a hump mould, a small conical press mould, which could be used to form hollow, high-relief surface detail on a form, and a bowl-shaped press mould.

Making and using a low-relief tile mould with a simple repeat pattern

Making a tile with a repeat pattern demands a little design work to be sure that the pattern will repeat correctly. Many beginners are daunted by the prospect of working on paper, but the key is to keep the design simple and to have a good idea of how you want the tile to look before you begin. As the design is worked out, you will need to modify the original idea a little for the repeat to be successful, but from this a truly inventive design should develop. The concept for the tile shown here was inspired by 1950s textile patterns, which are a rich source of ideas.

First decide what size mould you want to make. Remember that the smaller the tile, the less detail that can be modelled onto the surface. In this case, the tile measures 15 cm square. Begin by drawing the details inside the square that will not be affected by the repeat. Keep the design simple and imagine how it will work in relief. Draw a few lines from the contained part of the design out to the edges of the square – only a few, or the repeat will be too difficult to figure out.

1

5

When the pattern is complete and forms a good repeat, roll out a slab of smooth clay, using roller guides no thicker than 5 cm. Carefully cut out a 15-cm square from the slab and transfer it to a nonabsorbent board that is at least 5 cm larger. Save the spare pieces of slab for later. Make sure that the slab sticks to the surface well and that the edges have a slight inward bevel to avoid undercuts. Place one of the paper designs over the clay square and, using a pencil, transfer the pattern to the surface by tracing over the lines.

6

Roll a long thin coil of clay to build up some areas of the pattern to form the relief. Place sections of the coil over the lines to be built up, then model them onto the slab, being sure to avoid undercuts, which would trap the plaster and make it impossible to remove the tile from the mould. This is a somewhat awkward and time-consuming procedure, but it must be done well for the tile to work properly. Model all of the fine detail onto the surface in the same way.

7

When the fine relief detail is complete, draw in the lines more clearly using a pointed modelling tool. Use a roller guide or batten to keep the lines straight, and don't make them too deep to avoid creating undercuts. Holding the modelling tool relatively flat to score the lines will help. Use a soft brush to remove any tiny pieces of clay from the surface of the tile as they accumulate, and smooth the surface over with a finger regularly as each area is completed, because all marks in the clay will show in the plaster cast.

8

Use parts of the spare clay cut from around the tile to build up some of the areas within the drawn lines. Remember that the pattern in some of these areas continues over to form the repeat, so if a section at the bottom is built up, a corresponding area at the top will probably need to be built up in the same way. It should not be necessary to score and slip these pieces into place because the tile is only the model for the mould, but they must be blended well onto the base so that the plaster cannot get underneath when it is cast.

Divide the square into four smaller 7.5-cm squares by first folding it, then drawing in the lines with a pencil and a ruler. Draw a tiny circle in each central corner of the divided square where the lines cross in the center. This will allow you to move the individual quarters around but always have a reference to return them to the original design. Cut the square accurately into four with scissors or a craft knife.

With the square cut in four but still forming the original design, move the two squares on the left to the right of the remaining two. Now continue the drawn lines from the two repositioned squares so that they connect to the design on the original squares. Next, return the moved squares to their original position on the left, lining up the tiny central circles. Take the two upper squares and position them beneath the other two, and repeat the exercise, continuing the lines over from each square to connect to the pattern in the squares above.

Before committing the design to clay, tape the four quarters back together neatly with masking tape, then trace the design and make three copies. Put the copies together to view the repeat. If any lines were missed, go back to the original square, remove the tape from the back and rework the design to correct the error. Working in pencil at the design stage means that lines can easily be erased.

When the relief is complete, add any final details to the model. Here, some tiny holes are made around one of the leaf patterns, and a narrow strip of clay is gouged out between two lines to create yet another variation of level. The corresponding area on the other side of the tile is also gouged out to form the repeat. A couple of squares are stamped into the clay, using the end of a piece of wooden batten, to form additional details that were not included in the original design and dividing lines are impressed into some of the leaves to complete the tile.

Check that the surface of the model is smooth and free from specks of clay; then put it to one side and roll out a slab of clay about 13 mm thick to form a cottle for the tile. Cut the slab into four strips 20 cm long and 5 cm thick. Position the slab walls around the tile model, allowing a 25-mm gap all the way around, and secure them in place with a thick coil of soft clay. Mix up 675 g of plaster to 570 ml of water, using the method described earlier in the chapter (page 117). Pour the plaster mixture over the model.

Agitate a flattened hand gently over the plaster in the cottle to raise any air bubbles to the surface. Alternatively, lift the board slightly and tap it back onto the surface very gently several times. Burst any bubbles with a finger, then let the mould harden. When the plaster has heated up and cooled again, remove the cottle. Bevel the edges of the mould with a rasp blade, and dispose of the waste carefully. Wipe around the mould to remove any clay and plaster.

Carefully turn the mould over and bevel the rim to match the base. If the mould seems stuck to the surface, push it across and over the edge of the board to break the seal and provide a grip with which to lift it. Remove the model carefully, using your fingers rather than a tool to avoid damaging the surface. With the model removed, the mould is complete, but it must be dried out before use. Put it somewhere warm, in a position that allows the air to circulate, in order to dry it evenly. This should take only a day or two because the plaster is thinner than that of most moulds.

Making tiles from casting slip

Casting slip is a clay body in liquid form, enabling it to be poured into moulds so that repeat shapes can be made. The slip should not shrink too much when it dries and should have a good dry strength for handling.

When the mould is dry, you can begin to produce a batch of tiles. To do this with casting slip, first mix the slip to the right liquid consistency. Transfer the slip to a pitcher to make it easier to pour into the mould. Fill the mould with slip and replenish it from time to time to keep the surface level. Let the slip firm up in the mould until the clay shows no marks when it is touched. This can take any time from 30 minutes on, depending on a variety of factors.

The easiest way to judge that the tile is ready for removal is when the clay begins to shrink away from the edges of the mould. The clay used here is white earthenware (although it looks buff-coloured in its liquid state). It can be cast and removed from the mould in about one hour, depending on the surrounding temperature. This allows several tiles to be cast in a day, although the mould quickly becomes saturated when in constant use and must be dried out thoroughly after each session of casting.

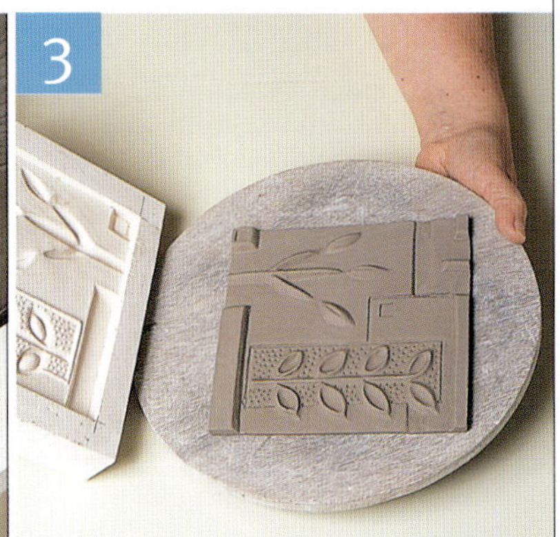

To remove the tile from the mould, place a bat over the surface and turn both over before lifting the mould off. It is much better to turn the tile out onto a surface than to try to lift it out with your hands, which risks distorting the shape. Once a tile is distorted, it will always fire to that shape, so it is important to keep it as flat as possible at all times. When the mould is free, the next tile can be cast in the same way. Dry the completed tiles slowly to prevent them from warping. This often happens when tiles dry out too quickly on one side; it can be avoided by placing them on a wire rack, which allows the air to circulate freely. The tiles must also be turned over regularly. An alternative is to dry the tiles very slowly between wooden boards, but check them from time to time and move them around so that they dry evenly.

Making tiles from soft slabs

Thoroughly wedge a large block of clay and form it into a square of approximately 15 cm. Place the block on a smooth work surface directly in front of you. Set the wire on the harp at an upper level that corresponds with a point just below the top of the block of clay. Stand the harp on the opposite side of the block, holding it firmly at the base of each side, and draw it back through the clay towards your body. Lift the first slab off the block and put it to one side. Adjust the wire down to the next level at each side of the harp and cut another slab. Continue to cut and adjust in this way until the entire block has been slabbed.

In addition to the methods described in the Slabbing section, slabs can be formed using a harp, which is the perfect tool for making tiles. A harp is a three-sided steel frame with ridges spaced equally along two sides, from which a cutting wire is stretched. Each ridge allows the wire to be adjusted to a different level, which in turn allows many slabs to be cut relatively quickly. The use of a harp to cut slabs is demonstrated here, but rolling the clay is an equally valid method, and it is not worth buying a harp unless you intend to use it extensively.

Before placing a slab in the mould, smooth over the surface on one side with a kidney or metal scraper. This is especially important if using grogged clay, whose texture can cause some loss of definition in pattern (unless, of course, this is the effect you want, in which case a tile with fine detail would not be appropriate).

Turn the slab over into the mould, so that the smooth side is face down. Using your fingers, push the clay into the mould, making sure that it fits into the corners and all the detail of the pattern. Marks in the surface are unimportant, but try not to push down too deeply below the level of the sides of the mould to avoid creating air pockets. Both hands can be used to fit the slab.

To trim off the excess clay, place a roller guide over the rim of the mould and draw it across the surface. Do this in several stages, working from the centre outwards, to avoid dragging the tile out of the mouldprematurely. Use both hands, with the thumbs gripping the sides of the mould for support. When all of the excess is trimmed away, either leave the tile in the mould until it starts to shrink away from the sides or speed the process with a hairdryer, so that the next tlle can be made quickly.

Turn the tile out of the mould in the same way as for the slip-cast version. Using slabs to make the tile offers you the choice of adding some coloured slip decoration at this stage. This could involve paper resist, some inlay or sponging and even freehand painting – masking areas in order to build up the design in a different way. Whatever its decoration, the tile must be dried slowly, either on a wire rack or between wooden boards, but a slip-decorated surface must be dry before a board is placed on top of it. The first tile is now complete, and the next one, it is hoped, in the mould. For decoration, the tiles often look best covered in a glaze that pools in areas of relief to give variations in colour, or with a flat glaze that allows the relief to show in shadow. Once the principles of tile making are learned, potters often make them as a sideline to their normal range because they are relatively quick to do.

Making a two-part mould

Making a mould with more than one part presents the beginner with a few technical challenges. Usually a solid model of the finished form must be built from which the mould is cast. The model can be built from clay or plaster, or an existing object can be used. The advantage of using existing items is that they usually require little preparation before casting, whereas clay and plaster models can take some time to make.

The object can be an everyday item; it is fun to seek out everyday objects from the kitchen and around the house that would serve as good models. The mould in this technique is a simple cylinder, made from a wooden rolling pin with detachable handles. The shape of the pin is perfect because its gently bevelled rims will give the base of a mould a neat, rounded finish.

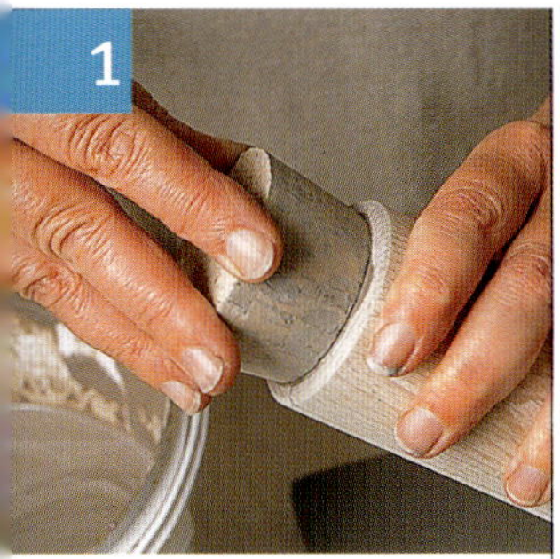

1

The preparation for making a mould in more than one part is crucial to the success of the finished item. A mould that is to be used for slip casting must have an opening through which the liquid clay can be poured, and the opening must be positioned where it does not affect the appearance of the form. The opening is usually made by inserting a plug of clay or plaster during construction of the mould, and is often referred to as a 'spare'. Here, the spare is a bottle cork slightly smaller in circumference than the end of the rolling pin. When the cylinder is cast, the cork will allow for a wall up to 6 mm thick. The cork is secured on the end of the rolling pin with slip, and is held in place for several minutes before surplus clay is removed with a damp sponge.

2

The next stage in the preparation of the model is to mark a halfway line down each side of the rolling pin. This must be measured precisely, using a soft tape measure and a ruler. The simplest method is to stand the rolling pin upright with the ruler against it and to draw the first line in pencil. The second line is then easy to measure from the first. The line must include the spare at the top to avoid undercuts when the model is cast in plaster.

3

Roll a thick slab of clay deep enough to secure the model without its rolling off. Use two blocks of wood, or stack several roller guides on either side of the slab to allow for the thickness. When the slab is the correct thickness, transfer it to a non-absorbent board. Cut the slab into an oblong that allows at least 38 mm on either side of the model. Press the rolling pin model gently onto the slab to settle it in place. Take care not to knock off the spare. There should be at least 25 mm of clay extending beyond the base of the model, but the spare should be lined up with one end of the slab.

4

Roll another slab of clay at least 13 mm thick and wide enough to extend 5 cm above the embedded model. Dry the slab wall to the point where it holds its shape without bending. Position the slab at the top end of the model so that it butts tightly against the spare. Secure the wall in place with a thick coil of soft clay, making sure that it cannot move. Hold the model in place with one hand as the wall is secured. Cut the slab wall to size, allowing a little overlap at each side for the supporting side walls to butt against.

5

Very carefully start to build up the level of clay around the model to the marked halfway line. This is most easily done by layering thin slabs of clay against the sides of the model up to the line, then carefully working the clay smooth and level. It can be tricky to work around edges, but this must be done precisely, so take as much time as necessary to get this right. Use a modelling tool for the finer detail. As each side is built up to the line, level and smooth the clay with a metal scraping tool, placing it carefully against the side of the model and drawing it away to the side.

At the base of the model and around the spare, you will need to use a modelling tool to level the clay to the line. It is important that the clay seals against the side of the model to prevent the plaster from running underneath. This also applies to the supporting walls, so make sure that the clay bed seals against the top supporting wall as well as the spare. Hold the top supporting wall in place on the outside as it is sealed on the inside.

When the model is fully bedded into the clay base, work over the surface several times with the metal scraper to make certain that it is level and smooth. This may seem excessive, but it cannot be stressed enough how important this stage of the process is, and it will save many problems later if it is done correctly. Potters are often discouraged from mould-making because they think it is too tricky and bothersome, but it is just a matter of taking the time to get the details right – and, like other techniques, it becomes much easier with practice.

Roll out another 13-mm thick slab, large enough to form the remaining three walls around the model. Dry the slab to the same stage as the upper supporting wall, then cut out three pieces the same height as before. Butt the two side slabs up to the top wall, being sure to hold it in place as the joints are sealed. Pack the base of each slab wall with a thick coil of soft clay to support it and seal any gaps through which plaster could escape. Fit the base wall so that it butts to the side walls, and again secure it in place. Seal the bed to the walls on the inside of the cottle, taking care not to make marks in the clay.

The amount of plaster required will depend on the size of the individual model and cottle, but in this case at least 1.2 l of water to 1.4 kg of plaster is needed for each half of the mould. Mix the plaster into the water, following the method described in Making a press mould (page 116). When the liquid plaster is ready, pour it over the model, making sure that it flows into the corners and levels out again. Lift the board slightly and tap it against the work surface to bring any bubbles to the surface of the plaster, then burst them with a finger. Leave the mould to set for a while and clean out the plaster bucket so it is ready to use again for the second half. Remember not to clean the bucket in the sink!

When the heating and cooling of the plaster is done, start to peel away the supporting coils on the outside of the walls. It should be possible to reuse the walls for the second half of the mould, so peel them from the plaster without distorting them. If there are scraps of plaster on the walls, scrape them as clean as possible; alternatively, reuse the walls the other way around.

While the mould is still in place on the board, bevel all the edges with a rasp blade to prevent them from chipping later. If the upper surface of the mould is not level, correct it with the rasp blade or a metal ruler. Dispose of the plaster in the rasp carefully, so that no traces remain to contaminate any clay. Similarly, wipe away any pieces from around the model and mould, and dispose of them in the trash. Even sweep scraps from the floor, if necessary. It is important to work cleanly with plaster.

Turn the mould over onto a clean surface with the clay bed still in place. Now carefully peel back the clay, leaving the model in the plaster bed. It should be possible to remove the clay bed in one action. When this is done, check around the edges of the model for any specks of clay that may be stuck there, and remove these carefully with a modelling tool; otherwise, they will be cast as part of the second half.

To be sure that the two halves of the mould will fit together correctly, locating keys, or 'natches', are marked in the plaster surface on either side of the model. These can be made by twisting a coin or other round object into the plaster surface to make a hollow. Here, a melon ball maker – a useful tool for a potter! – was used to form the natches. Three natches are carved on each side, halfway between the model and the outer edge of the mould – one at each end and one in the middle.

Before casting the second half of the mould, the surface of the first half must be coated with a separator to prevent the plaster from sticking to it. A soft paintbrush is used to apply soft soap liberally over the surface of the mould and the top of the model, and a little way down the model's sides. Mould-maker's releasing agents, petroleum jelly or oil can also be used for this purpose. After applying the first coat of soft soap, wipe it away gently using a damp sponge. Don't rub the soap; a thin coat needs to remain on the surface. Now repeat the process twice more, painting the soap on, then gently wiping it off again. At least three such applications are necessary to prevent the two halves of the mould from adhering.

Fix the mould onto a board with a little soft clay to prevent it from moving as the walls are rebuilt around the sides. Make sure that the mould is level and secure, then fix the top wall back into place, securing it on the outside with a thick coil of soft clay. It is essential to seal any gaps between the first half of the mould and the newly positioned walls; if not, plaster will find its way through, and the two halves will be almost impossible to separate. With this in mind, check that the walls seal against the plaster of the first half, or fill the gaps with a little soft clay.

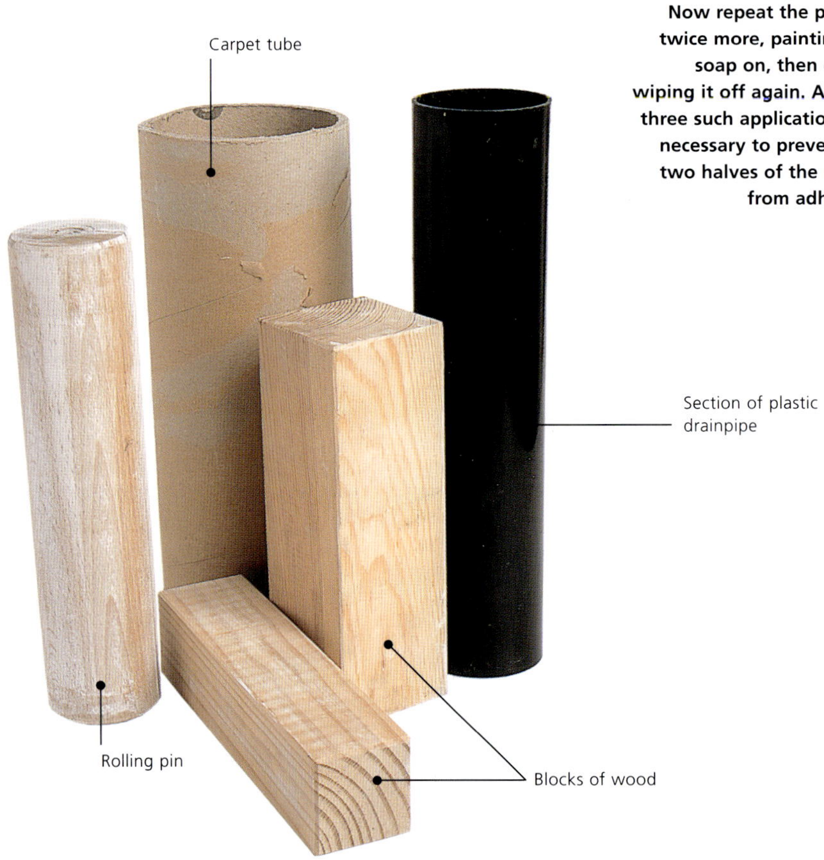

Here is a selection of objects that could be used to make simple two-part moulds. It is helpful for beginners to practice making moulds from found objects to gain an understanding of the principles of working with plaster. Many plastic objects are made in moulds and are perfect for casting because the seams are obvious and therefore provide ready-made dividing lines. Practise a little with such objects before committing yourself to a final piece.

Build up the walls around the rest of the model, taking care to seal the supporting coil to the board and the wall. It will be necessary to seal up to the top of the corner joints to prevent plaster leakage. Hold each wall firmly in position as the coil is fixed into place on the outside. When all of the walls are secured, check that no specks of clay fell onto the first half of the mould or the model. Remove them carefully if they did, to prevent them from being cast into the second half.

Mix the same amount of plaster to water as for the first half, and pour the mixture into the cottle. Carefully tap the mould on the work surface to bring the air bubbles to the surface and then burst them. Leave the mould to heat up, then cool down again, before removing the cottle. Bevel the edges of the mould and level the surface, if necessary, as for the first half, taking care to dispose of the plaster safely. Throw away all of the clay used to make the mould unless it can be used to make another mould, in which case store and label it meticulously.

Moulds with two or more parts are often difficult to separate, because the various parts form a strong seal. When the spare is removed, however, the seal is usually broken. The spare in this example is easily extracted with a corkscrew, though care is taken not to screw into the wooden model. A spare made of clay should be scooped out with the fingers rather than a tool, to avoid damaging the mould.

When the spare is released, the two halves of the mould should come apart easily, especially if they were soft soaped correctly. If you have difficulty separating the sections, wrap the mould in a towel and give it a little tap with a rolling pin, or position a metal kidney or scraper on the joint along one side of the mould and give this a gentle tap with a hammer. Don't tap with a rolling pin because the kidney will damage the surface. It should not be necessary to use much force to separate the halves, but if this is unsuccessful, allow the mould to dry out a little before trying one of the separation methods again.

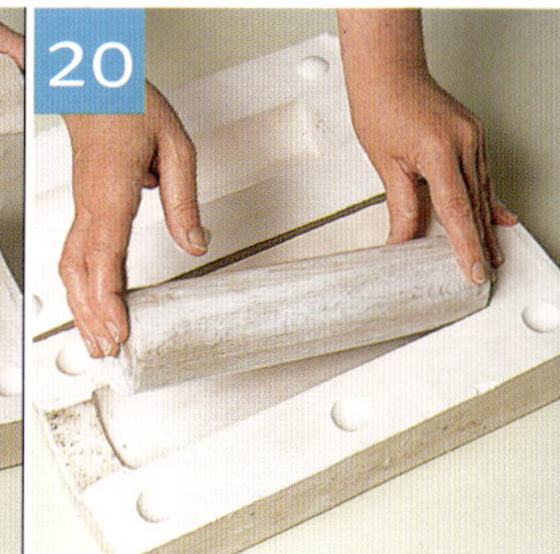

The mould is now complete, in two perfectly matching halves. It should not be necessary to clean the inside of the mould, but if you want to do so, simply wipe it with a damp sponge. Reunite the two halves and put the mould somewhere warm to dry out thoroughly before use. Keeping the sections together and turning the mould over from time to time helps achieve even drying. When the two halves are separated, releasing the model from the mould can be simple.

Tips for success

- Mould making can be quite daunting for the beginner, so it is a good idea to start making moulds from found objects that are easy shapes to cast. Square shapes are good because they have no undercuts. Similarly, two-sided objects are a good choice because they have a natural halfway mark to cast to.
- When casting wooden objects, you may encounter problems releasing them from the mould after they have been cast, because wood absorbs water and expands slightly. The simple solution is to allow the mould to dry off a little with the model in place; it should shrink back to size, allowing for easy release.
- It is vital to measure and draw the halfway line on the model accurately to avoid the possibility of undercuts. If this was not done properly and the model sticks in the mould, there is no alternative but to break the mould and start again.

Press moulding from a two-part mould

If you run out of casting slip or want a different surface quality, a mould made for casting can be used as a two-part press mould. Joining the two halves of a small mould successfully can be difficult because the interior of the shape cannot be reached by hand, but this should not be a discouragement. Although the press-moulded form does not have the pristine surface quality of the cast version, it offers the potter the opportunity to make a more individual piece.

Roll a slab of clay using roller guides no thicker than 5 mm. Make the slab large enough to fill both sections of the mould, using about 675 g of clay. Cut the slab in half and ease one section into each half of the mould using a damp sponge. Make sure that the clay fits properly into the curve of the base, but it need not extend into the spare at the top. Trim away the excess using a roller guide, as demonstrated in the section on press moulding (page 139). Leave both sections of clay to firm up in the mould. When they are able to hold their shape, turn them out onto a bat. A good indicator of dryness is when the clay starts to shrink away from the plaster wall. The drying process can be sped up with a hairdryer, if necessary.

The sections are vulnerable to distortion at this stage, so handle them gently.

When the sections of clay are sufficiently firm, turn them out of the mould sections onto a bat.

To make certain of a good joint, score the edges of each section with a knife in a cross-hatch action. Allow the sections to rest gently in one hand as they are scored, keeping the fingers well away from the knife. Set the scored sections aside. Make some slip by crushing some dry scraps of the same clay to powder. A mortar and pestle is useful for this task. Add enough water to the clay powder to reconstitute it to the thickness of cream.

Using a brush, apply the slip liberally to the scored edges of each section. Now fit the sections together in an upright position, checking that the joints line up. Any slip that oozes out at the sides can be cleaned up later. Hold the two sections together for a few minutes to make sure the seal is good. Check that the joint on the base is also correct. If the joint looks at all insecure, separate the two sections slightly, apply more slip, and ease them back together again.

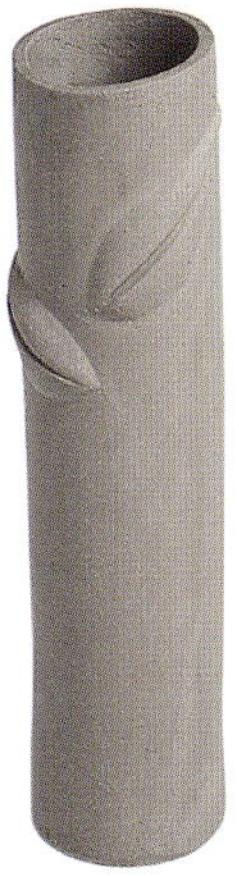

Clean up the joints on both sides of the form, using a metal kidney to remove the excess slip and smooth the surface. Finish off by working a rubber kidney over the same area. It is impossible to reach a hand inside this form to neaten the inner surface, but this can be accomplished by using a damp sponge tied to the end of a long paintbrush. Do not overwork the sponge on the inside or use an excessive amount of water because this would weaken the form and force the joint open again.

Cut the rim to the required shape using a potter's knife. Here the rim is cut on a diagonal to add interest to an otherwise basic cylinder form, but you could introduce shaping and cutaway details for a more decorative effect. When the rim is the required shape, neaten it and round it off, using first a metal then a rubber kidney. Spend time making the rim as neat as possible – it is an important feature.

As a finishing detail, the form can be decorated with sprigs. Here, one of the sprig moulds made later in the chapter (page 132) is used to create a simple leaf design. The decoration can be as simple or elaborate as you choose. Apply the sprigs (page 140), making sure that no air is trapped beneath them. Coloured slip decoration, if required, can also be done now before the form dries out any more. The form is now complete and should be dried carefully before bisque firing. The simple cylindrical form offers not only great scope for decoration but also the opportunity to make more adventurous shapes. For example, several sections could be put together in a faceted style and fitted onto a slabbed base to make a larger form, or multiple sections could be placed side by side horizontally and fitted together to make a ridged dish. A little creative thinking is all that is needed.

Using a two-part mould with casting slip to cast a form

Using liquid clay in the form of casting slip is the standard industrial method of mass-producing ceramics, and it is increasingly used by studio potters who want to repeat standard forms but decorate them individually. Combining the industrial and studio approach in this way gives the potter creative freedom while speeding up the making process considerably.

It is much easier for beginners who are still at the experimental stage of slip casting to buy ready-made casting slips in plastic buckets from a pottery supplier than to make their own. A good first choice is an earthenware slip – preferably a white one, because this enables a wide variety of decorating finishes. Ready-made slip should be exactly the right consistency for use, but it must be thoroughly stirred before being poured into the mould, to return it to a fully liquid state. The two sections of the mould are secured together with special bands from a pottery supplier, or with cinch straps. When the mould is secured, pour the slip into it in a continuous stream until it reaches the rim. Use a pitcher for this to avoid struggling with a weighty bucket over a small opening. Make a note of the time for future reference.

Allow the slip to stand in the mould for up to 10 minutes, adding a little slip from time to time as the plaster absorbs the moisture from it. How long the slip must be in the mould depends upon a number of factors, such as the type of slip (earthenware or stoneware); how thick the potter wants the walls to be for subsequent treatments; and the size and shape of the mould. The thickness of the wall can be seen to some extent as the slip is absorbed, but ultimately the correct thickness can be gauged only with experience and a keen eye, but this develops quickly, since casting is a relatively speedy process. When the slip has been in the mould for the required amount of time, pour it out slowly back into the bucket.

Place two roller guides over a shallow tray with another guide across them. Turn the emptied mould over so that it sits on the guides at a slight angle, as shown in the photograph. This allows the remainder of the liquid slip to drain out, and the angle prevents the bottom of the form from slumping. Leave the mould in this position until the slip has stopped dripping, then turn the mould over and leave the form to dry out. The timing again depends on the slip used and other variables, but with practice you will soon be able to gauge the process. As a very general guide, the form will take at least 30 minutes before it is dry enough to remove, but the time will increase the more often the mould is used and the wetter the plaster becomes.

Before removing the form from the mould, the spare clay must be cut away from the neck. Using a potter's knife and holding the mould firmly in place with one hand, cut the spare clay in a neat downward action around the rim. Try to avoid cutting into the plaster by resting the side of the knife against the mould as the clay is cut. Lift the spare clay out of the mould carefully to prevent it from falling inside. The rim of the form should now be the same thickness as the wall and will need minimum attention to neaten it when the cylinder is removed from the mould.

5

Very carefully remove the bands holding the mould together, then separate the two halves. If there seems to be some resistance, let the mould stand a little longer; then try again. When the mould separates, the cast form remains in one half. Lift the cast out of the mould with great care in order not to distort the shape. Put the cast onto a wooden bat and let it dry out completely. Put the mould back together and make the next cast.

6

When the cast is completely dry, it can be fettled (a term used to describe the neatening up and finishing of a slip-cast form). Stretch a piece of chamois leather over a wooden bat and secure it to the back so that it does not move. Dribble a little water onto the chamois from a sponge, then turn the cast onto its rim and move it in a circular motion over the wet surface. Use both hands to hold the cast as the rim is fettled. Using a chamois in this way is by far the easiest way to level and finish the rim. Check that the rim is flat and even, then finish by wiping around it with a damp sponge. Using water on a dry cast surface does not damage the form.

7

After fettling, check the surface of the form for any blemishes. The halfway marker lines down each side will be obvious, so scrape them back very gently with a metal kidney. Scrape just enough to remove the excess – too much would affect the outline of the form. Hold the form gently but firmly in one hand and scrape with the other. Remember to include the base.

8

To finish the form, wipe the surface with a damp sponge regularly rinsed out in clean water. This will refine the surface, removing all trace of the halfway lines and any other small blemishes. Provided you do not saturate the surface, the water will do no harm. The form can now be allowed to dry out again, and you can repeat the process with the next cast. The first of many cast cylinders is now ready to be fired and finished in the potter's preferred style. It should be possible to cast up to six forms a day from one mould, working until the mould becomes saturated. After this, the mould would need to be dried out before reuse, but the scope to mass-produce with many moulds of different sizes and shapes is endless.

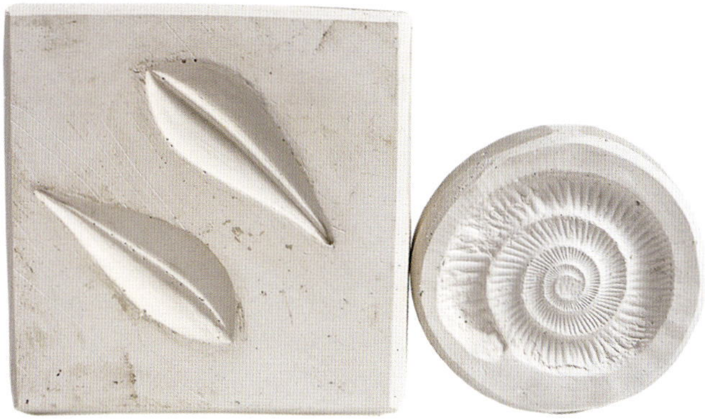

Sprig moulds are technically a form of decoration, since they are added to a finished form to provide low-relief detail.

Sprig mould

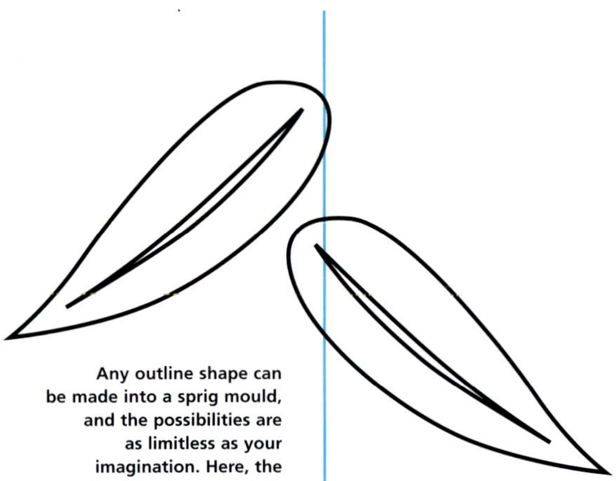

Probably the most famous example is Wedgwood's jasperware, which has white sprig work on a coloured background (usually blue or green). Sprigs can be cast from a clay model or from found objects, and this project demonstrates how to make both kinds. Sprigs are quick and easy to produce, and it is a good idea to make several at a time so that you have a selection to choose from. Generally speaking, the clay you use for sprigs should be the same as the body clay, or a stained version, to avoid possible shrinkage problems. It is usual to discard the first cast from a new mould because it can pick up any specks of plaster left behind on the surface and cause the work to explode when fired. This also applies to slip casting.

Any outline shape can be made into a sprig mould, and the possibilities are as limitless as your imagination. Here, the sprigs have been made in the shape of leaves pointing in different directions to give some flexibility to the way they can be arranged on the pot. The most important factors in the making of sprigs are to not make them too thick and to keep the modelled surface as simple as possible to avoid undercuts.

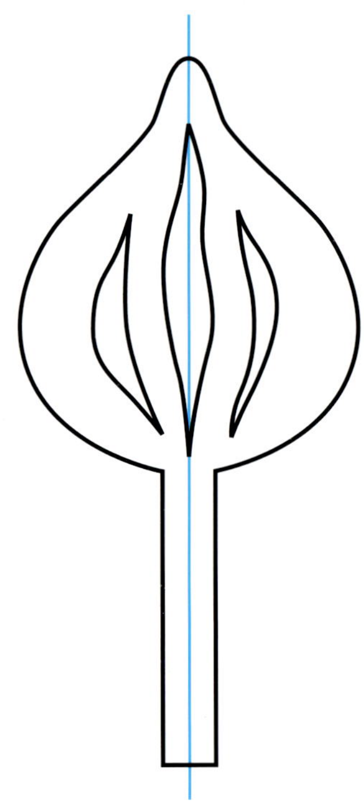

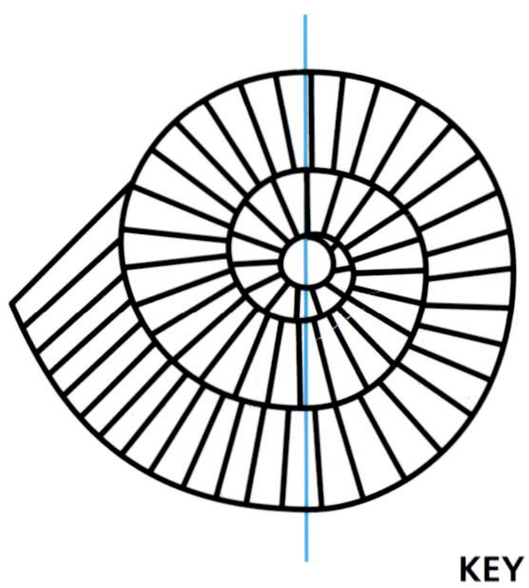

Found objects can be used to make sprigs, as with the ammonite in the demonstration. However, it is possible to model the same shape using a thick coil of clay rolled into shape if the real thing is not available to cast. The modelled detail should be simplified to avoid undercuts.

KEY

Pulling, lifting and supporting movements

Pushing, shaping and reinforcing movements

Decide on the shape of the sprig, draw the outline on a sheet of paper or cardboard and then carefully cut out the template. Position the template on an old tile or nonabsorbent board, and draw around the shape with a marker pen. The design here is repeated to create a left and right version. To do this, the template is simply turned over for the second model. This is necessary because the leaf has a slight twist at the end, but a model that is perfectly symmetrical will not need a repeat version.

After drawing the outline on the board, fill in the space with a tiny amount of clay. Using a modelling tool, model the clay carefully to fit the outline. It is important to make sure that there are no undercuts in the model that would allow the liquid plaster underneath, because this would prevent the sprig from being released. When the shape of the model is correct, smooth over the surface with a finger to remove all marks, then add any additional details required. In this case, a central line is made in the leaf by impressing the edge of a piece of batten in the clay. This dispenses with the need for additional modelling to remove undercuts because the wood makes a V-shaped impression.

1

2

Other ideas for templates

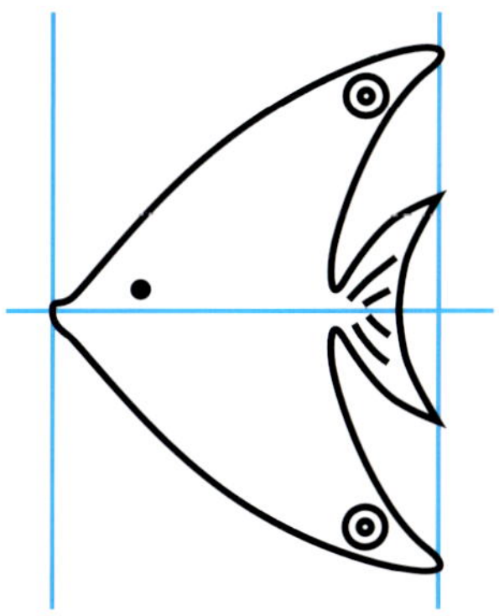

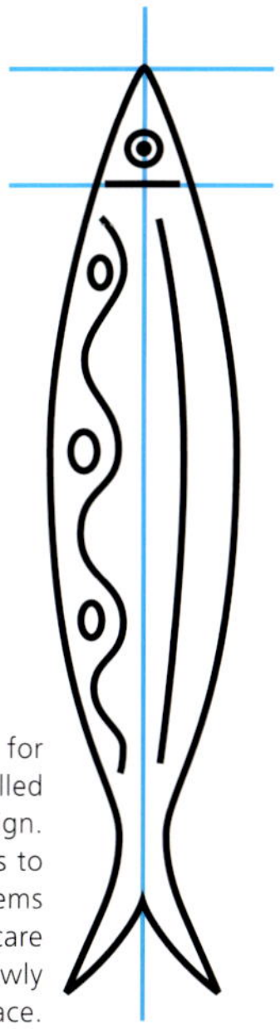

Sprigs with thin details such as stems or legs can be quite tricky to remove from the mould; therefore, the potter should try to avoid them if possible. If these details are essential to the design, however, they are best made as separate sprigs and added on. Simple single sprigs can be put together on the surface of a form to make a different image. For instance, leaf stems can build together to form a flower head.

Mirrors with a fishy or seaside theme work very well for bathrooms, and simple sprigs of sea life can be modelled and cast, along with seashells to build up a lively design. Not all sprigs need to be small – many potters use sprigs to decorate the surface of large-scale ceramics – but problems can arise if the section of the sprig is very thick. Extra care should be taken, therefore, to dry the finished form slowly to prevent the sprigs from cracking away from the surface.

Soft soap the object to be cast three times, wiping the soap off carefully with a sponge after each application. If you have any doubts about the reliability of the surface on which the first sprig was modelled, soft soap that also, following the same procedure. Take care not to create undercuts in the models when wiping away the soap, and correct the problem if it happens by remodelling the shape. It is only important for the object, and possibly the board, to be soft soaped – avoid the clay wherever possible.

Roll another thick slab of clay to form the wall around the modelled sprigs. Again, the wall must be about 38 mm wide to allow for a 25-mm thick mould. Fix the walls onto the tile or board, if possible. A margin around the model of at most 13 mm is sufficient. Secure the walls, as before, with soft clay, making sure that there are no gaps. Before mixing the plaster to make the moulds, cut out two small pieces of scrim to reinforce them while the plaster is poured in. (Scrim is a webbing material used in building work. It is obtainable from building supply centres.)

You can also use a found object for casting – a sea shell, button, old piece of jewelry or any item that can be cast without presenting a problem of undercuts will do. Here, an ammonite is used. Embed the object in clay on another tile or board and build up the level around the shape so that the sprig, when cast, will not be too thick. Model the clay around the object with a rubber kidney to form a level shelf about 13 mm wide, taking care to avoid undercuts.

3

4

5

Tips for success

- Holes in a mould caused by bubbles in the plaster can be filled by being sprayed with water and then carefully filled to the brim with a sprinkling of plaster. When the plaster begins to set, the area can be scraped over with a kidney or modelling tool to smooth it off to the same level as the rest of the mould.
- Soft soap – a special liquid soap used in mould-making – is obtainable from pottery suppliers and needs to be diluted. Use 50 per cent boiling water to 50 per cent soap, and store the mixture in a screw-top jar.
- If you find it is too difficult to model fine detail onto a tiny sprig, scale the sprig up to a manageable size and then dry and fire it, either to bisque or to the clay's top temperature, depending on the reduction in size required. The model can then be cast in plaster with all the detail in place.

Roll a thick slab of clay wide enough to form a wall around the model. The wall must extend at least 38 mm above the model, since the mould needs to be about 25 mm thick. Secure the wall in place with a coil of soft clay and check that there are no gaps through which the liquid plaster could escape.

Make a plaster mix following the method described earlier in the chapter (page 117). For these two small moulds, 285 ml of water to 340 g of plaster should be enough, but double this if you are unsure, disposing of any surplus in the rubbish bin and not the sink. Remember to skim off any bubbles from the surface of the plaster into a plastic bag, then pour the plaster over the models, filling each cottle almost to the top.

Agitate the surface of each mould with your fingers to bring any remaining bubbles to the surface. Alternatively, lift the moulds at one edge and tap them back onto the work surface very gently a few times. Burst any bubbles with a finger. It is important to work quickly at this stage because the next procedure must be completed while the plaster is still liquid.

All kinds of objects can be cast in plaster to make interesting sprig molds. The selection here includes buttons and old earrings, sections of wooden moldings, shells, and a fossil ammonite.

Carefully place the pieces of scrim cut out earlier over the surface of each mould, then gently ease them just under the surface. The scrim acts as an extra reinforcement for what is essentially a very thin section of plaster. It is not strictly essential but can prolong the life of the mould, which is otherwise vulnerable to breakage. The moulds can now be allowed to harden in the usual way.

To remove the cast object from the mould, peel away the cottle, then cut through the clay bed at board level so that the entire piece can be lifted to provide a better grip to separate the parts. Carefully ease the mould off the model. This should not be difficult if the model was soft soaped fully, but a gentle tap may be necessary to release a solid object. Bevel the edges around the mould using a rasp blade, and dispose of the plaster in a rubbish bin to avoid contamination.

Use a similar method for the mould made from modelled clay. Peel off the cottle and bevel the bottom edge of the mould with the rasp blade. Lift the mould off the board and bevel the upper edge. If the model is still in the mould, ease it out with a finger, or press a ball of soft clay onto the surface and lift the model out. Don't use sharp tools, which could damage the surface of the mould. Wipe around the moulds with a damp sponge to remove any traces of clay, then dry them thoroughly before use. Sprig moulds can be used to create a single detail on a form, or to cover the entire surface in low relief. Join them to the surface of a leather-hard form, using water or slip.

A selection of sprig moulds and the clay sprigs cast from them. Only a small section of the shell at the top left could be cast in plaster, and then it had to be set at an angle to avoid undercuts.

The method for making this simple cylinder vase is demonstrated on pages 128–129. After bisque firing, the vase was dipped in a transparent crackle glaze before being Raku fired. To create the veining on the leaves and the stem, paper resist lines were applied to the form before it was dipped in the glaze. The paper resist was removed before firing to leave the area unglazed and to allow for the absorption of smoke during the post-firing reduction phase (see page 33) of the Raku process. A bisque-fired ammonite sprig stands next to the form. These make useful stamps for decorating slabs of clay.

Making a dish from a press mould uses techniques described in earlier sections of the book, but the additional technique of placing a single sheet of clay in a mould demands a slightly different approach.

Dish with sprig decoration

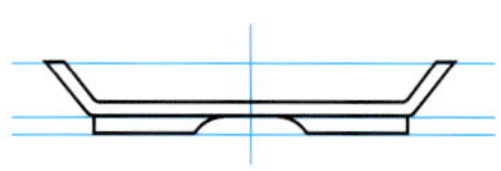

An open, shallow dish is always a useful addition to any kitchen. This simple square shape is good for many methods of decoration, from sprigs to slips and glazes. Simple feet give the form some lift and a convenient point to glaze to.

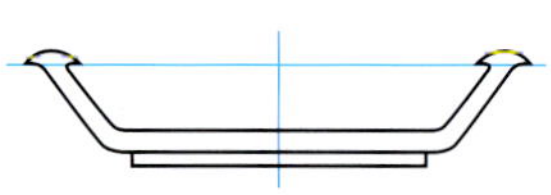

Once the basic shape has been made, the sides can be extended by the addition of flattened coils to make a deeper dish. The rim can be finished off with an extruded or handmade coil to form a decorative flange, and a wider foot ring can be added for greater stability.

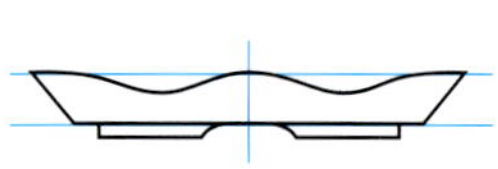

The look of the basic dish can be altered radically by cutting the rim to a different shape. It is always best to cut a template of the shape from cardboard so that it can be repeated exactly on all sides of the dish. Undulating rims always look appealing and once cut can be further enhanced with a flange.

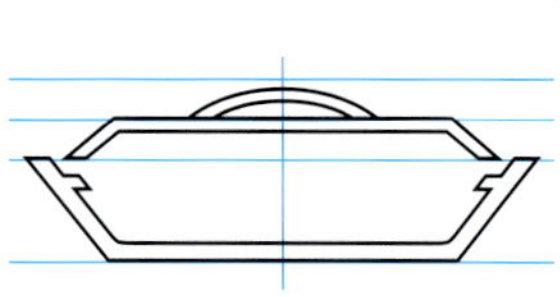

The same basic form can be turned into a lidded dish by making two dishes, building the base one up with a flattened coil, and using the lid to add a locating rim on the inside. The lid can then be fitted with a handle or handles. If firing to stoneware, the base would probably be best left without a foot ring because of the added weight above it.

A grogged stoneware clay was used to give some strength to this form because it is wide and open. The making of a sprig mould is demonstrated earlier in this chapter (see page 132), so if you want to add the sprig decoration, make the sprig mould first and allow it to dry before making the dish.

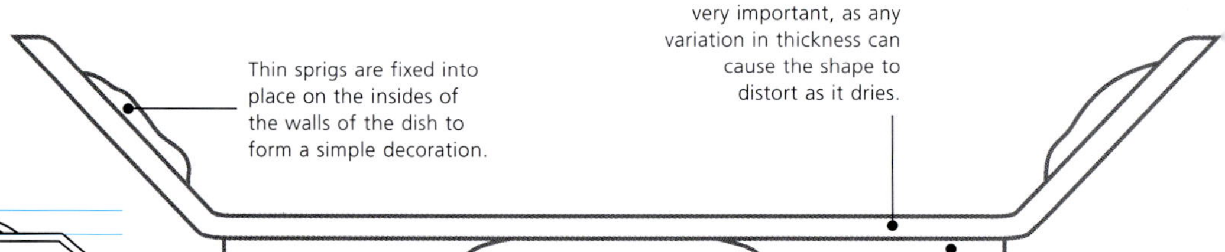

KEY

Pulling, lifting and supporting movements

Pushing, shaping and reinforcing movements

Using 5-cm thick roller guides and following the technique demonstrated on page 86, roll out a slab of grogged clay large enough to fit the mould (about 900 g). Lift the clay carefully over the mould and allow it to slump naturally into the shape as far as possible, supporting the slab with both hands as it is eased into place. Do not push the clay into position with your fingers because they will make unnecessary marks and possibly tears. The slab should fit the mould with a little spare lapping over the rim.

When the slab is in place in the mould, ease the clay into the corners using a damp sponge in a gentle dabbing motion. Lift the slab at the edge to ease the clay into the angle and avoid stretching it out of shape. Work around each corner in the same way until the slab properly fits the mould. Do not smooth the surface of the clay too much because this would bring the grog to the surface, giving the dish a rough texture that is unpleasant and difficult to cover with glaze.

Trim off the excess clay folded over the rim of the mould, using one of the roller guides. Set the guide flat on the mould rim and draw the clay towards your body. Take the excess away in small sections – removing it all at one time could drag the clay out of the mould. Always use wooden tools for this task to avoid scratching the mould and contaminating the clay with plaster. Put the spare pieces of slab aside for later use.

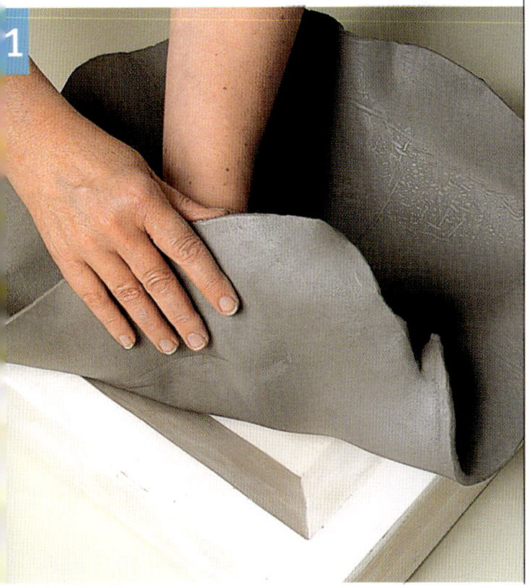

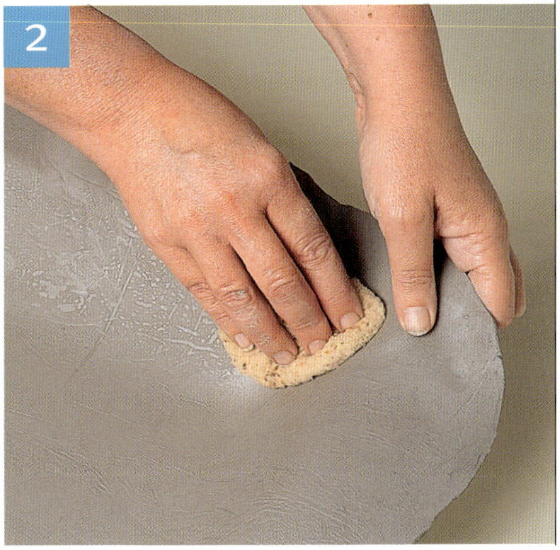

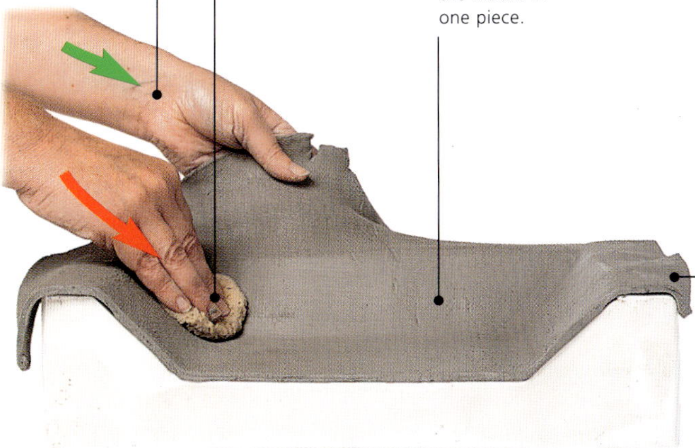

When all of the excess is removed from the rim, smooth the inner surface of the dish carefully, using a rubber kidney. This will help to compact the grog in the clay and form a better surface for glazing. Take care not to make cutting marks in the clay from the kidney. To finish off the interior of the dish, run a finger along the inner edge of the rim to soften it slightly and round it off.

Make a sprig by placing a small, thin slab of clay in the mould, working it in well for good definition. Trim away the excess clay as you did for the large mould; then score the back of the sprig in a cross-hatch action before lifting it out with a ball of soft clay. Decide where the sprig will be positioned in the dish and mark the outline by holding it in place and then drawing around it. Score and slip the marked area and the back of the sprig using a toothbrush and a little water; then fix the sprig into position carefully, making sure it does not slide out of place.

Trying not to press too hard so that the definition of detail is lost, press the sprig from the centre towards the edges to ease out any trapped air and excess slip. When the sprig is firmly fixed, repeat the process to fit the number of sprigs required. You may want to decorate the dish with a variety of sprigs to reflect a theme – shells and the seashore, or flowers and gardens, for example. Sprig moulds are easy and quick to create, so it is possible to make several at a time to express a design theme.

When all of the sprigs are in place, work carefully around each one with a modelling tool to remove any slip that squeezed out and to seal the edges, so that the sprigs look integral to the form. Sprigs should never look 'added on' but should appear to emerge from the clay wall as an innate part of the entire piece. Before deciding how many sprigs to use in a form, consider the object's intended purpose. A lavishly decorated interior will be hidden in a dish for serving food, for example.

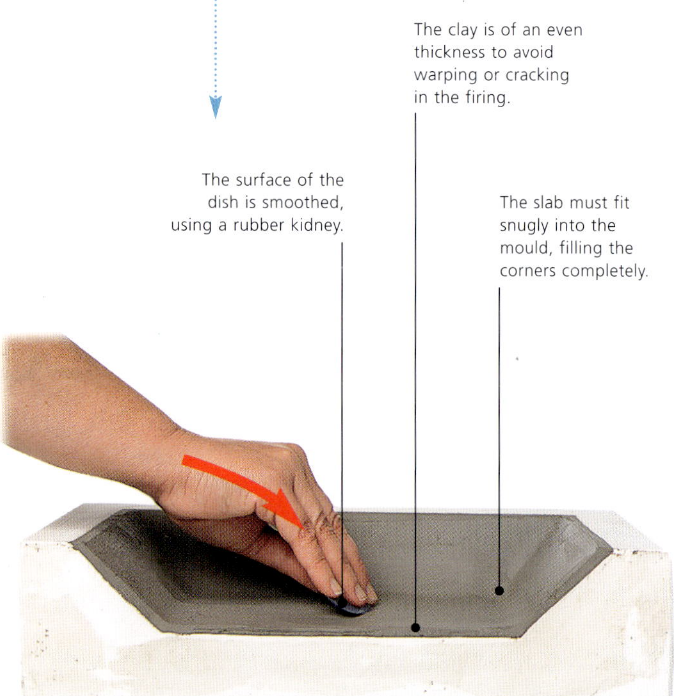

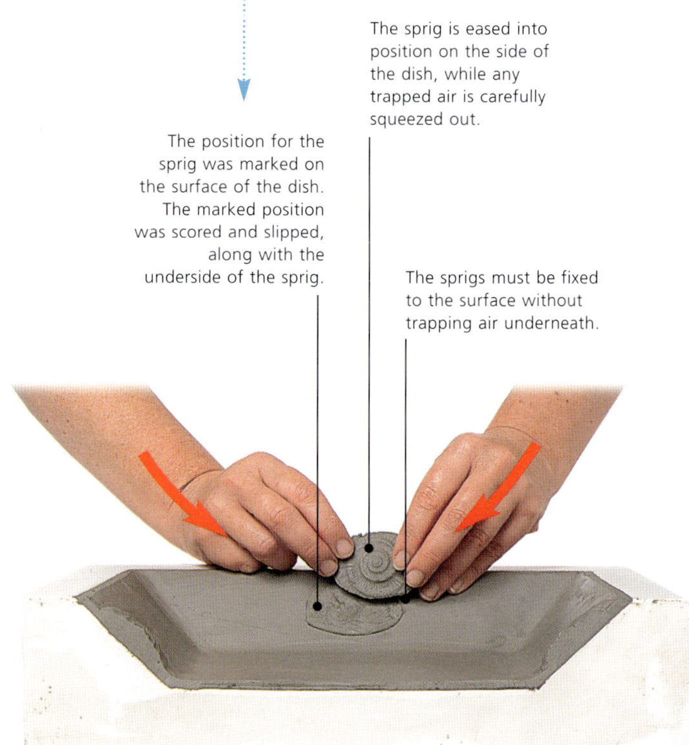

Roll out a long slab of clay, using the same size roller guides as for the main body of the dish. Cut a long strip of clay from the slab, measuring the same width as the roller guide, then cut this into eight equal pieces, each about 5 cm long. Cut one end of each strip diagonally, so that when two sections are fitted together they form a right angle. Check that the dish is dry enough to support its shape; if not, dry it to the correct state using a hairdryer. Then turn it out of the mould by placing a board over the top and turning mould and board over in one gentle action.

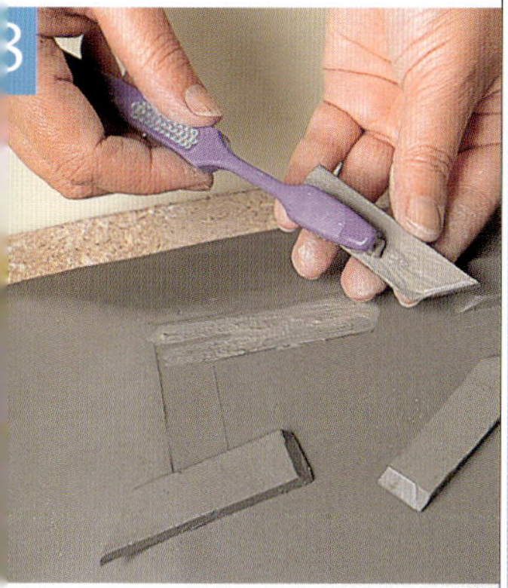

Position the strips fractionally in from the edge of the base so that they form a corner foot ring. Mark the position of the strips on the base, score and slip the marked area and the underside of each section, and fit them into place. Fitting the foot ring into the corners gives the dish a slightly Eastern look, but the ring could just as easily be fitted all around the base. Wipe away any slip that squeezed out from around the joints, using a barely damp sponge. Before turning the dish back over into the correct position, cut a square of clay from the leftover scraps of slab, roughly the size of the interior space of the foot ring, and position it to support the base of the dish as it dries. Place a bat over the base and turn the dish the right way up. Neaten the rim of the dish using a metal kidney to round off the edges; then finish off with a rubber kidney or finger to soften the outline.

The dish has been covered in an iron rich, red/brown stoneware glaze. The ammonite sprigs on the sides had a secondary sponging over with a little reactive glaze to highlight the surface detail and form a contrast to the rest of the dish. This works well to give the sprigs an aged look. Dishes like this, which are likely to be used domestically, look much better if glazed in simple fashion. Always consider the purpose of a form before glazing it, because elaborate decoration is lost when a dish is filled with food.

Agate is a term for the swirls and patterns that occur when pieces of clay are stained in different colours and then wedged loosely together.

Simple agate bowl

Because porcelain agate can be difficult to handle, it is better to form the shape in a simple open mould that will allow the bowl to be built up quickly. Bowls with no definite base can look very attractive as the form finds its own balance and can sit on the tiniest area of clay. The same form can be vulnerable and unstable, however.

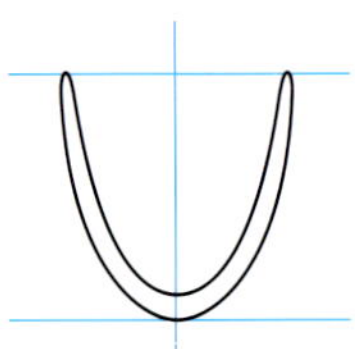

The addition of a simple foot ring can lift the basic shape and give it more stability. This can be added in the form of a coil or slabbed strip curled into a ring. It can be joined on and then carved or cut away in sections to open it up a little. Whatever finish you choose, it is important to balance the base with the rest of the form so that the body does not look top-heavy.

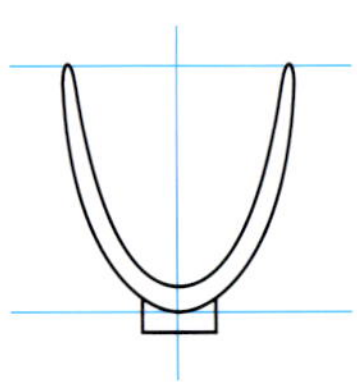

Two bowls can be joined to make a vessel form. This would require a plain section of porcelain in the centre to make joining the two halves easier. One of the bowls would also require an opening at the top so that a hand or tool could fit inside to reinforce the join. A decorative coil on the rim and a simple foot ring would finish the form, but you also need to consider the positioning of the agate with respect to the coil and foot ring.

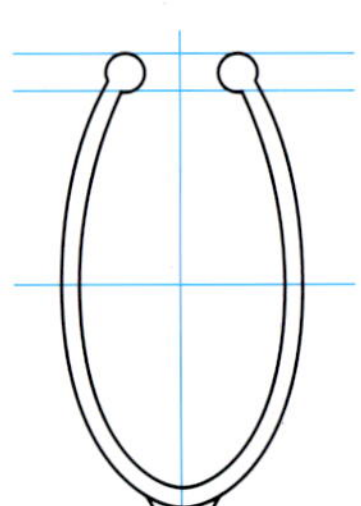

Continuing on from the vessel form, the shape can be built up further into a bottle form by coiling the last section. Again, this would be difficult to do in agate. It is, therefore, best finished in plain porcelain with the coloured agate more selectively positioned throughout the form.

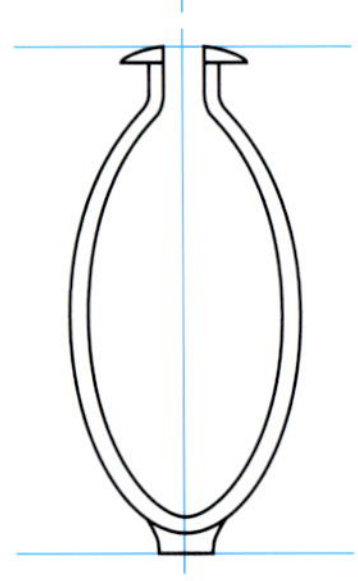

The resulting clay mixture resembles the geological structure that is formed in layered silica minerals. Porcelain is the clay of choice for agate because it combines smoothness with strength and good colour response, offering the potter the scope to create thin-walled pieces of ceramic with fine detail. In this project, four colours are used to stain individual blocks of porcelain, which are then combined with some unstained clay to make the agate. Porcelain can be tricky to work with, but the simple construction of the bowl offers you an excellent opportunity to practice the technique before attempting a more challenging project.

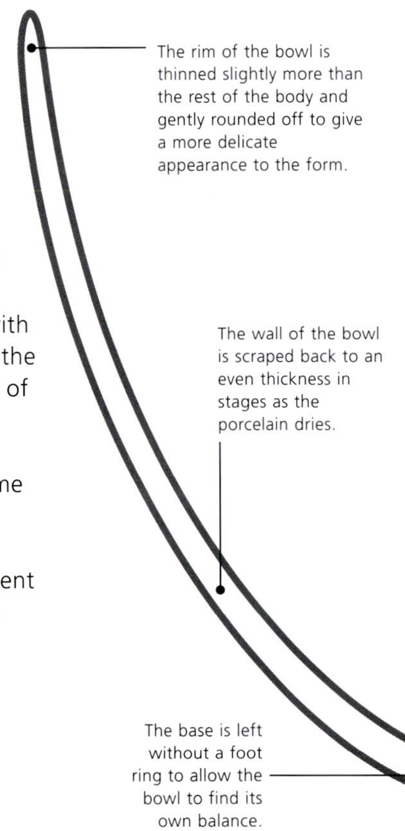

KEY

Pulling, lifting and supporting movements

Pushing, shaping and reinforcing movements

Using the method described on page 13, stain at least four differently coloured batches of porcelain. Now mix three of the colours with some unstained porcelain by layering each colour together and then loosely wedging them. Don't overdo the wedging – a little makes a good agate pattern, and the pattern also evolves as the clay is handled. Now mix another combination of three colours to include the one omitted from the last batch, again with some white. From each different batch of agate, form a number of marble-sized balls – about 12 of each, although the number depends on the size of the mould in which the bowl will be formed. Make an equal number of plain porcelain balls. Keep the balls on a nonabsorbent surface and cover them with plastic to prevent drying.

Squash one of the agate balls into the base of the mould. Then work the plain clay balls slightly over and around the agate base to form a ring. Build up the agate pattern at the next level by alternating the coloured balls to form another ring. Overlap and squeeze the colours together well. Do not be concerned if the pattern looks messy at this stage; it can be amended later, and a certain random blending is, in any case, part of the design.

Continue to build up the layers of agate over plain clay to the rim of the mould. The final layer should be of agate, and it should overlap the rim considerably in order to be trimmed off neatly. When this level is reached, work back over the layers to check that they are all well blended. The mould will dry out the porcelain very quickly, so it is important to blend the clays thoroughly before this begins to happen.

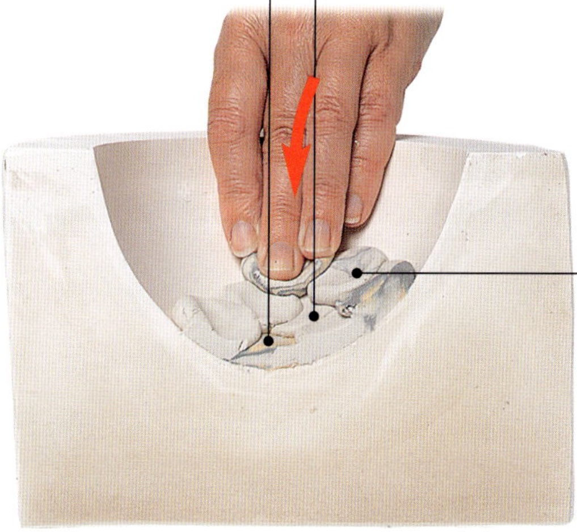

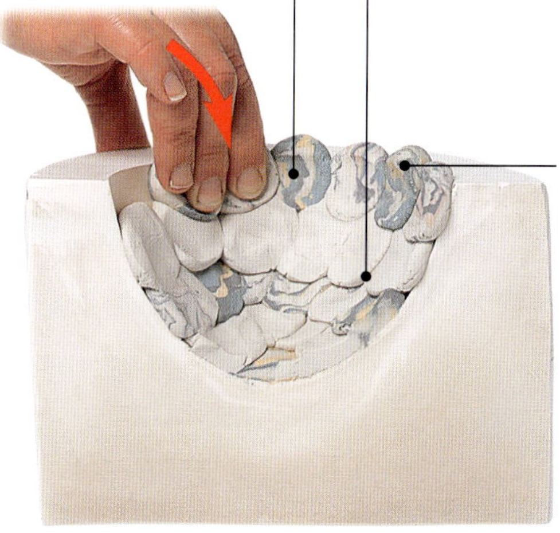

Trim off the excess at the top of the mould, using a roller guide held flat on the rim. Trim small amounts at a time to avoid breaking the wall, and draw the guide back towards your body each time, rotating the mould as you go. If the trimmed-off pieces of agate are still soft enough, they can be reused to make another form, so transfer them to some plastic and wrap them well until needed. If they seem too hard, they can be softened again by being wrapped in a damp cloth and placed inside a plastic bag for about 30 minutes.

Allow the bowl to dry off a little in the mould; then very carefully begin to scrape back the surface with a metal kidney to reveal the swirls of agate layered against the white of the porcelain. It may be necessary to scrape the surface in stages as the clay dries, because porcelain has an optimum time for scraping and carving and can be difficult at other moments. Do not apply too much pressure as the inside is scraped to avoid causing cracks along the lines where the balls of clay were squeezed together.

Carefully lift the bowl out of the mould and finish off the rim by bevelling it neatly, using a metal kidney. It is essential to support the wall of the bowl with one hand as the rim is neatened and to avoid applying too much pressure, which could distort the shape and cause the clay to crack. This is the most delicate stage of the process and requires patience. The bowl is now essentially finished. The lines where the balls of clay were squeezed together can be left on the outside to form part of the design. Alternatively, the outer surface can be scraped back in the same way as the interior, taking great care in the handling of the form. Dry the bowl very slowly, loosely wrapped in soft plastic, inside the mould. After bisque firing, the bowl surface can be further refined with fine sandpaper before its final surface treatment.

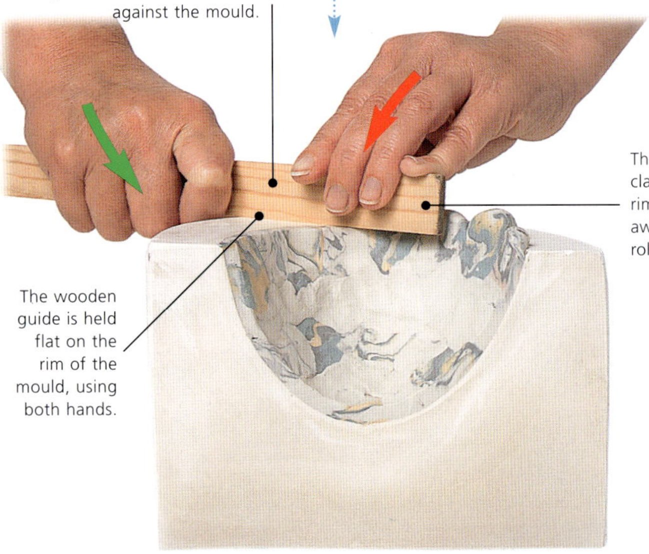

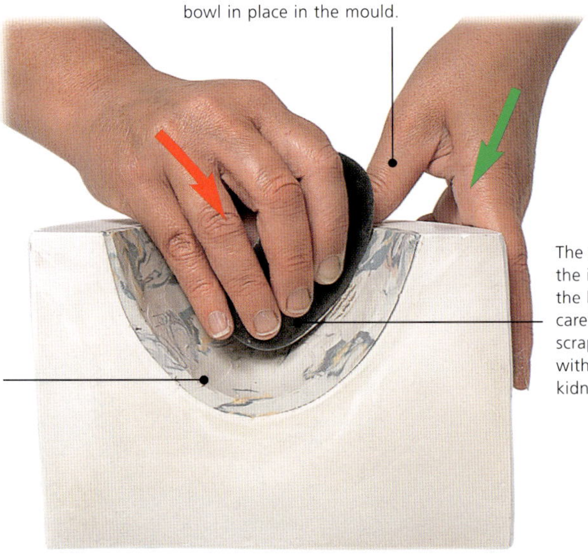

After the bowl was dried out slowly over a very long period, it was bisque fired to 1,000°C. The surface was then refined further, using wet and dry paper before it was glazed in transparent glaze. The bowl was fired to 1,280°C in an electric kiln. The glaze softens the various colours in the porcelain nicely, but the bowl could be fired without glaze as the clay is vitrified at this temperature anyway, making it impermeable to water.

This project uses the remainder of the porcelain stained for the preceding project to achieve a different effect.

Laminated porcelain dish

The simplest shape to start with is a square moulded over a hump mould to form a dish. The dish is lifted by the addition of a simple foot detail reflecting the agate pattern on the inside surface. Making simple dishes like this allows you to experiment with pattern without compromising on form, as the one should not detract from the other.

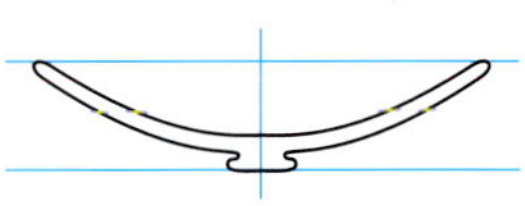

Inlaid agate sheets can be made up and allowed to stiffen a little for use in simple slabbed forms such as boxes. The same techniques as those described in the project on porcelain boxes (pages 102–107) should be followed to construct the parts.

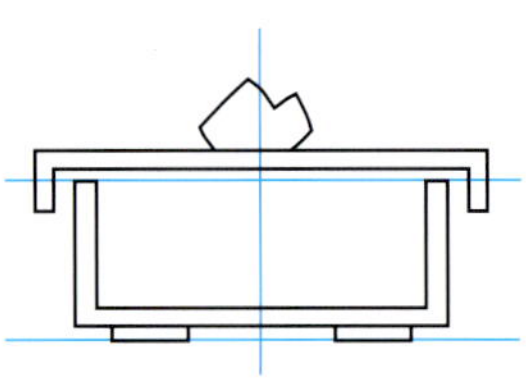

Another possibility for inlaid agate sheets is to wrap the slab around a template to make a cylinder vessel. A plain porcelain slab should be used for the base and consideration given to the positioning of the agate pattern to avoid spoiling it where the sides are joined.

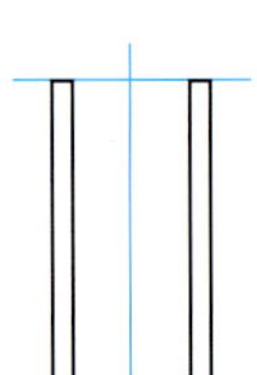

Other two-sided forms can be constructed from the inlaid slabs using techniques described in other sections of the book because this is really a slabbing technique.

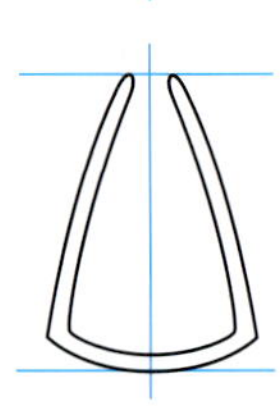

The technique of lamination involves rolling sheets of coloured porcelain, which are then layered on top of one another and rolled again. The slab is then cut and layered again to form as complex a combination of layers and patterns as the potter chooses. This project demonstrates simple lamination, which is then used as an inlay to decorate a sheet of plain porcelain, but it provides a starting point for more ambitious designs.

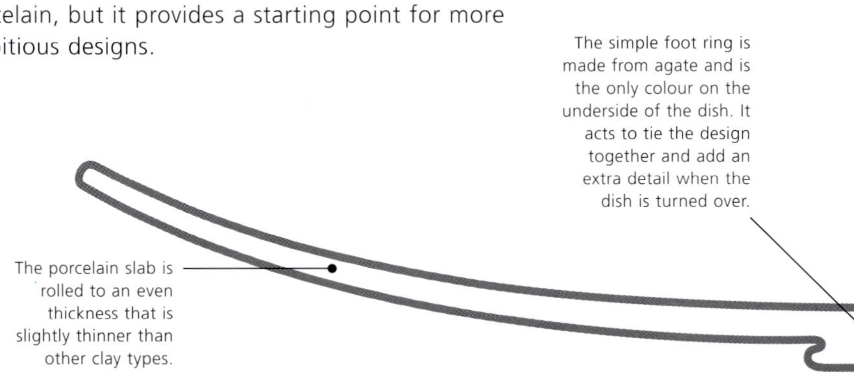

KEY

Pulling, lifting and supporting movements

Pushing, shaping and reinforcing movements

Roll three or four small slabs from the coloured porcelains left over from the agate bowl project. Each slab should be about 6 mm thick, and they should all be cut to the same size. On a clean sheet of fabric, layer the colours on top of one another. The surface of each layer can be scored and slipped with a toothbrush and water for adherence, but wash the brush thoroughly between each layer to prevent colour contamination.

Place another sheet of fabric over the stacked slabs, and roll them out again to 6 mm thickness. Use roller guides if necessary. The layers will distort somewhat in the rolling so that some colours will be obvious around the edges, but the slab will eventually be trimmed and these sections discarded. It is much easier to roll and laminate porcelain between sheets of fabric rather than plastic because fabric is absorbent and prevents the clays from sticking.

Using a ruler or a roller guide, cut as many strips as possible from the slab of laminated clay. Discard the sections cut away at the edges of the slabs. These can be used to make more agate, if required, but they must be well wrapped to prevent them from drying out. Now layer the strips again, using the toothbrush and water to seal them. This process can be repeated as many times as required, but each time the layers are rolled, the strips become thinner and the detail finer. Is this case, just two strips are re-layered to keep the strips wider.

1

2

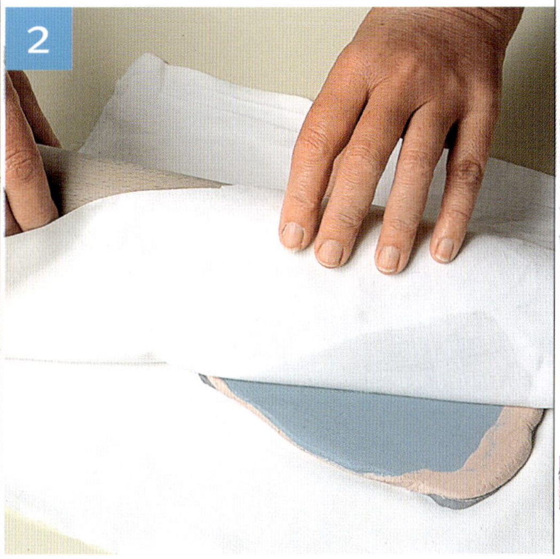

3

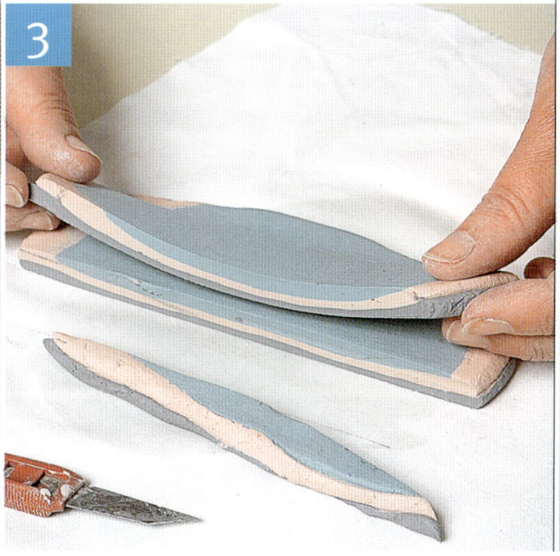

Different effects can be achieved by laminating the coloured clay blocks in varying thicknesses. These can be totally random or the blocks can be sliced and layered to form repeats. If the blocks are rolled out again, each strip will be thinned but the variation in thickness of each colour should remain.

An alternative to layering the colours a second time is to roll them into a coil. This can be done with one of the strips to contrast with the layers in the inlay. Before rolling up a strip, cut off the obscured section of clay at each end; then roll as tightly as possible to avoid trapping air between the layers. Then roll the coil between your palms to thin it out a little and squeeze out any air.

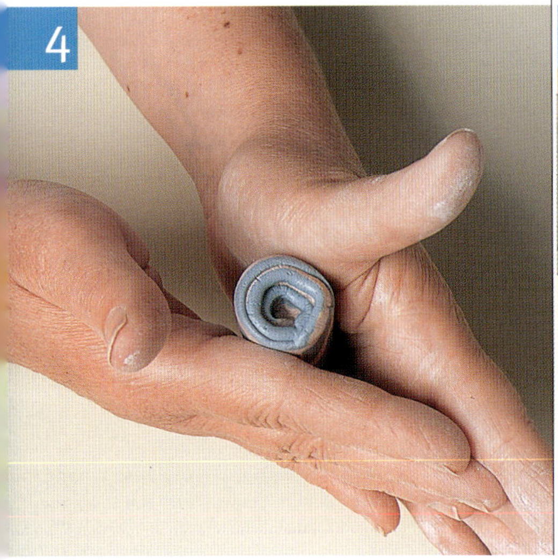

At this stage, you can view the pattern by cutting the coil in half. Alternatively, you could shape the coil by tapping it onto the work surface to make four sides for a square, or three for a triangle, and so on. After the coil is cut to check the pattern, it is better to slice additional sections from that point rather than starting again at the end, where the patterning may be slightly different. When work on the coil is finished, wrap it in soft plastic, along with the laminated strips, until ready for use.

Another way of using up extra strips and discarded pieces of clay is to layer them and then form them into a twisted coil. To do this, hold the strips at each end and twist the clay in opposite directions. The twisted coil is then rolled to squeeze out trapped air and even out the shape. Again, the coil can be shaped, if required. The more you experiment with the technique, the more creative you will become in using all of the clay pieces – and it can become an irresistible challenge not to waste a scrap!

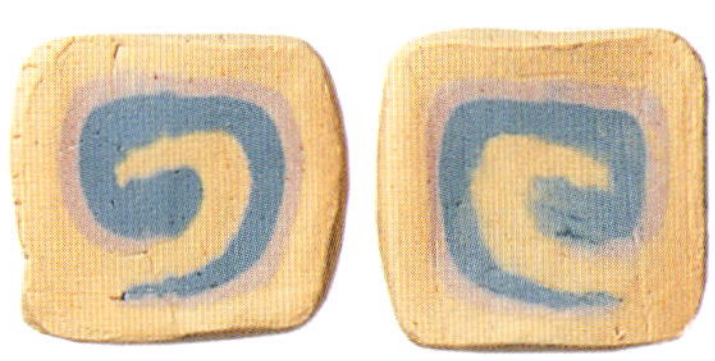

Many combinations of patterns can be achieved by rolling and then shaping the laminated clay. The coils can be made triangular by simply tapping out three sides, or square by tapping on four sides. The shaped sections can be cut and reassembled many times to make even more patterns. Try making and firing little test pieces for future reference.

On another sheet of clean fabric, roll a slab of plain porcelain about 3 mm thick. Use roller guides, if available in this size; otherwise, roll the slab freehand very carefully and evenly. Cut out a paper template corresponding to the size of the dish – in this case, 15 cm square. Don't make it too large because porcelain can easily warp in the firing, and the larger the form, the greater the likelihood of distortion. Place the template over the porcelain slab and score the outline onto the surface. It is not necessary to cut the shape out at this stage. Now cut a strip from the laminated block of colour, brush a little water or plain porcelain slip on one side, then place it on the slab inside and next to the scored outline.

Continue to build up a pattern on the surface of the slab by cutting thin sections from the laminated strips and arranging them around the edge of the square. When you are finished, fill in the space between the strips with equally thin sections from the laminated coil. You can continue making the pattern as intricate as you like, but a first attempt is best kept simple and abstract so that you can gain an idea of how the process works.

Complete the surface of the slab by filling in any very bare areas with tiny details from another laminated shape. The pattern here was designed to look relatively free, but the next stage in the process flattens and distorts the shapes somewhat, so this must be borne in mind as the pattern is built up.

Tips for success

- Keep all stained clays separate before laminating them, to avoid danger of cross-contamination.
- Prepare a good selection of laminated sizes and shapes to build up the pattern on the surface slab. Make too many rather than too few because you won't want to stop and make more halfway through the construction process.
- Don't waste any clay! It can all be used either by laminating scraps and re-rolling them or by simply mixing bits to make agate. Remember that oxides and body stains can be expensive.
- Make a series of test pieces before making your finished form. Measure the amount of oxide or stain added to each batch of clay, then fire the samples to different temperatures to see how the colours respond. Use these as reference for future work.

Place another sheet of fabric over the patterned slab and roll it back to at least 3 mm thickness. Roll the slab in one direction, then rotate it 90 degrees and roll again to maintain the square shape. Remove the top sheet of fabric, then roll the slab a final time in whichever direction is needed to return the shape to an approximate square. Slabbed porcelain looks best when thin, but beginners should roll the slab only to the point where they are confident of handling it easily – it's better to have a slightly thicker slab with an interesting surface pattern than one that is too difficult to use creatively.

After rolling the slab to the required thickness, position the template over the surface and carefully cut out the shape, using a sharp knife and a roller guide for extra support along the edges. It does not matter if colour extends beyond the edges of the template – this will nicely frame the design. Remove the excess as each side is cut, but leave the finished square in place on the fabric. Do not attempt to lift it off; doing so would distort the shape.

Lift the cut slab, still in place on the sheet of fabric, and position it over a hump mould. Don't remove the fabric until the square is in the correct position on the mould's centre. When the fabric is removed, you will see that the pattern of the weave has transferred to the clay surface. This can either be left to form a feature of the dish or be smoothed away with a rubber kidney. Round off the rim of the dish. Make a foot for the dish by squaring off the remaining section of laminated coil, then cutting four 6-mm-thick sections and joining them together with some slip. Roll the sections slightly to bond them, then cut them into a 38-mm square. Score and slip the position for the foot on the dish and the underside of the foot before fixing it in place.

10

11

12

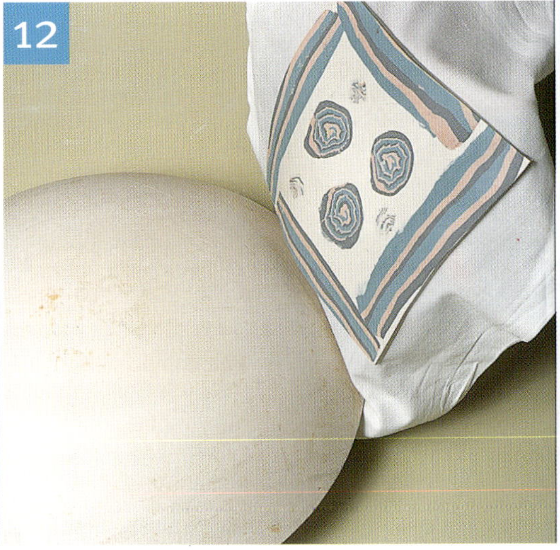

A cross section of the foot shows the four sections of laminated coil joined together to create an attractive design.

The dish was left on the mould until it could be handled easily without distorting the shape. It was then taken off and allowed to dry out slowly to avoid cracks. The surface of the dish was very carefully refined with wet and dry paper after bisque firing. Because of the thinness of the clay section, the dish must be handled very carefully at this stage to avoid breakages. To minimize the possibility of warping, the dish was fired to 1,280°C on a bed of placing sand (a silica sand used to stop clay from adhering to the kiln shelf) inside a larger unglazed but pre-fired dish. Without a glaze covering the surface, the coloured porcelain looks much deeper and richer but the clay has vitrified, making it very hard and impermeable to water. The design of this dish (above) is a slight variation on that of the dish shown on pages 147–150.

This project combines several techniques demonstrated earlier in the book to make a single form in three parts.

Double-walled bowl

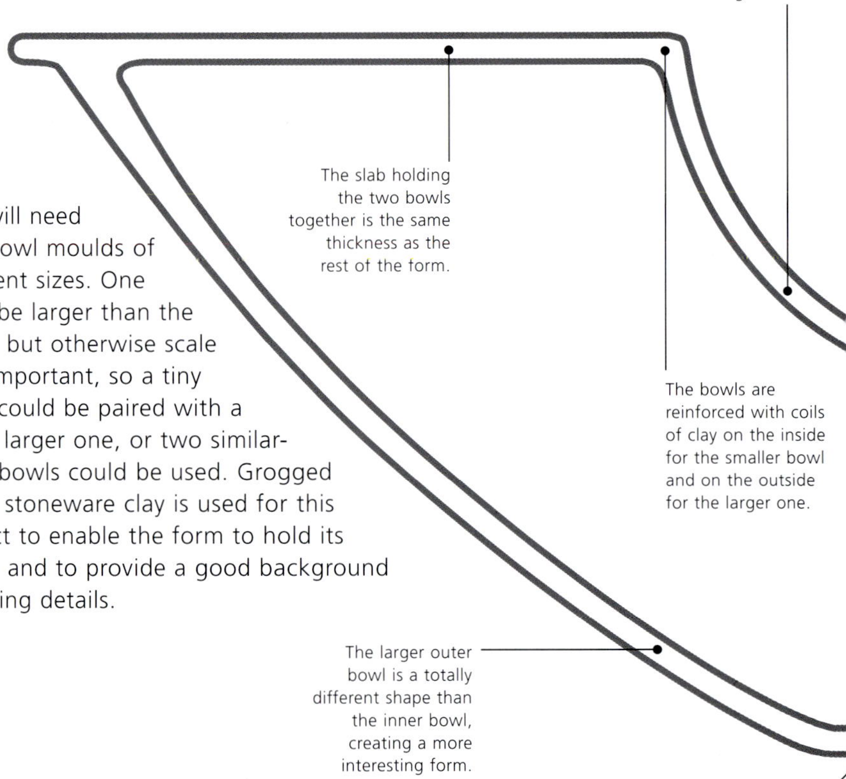

The basic form uses two different bowl moulds, which allow for one to fit inside the other. The bowls can be close in size or radically different, depending on the effect required.

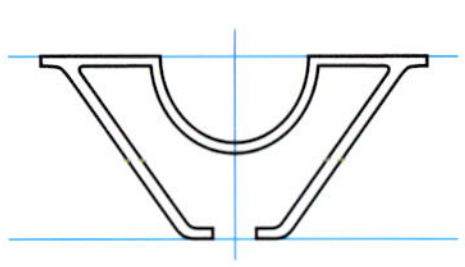

Much larger bowls can be made using the same technique but by building the bowls up with flattened coils. It is not always necessary to cut a hole in the base of the outer bowl, provided a small hole is pierced somewhere in the form before firing to allow for the release of air. The hole in the base does, however, allow the inner bowl to be supported by a lump of clay while you work to finish off the inner rim.

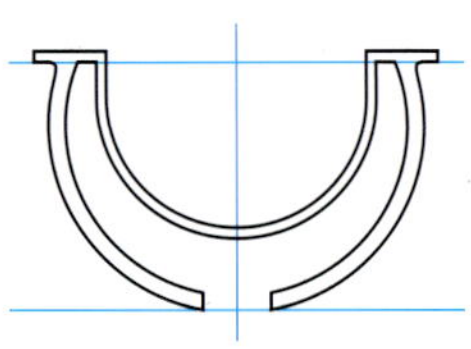

The inner bowl need not be centred over the outer bowl. In shallower bowl forms, the inner bowl can look good offset to one side, giving the form a more contemporary feel.

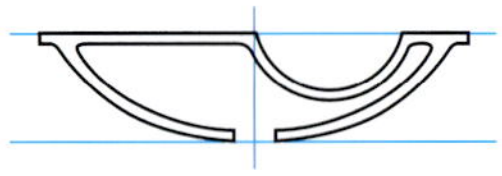

You can fit several bowls of varying sizes inside the outer one. Try one large bowl and two slightly smaller ones to balance the overall form.

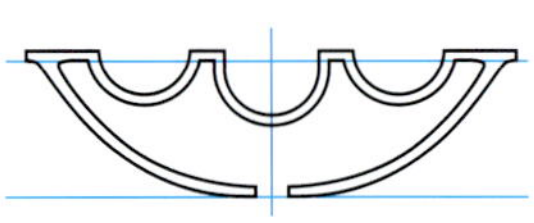

You will need two bowl moulds of different sizes. One must be larger than the other, but otherwise scale is unimportant, so a tiny bowl could be paired with a much larger one, or two similar-sized bowls could be used. Grogged white stoneware clay is used for this project to enable the form to hold its shape and to provide a good background for firing details.

KEY

Pulling, lifting and supporting movements

Pushing, shaping and reinforcing movements

Select two bowl moulds that allow one form to sit inside the other. Roll a slab of clay using the method described in Slabbing (page 86). It should be large enough to fill both moulds and no thicker than 6 mm. Line both moulds from the slab; you can use two pieces of slab, joined together, for a single mould. Smooth off the surfaces well with a rubber kidney. Let the clay dry naturally to the leather-hard stage, or speed the process using a hairdryer. The bowl should be ready to be turned out of the mould when the clay starts to shrink away from the sides.

Turn the smaller bowl out of the mould onto a bat. Reinforce the joint between the two pieces of slab with a thin coil of soft clay. Scrape the excess away from the reinforced area and smooth it over with a rubber kidney. This side of the bowl will not be seen, but it is good practice to finish all surfaces, and this maintains an even clay section. Repeat the process with the second bowl, bearing in mind that this surface will be visible, so it must be as neat as possible.

Draw a small circle on the base of the larger bowl and cut it out carefully. Because the area between the bowls would otherwise be sealed off, this hole allows the escape of air and also helps the potter to handle the bowl at key stages. Neaten the hole by smoothing the rim with a rubber kidney.

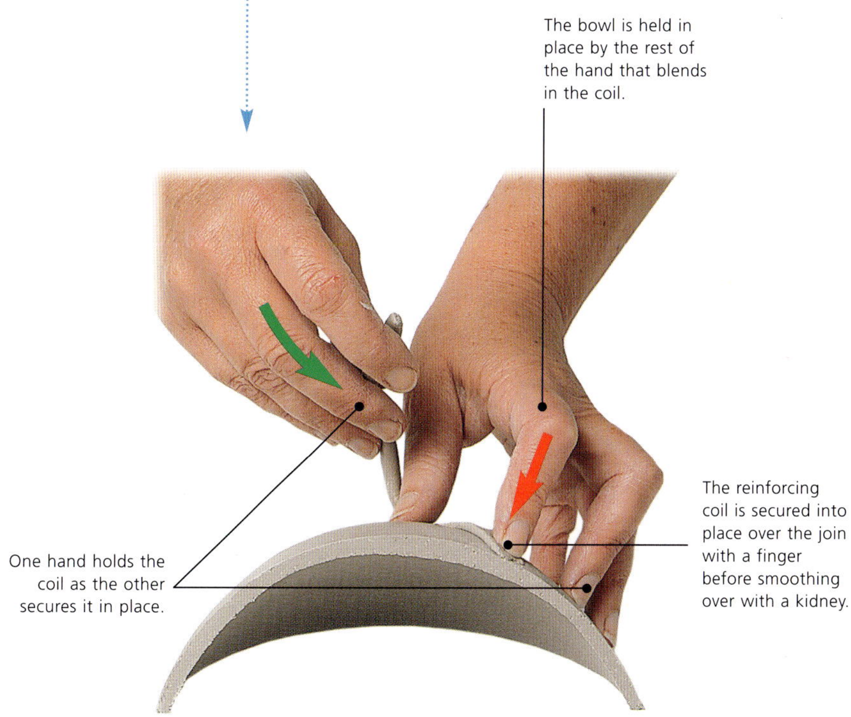

Roll another slab of clay, using the same size roller guides as for the bowl slabs. The slab needs to be slightly larger than the circumference of the larger bowl. Cover the slab with a sheet of embossed wallpaper or a fabric with an open, textured weave, which will create a pattern in the clay. Roll the texture onto the slab to form a deep impression. Check the effect by lifting a small area of paper or fabric; if it needs improvement, you can replace the paper or fabric accurately and roll again.

Lifting the larger bowl carefully, position it over the textured slab and mark an outline 13 mm wider than the circumference of the bowl. Remove the bowl carefully, return it to a bat and then cut out the circle from the textured slab. Although much of the texture will be cut away to accommodate the inner bowl, you should now gain a good idea of how the surface will look in contrast to the rest of the form.

Turn the slab over onto a wide bat, with the smooth side of the slab up. Position the smaller bowl in the centre of the slab circle, and score the position gently in the clay. Remove the bowl carefully, return it to a bat and cut out the circle – this time allowing 6 to 13 mm extra inside the scored line, making the cut-out circle smaller than the one scored. The circle is smaller, therefore, than the circumference of the rim of the bowl.

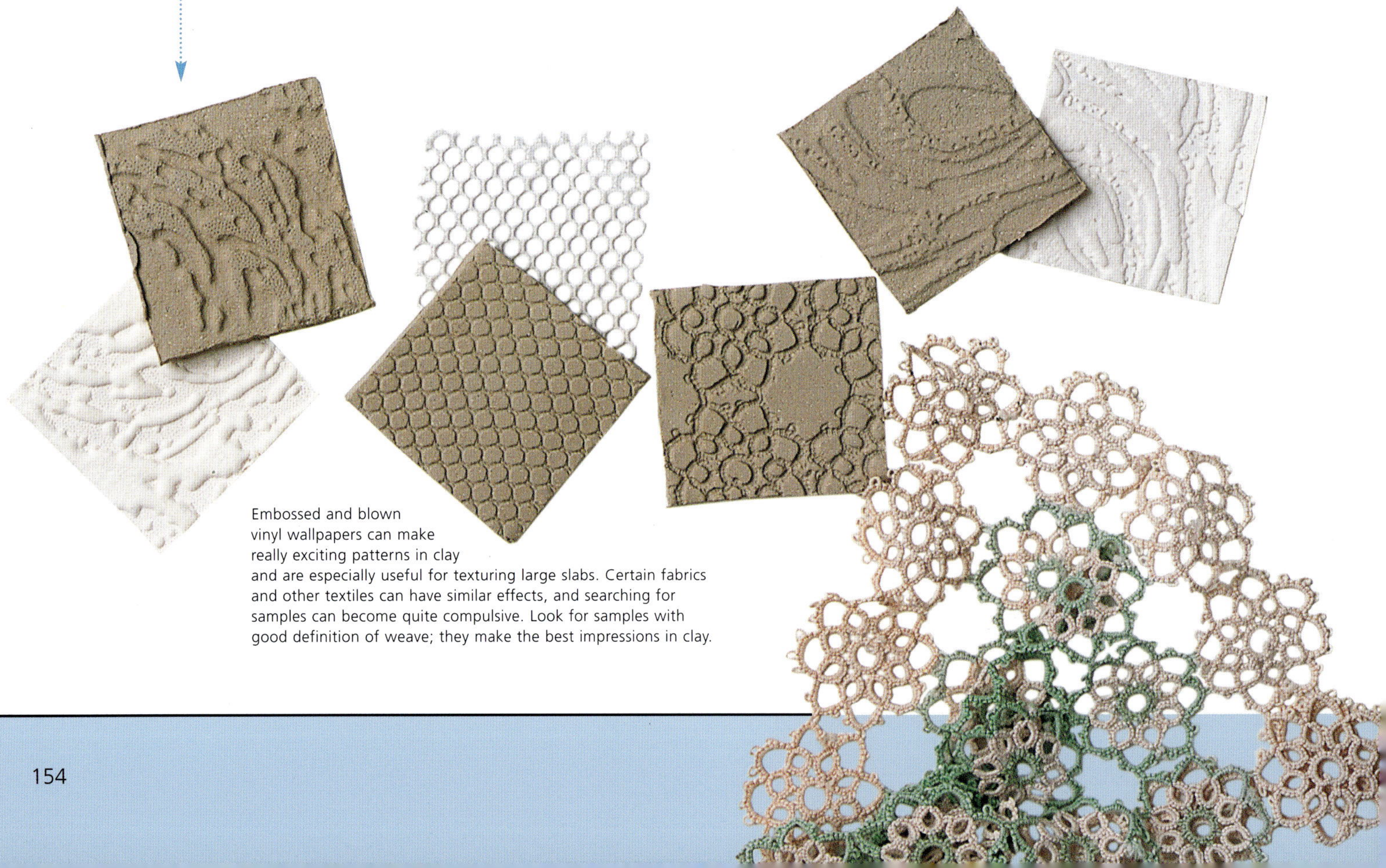

Embossed and blown vinyl wallpapers can make really exciting patterns in clay and are especially useful for texturing large slabs. Certain fabrics and other textiles can have similar effects, and searching for samples can become quite compulsive. Look for samples with good definition of weave; they make the best impressions in clay.

Score and slip the area on the slab between the scored line and the cut-out circle. Using a toothbrush and water, work the surface up well to make a generous amount of slip. Score and slip the rim of the smaller bowl in the same way, then fix it into position on the slab. Hold the bowl in place for a few seconds, applying gentle but firm pressure, to allow the two surfaces to bond together.

Roll a thin coil of soft clay and reinforce the joint around the rim of the bowl. Press the coil into place with a finger first, then use a modelling tool to neaten the joint. Although this area will not be seen, neglecting it could cause a problem at a later stage or in the firing, and it is always good practice to finish a form in its entirety.

Score and slip the outer rim of the slab circle in the same way as the inner one, and also the rim of the larger bowl. Make sure that the bowl is correctly positioned on the slab with an equal margin all the way around, then hold it in place for a few seconds to bond the two surfaces and squeeze out any air or excess slip.

The inner circle of clay is cut out slightly smaller than the circumference of the rim of the bowl to allow for some movement when the bowl is secured.

The bowl is held in place on the slab for a few seconds to bond the two surfaces securely.

The inner bowl is secured onto the slab base after scoring and slipping the two surfaces.

Reinforce the joint with a slightly thicker coil of soft clay. This coil must be blended in very neatly so that the bowl and the textured rim appear integral. Use the rounded end of a rubber kidney to blend one surface thoroughly into the other. All of the joints in this form must be reinforced especially well because they must bear the weight of other parts of the construction – so be meticulous.

Before turning the bowl over to complete the top, the inner bowl must be supported in case its weight causes it to sag into the larger bowl. To do this, form a thick coil of clay that will just fit inside the hole in the bottom of the larger bowl and sit on the inner bowl. Surround the coil with soft plastic to prevent it from sticking to the surface of the inner bowl and to provide a means of lifting it easily in and out. Then set the coil in position and cut it level with the base. Place a bat over the base, then turn the bowl over, sandwiched between the two bats, only removing the larger bat when the bowl is safely on the work surface. Use a craft knife to carefully trim away the excess slab from around the rim of the inner bowl, taking care not to cut into the body of the bowl.

Smooth the joint on the rim of the inner bowl into the slab, using a metal kidney or wooden modelling tool. Work over the surface thoroughly to remove any traces of the joint. Finish off with a rubber kidney to refine the surface completely. Hold the bowl in place with one hand as the surface is refined, and rotate the bowl on a turntable if it helps. Don't apply too much pressure, which could strain the joints even though the sections are supported.

Finish off the bowl by trimming the outer rim with a rasp blade to remove any irregularities in the shape. When this is done, refine the edge with a kidney and run a finger over it to soften it. The bowl is now complete but must be dried upside down to keep the slab rim flat. Place the large bat over the surface and turn it back over; then remove the coil support. The bowl can also be bisque fired in this position, but be careful when handling the dry form because it will be much more fragile. The finished bowl can now be decorated with coloured slips or simply bisque fired for later glazing. The technique enables the potter to make a variety of bowls of differing scale and proportion, depending only on the selection of moulds.

The joint is reinforced with a coil of soft clay, which is secured in place using a finger before finishing off with a modelling tool.

The inner bowl was reinforced in the same way as the outside one and just as neatly.

The hole in the base of the outer bowl allows for the escape of air and easy handling.

The larger bowl is secured onto the slab base and over the smaller bowl.

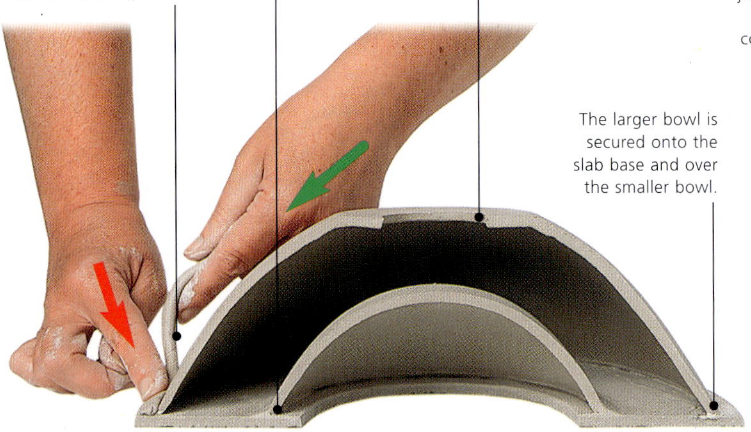

After the excess is trimmed away, the joint is neatened with a metal kidney to compact the clay and seal the seam.

The rim of the inner bowl is smoothed with a wooden modelling tool.

One hand holds the bowl gently in place as the other works on the surface.

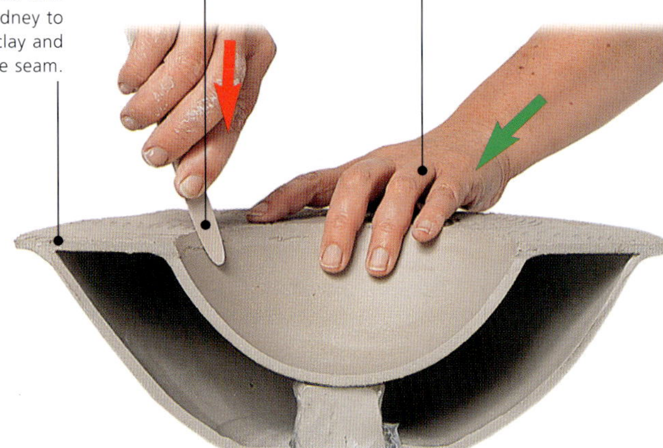

Before bisque firing the bowl to 950°C, several coats of decorating slip were applied to the moulded surfaces, which were then burnished. The bowl was then smoke-fired in newspaper after a grogged clay slurry was applied to the surface to act as a resist. For contrast, the textured rim of the bowl was not covered in resist and it blackened in the firing. A post-firing coat of beeswax was applied to seal the surface and restore the shine.

Index

A

agate bowl, project 142–145
air bubbles, forcing out 29, 30, 86, 88, 100, 116, 121, 125,135
ammonites 132, 136
architectural features 85

B

ball clays 10
banding wheel 9
base, fixing 96, 99
basket, coiled, project 40–45
beeswax 71, 77, 157
bertonite 10
bevelling 126
bird, modelling project 72–77
bisque firing 83, 145, 156
bow harp 8
bowls
  coiled, project 28–33
  double–walled, project 152–157
  moulded agate, project 142–145
  pinched
    bowl set, project 78–83
    joining to make pebble 64–65
  pinching 60–63
  shapes 28
boxes 85
  lidded, using firm slabs 86–91
  porcelain, project 102–107
brushes 9
butt–joining 110
butter dish, project 108–113

C

casting slip
  making tiles from 122
  using two–part mould with 130–131
chamois leather 131
china clay 10
clay 10–14
  ball 10
  chemistry 10
  china 10
  colour 10
  colouring 13, 143
  consistency 13
  digging 10
  drying 25, 31, 38, 55, 65, 87, 95, 112
  earthenware 12
  slip 130
  flattening 29
  frostproof 98
  Keuper red 46
  nonplastic (short) 10, 13
  peeling plastic from 86, 93
  primary 10
  ready–made 11
  reclaiming 14
  refining 10
  residual 10
  rolling on tube 94–95
  secondary 10
  sedimentary 10
  short 10, 13
  shrinkage 11
  stoneware 12, 78
  storage 13, 49, 89
  terra–cotta 10
  testing 10
  types 10, 12
  wedging 14
clay gun *see* extruder
coiling 17–57
  correcting shape 21, 27
  filling gaps 32
  fitting rims 37
  flattened coils 24–27
  projects
    basket 40–45
    bowl 28–33
    dish 34–9
    garden sculpture 52–57
    surface decoration 46–51
  rounded coils 18–23
coils
  decorative 32–33
  flattening 24
  patterned 34–36, 148
  reinforcing joints with 49, 54, 88, 90, 96, 111, 155, 156
  rolling 18, 24
colourants, safety 7
colouring 13, 143
coral, as stamp 92–93
cottle 117
crackle glaze 136
craft knife 8, 111
cutting wire 8

D

decoration 85
  coils 32–33, 34–36, 138
  pierced 63
  repeat patterns 120–121
  sprigs 100
    mould for 132–137
    shapes for 132–133, 135
  stamping 92–93, 94–95
  surface, project 46–51
  underglaze 83
  using embossed wallpaper 108, 109, 154
dies 47
  cleaning 48
dishes
  butter, project 108–113
  coiled, project 34–39
  laminated porcelain, project 146–151
  moulded, with sprig decoration 138–141
distortions, correcting 21, 27, 62, 67
double–walled bowl, project 152–157

E

earthenware clays 12
  slip 130
edges
  bevelling 126
  butt–joining 110
  mitring 89, 98, 103, 104
  scoring 88, 104
extruders 47
  cleaning 48

F

feet
  attaching 38, 114
  laminated 150
fettling 131
firing 12
  bisque 83
  glaze 83
  Raku 39
  smoke 71, 77
flattened coils 24–27
foot ring 62
found objects 132, 134, 135
frostproofing 98

G

garden sculpture, project 52–57
glaze firing 83
glazes 12, 141, 145
gold leaf 51

H

handles
  adding 44–5, 83, 112–113
  curled 112–113
harp 8, 122, 123
health and safety 7
hole cutter 8
household objects, used to make two–part moulds 124, 126

I

iron 10
iron oxide 57

J

joints
  butt–joining 110
  mitred 89, 98, 103, 104
  reinforcing 49, 54, 88, 90, 96, 111, 155, 156
  rejoining 89, 105, 128

K

kaolin 10
Keuper red clay 46
kidneys 8
kneading 15
knives
  craft 8, 111
  potter's 111

L

lamination 146–147
  test pieces 149
lids
  fitting 89–91, 106
  locating strips 91
  onion–dome 106–107
lustre 51

M

manganese dioxide 51
marbled effect 77

metal kidney 8
mitring 89, 98, 103, 104
modelling
pebble 64–65
projects
pinched bird 72–77
pinched pod 66–71
tools for 9
moulding 115–157
dish with sprig decoration 138–411
low–relief tile mould 120–121
press mould 116–119
press moulding from two–part mould 128–129
projects
agate bowl 142–145
double–walled bowl 152–157
laminated porcelain dish 146–151
tiles
from casting slip 122
from soft slabs 122–123
using single sheet of clay 138–141
moulds
discarding first cast 132
household objects used to make 124, 126
low–relief, making 120–121
press moulds, making 116–119
removing bowl from 31
shapes 119
sprig 132–137
two–part 124–127
casting form with casting slip 130–131
press moulding from 128–129

N
natches 126

O
ox-head kneading 15

P
paddling 61, 68, 73, 80
paint scraper 8
paper resist 136
patterns *see* decoration
pebble, joining bowls to make 64–65
pierced design 63
pinching 59–83
correcting shape 62, 67
joining bowls to make pebble 64–65
projects
bowl set 78–83
clay bird 72–77
clay pod 66–71
simple bowl form 60–63
plaster
disposing of 118, 135
mixing 117–118
ratios 117
pod, pinched, project 66–71
porcelain 12, 92, 142
decorating with coils of 46–51
firing 149
handling 103, 104
projects
boxes 102–107
laminated dish 146–151
post–firing reduction 33
potter's knife 111
potter's needle/pin 8, 65, 69
printing blocks, as stamps 95
projects
butter dish 108–113
coiled basket 40–45
coiled bowl 28–33
coiled dish 34–39
garden sculpture 52–57
laminated porcelain dish 146–151
moulded agate bowl 142–145
moulded double–walled bowl 152–157
pinched bird 72–77
pinched bowl set 78–83
pinched pod 66–71
porcelain boxes 102–107
surface decoration 46–51

R
Raku firing 33, 39
rasp blade 8, 119
reinforcements 49, 50, 53, 54, 55
releasing agents 126
relief, low, mould for 120–121
rims
cutting 129
fitting 37, 43–44, 97, 101
levelling 23, 27, 31, 44, 131, 156
refining 27
scoring 64
rock, weathered, as stamp 94
roller guides 9
using 100, 144
rolling pin 9
using 86
rounded coils, using 18–23

S
safety 7
sarcophagi 85
scrim 134, 136
sculpture, garden, project 52–57
shaping, tools for 9
shells, as stamps 95
shrinkage 11
slabbing 85–113
projects
butter dish 108–113
porcelain boxes 102–107
rolling clay on tube 94–95
texturing clay 92–93
using firm slabs 86–91
using large slabs 98–101
using soft slabs 92–97
slabs
coloured, making laminated porcelain dish from 146–151
dried out, softening 89
firm, making lidded box with 86–91
large
forming 98
making window box with 98–101
moulding tiles from 122–123
single, moulding with 138–141
soft
building vessel with 92–97
making tiles from 122–123
turning over 86
slaking down 10
slip 71
casting
making tiles from 122
using two–part mould with 130–131
earthenware 130
preparing 104
ready–made 130
slurry 71, 77
smoke firing 71, 77, 157
soap, soft
coating mould with 126, 134
preparing 134
spare 124, 127
spiral kneading 15
sponges 9
sprigs 100
fastening to surface 140–141
mould for 132–137
shapes for 132–133, 135
staining 13, 143
stamping 92–93
tools for 9
stamps 38, 92–93, 94–95, 136
stoneware clays 12, 78
stroking 65, 67
surface decoration, project 46–51

T
tableware 85
terra–cotta clays 10
texturing 92–93, 108, 109, 154
tools for 9
tiles 85
making
from casting slip 122
from soft slabs 122–123
mould for 120–121
tools 8–9
toxic materials 7
tray, project 82–83
turning tools 8
turntable 9

W
wallpapers, creating pattern with 108, 109, 154
waterproofing 51
weaving 44
wedging 14
window box, making, with large slabbing 98–101
wood blocks, as stamps 94
wooden ribs 8

Credits

Quarto would like to thank and acknowledge the following for supplying pictures reproduced in this book:

Key: l left, r right, c centre, t top, b bottom

J.W. 12 cl
Jill Hampson 12 c

Author's acknowledgements

I would like to thank everyone who supported me during the writing of this book, including my family, but particularly my good friends, Chris Mills and Jill Hampson, for the use of their kilns and for their technical advice. A special thanks goes to Ian Howes for his sensitivity and humour during photography; his experience made the project easier to complete and good fun.

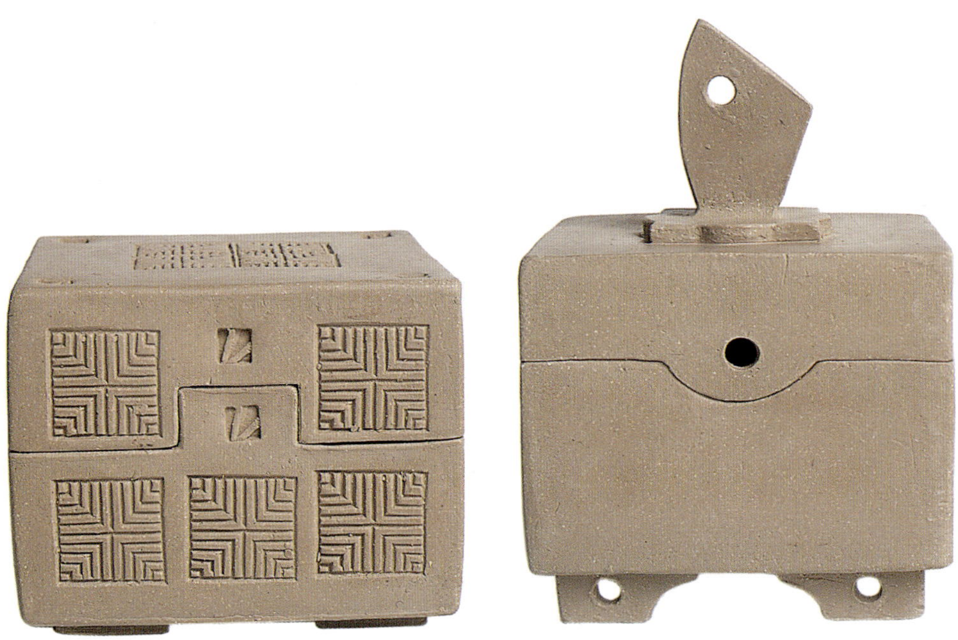